*Business Ethics*

# Business Ethics

*Tom Sorell and John Hendry*

Butterworth-Heinemann
Linacre House, Jordan Hill, Oxford OX2 8DP
A division of Reed Educational and Professional Publishing Ltd

&. A member of the Reed Elsevier plc group

OXFORD  BOSTON  JOHANNESBURG
MELBOURNE  NEW DELHI  SINGAPORE

First published 1994
Reprinted 1996

**British Library Cataloguing in Publication Data**
Sorell, Tom
  Business Ethics
  I. Title II. Hendry, John
  174

ISBN 0 7506 1705 5

Typeset by Deltatype Ltd, Ellesmere Port, South Wirral
Printed and bound in Great Britain byAthenæum Press Ltd,
Gateshead, Tyne & Wear

# Contents

*Preface*                                                                                          ix

*Companies*                                                                                        xi

PART ONE   STARTING POINTS IN BUSINESS ETHICS                                                        1
1   **Scandals and codes**                                                                          3
   The scandalous and the unethical                                                  6
   Essentialist and generalist approaches to business ethics                         8
   Moral codes in business                                                          11
   The limitations of codes                                                         14
   Beyond moral codes                                                               15
   Problems of motivation                                                           16
   Keith Erskine and Securicor                                                      17
   More applications of philosophy                                                  19
   Weighting principles: the Jones Bros. case                                       19
   Morality and constraint: meta-ethics and Royal Dutch/Shell                       22
   Summary                                                                          26
   References                                                                       27

2   **Narrow and broad business ethics**                                                           28
   The justification of breadth                                                     29
   Is corporate social responsibility in the corporate interest?                    31
   Self-interest and morality: the need for moral theory                            34
   Kant and Kantian theories                                                        35
   Kantian morality and business ethics                                             37
   Utilitarianism                                                                   40
   Aristotelianism                                                                  42
   Neo-aristotelianism                                                              44
   Applications of virtue theory in business                                        46
   Ethical egoism                                                                   47
   Moral theory and the presumption against self-interest                           49
   Broadness, narrowness and moral priorities                                       51
   Summary                                                                          52
   References                                                                       53

PART TWO   NARROW BUSINESS ETHICS                                 55
3  **Consumers**                                                   57
   Consumers as kings, consumers as victims                        57
   Consumer demands with moral costs                               59
   The commercial expense of consumer protection                   63
   The case of consumer credit and indebtedness                    65
   Uncontroversial protections                                     72
   'New' or 'ethical' consumers?                                   78
   References                                                      82

4  **Employees**                                                   85
   The employment contract                                         85
   Responsibilities within employment                              87
   Fairness between employees                                      89
   Maastricht                                                      90
   Moral demands and economic and political costs                  93
   Informing and consulting employees                              94
   Moralizing the economic objections                              96
   Political objections                                            97
   Objections in the spirit of the directive                       98
   Equal treatment                                                 98
   A logic of equality in EC treaties                              99
   The logic of equality and the aim of European integration      102
   Good practice in equal opportunities                           103
   Positive discrimination: to follow the American lead?          104
   Good practice illustrated                                      107
   Good practice in employee consultation                         109
   Other issues in European employment ethics                     111
   References                                                     111

5  **Shareholders**                                               113
   Obligations of shareholders                                    115
   Small versus institutional shareholders                        121
   The conditions of shareholder responsibility                   124
   Management buy-outs                                            126
   Ethical investment                                             129
   Shareholding as a desirable form of ownership                  135
   References                                                     137

6  **Other businesses**                                           138
   Suppliers as stakeholders                                      138
   Suppliers as creditors                                         139
   The principle of paying at the agreed time                     140
   The able and willing creditor                                  141

Multiple debts, and relative urgency 143
Debts and other liabilities 144
'Phoenixing' and the ethics of limited liability 144
Relations with competitors 147
The abuse of a dominant position 149
Degrees of aggression in competition and the need for restraint 151
Altruism and good practice 153
Competition and co-operation 155
References 156

PART THREE   BROAD BUSINESS ETHICS 157
7  Business, state and society 159
Whose responsibility? 160
The Dragon Award entries for 1992 161
The ethics of privatization I: for-profit public services 163
The ethics of privatization II: sales of state-owned business 173
References 177

8  Green business 178
Environmental issues in Western Europe 179
Conventional green initiatives in business 181
Less conventional green initiatives 183
The moral value of 'green' business 185
The weighting of environmental factors in business 187
Business ethics and environmental ethics 188
References 191

9  Development and the ethics of capitalism 193
The argument from realism 193
Capitalism, warts and all? 194
Scepticism about realism 199
Development ethics and businesses 201
The ethics of development in Eastern Europe 204
References 208

10 International business ethics 210
Moral absolutes, ethnocentricity and cultural relativism 212
Characteristic types of ethical dilemma 215
Criteria for judgement 217
Political considerations 222
References 223

Index 225

# Preface

This book is intended to contribute to business ethics in more than one way. First, we have tried to write it in a style that business people and students of business will not find too dry and abstract. Moral theory is expounded, but not at excessive length. Philosophical material is brought in, but without a lot of jargon. Everywhere there are references to real cases, real businesses, real laws, and real regulatory institutions. Moreover, justice starts to be done in this book to the idea that 'business ethics' is not just about big business: builders, restaurants and driving schools are as visible in these pages as big retailing multiples and huge manufacturers. We have approached the subject from the perspective of business and social practice in Britain and Western Europe: the overwhelmingly American mould of most business ethics writing is broken here. Finally, we have tried to be timely. This book acknowledges many recent developments in both Western and Eastern Europe that have affected popular expectations about business practice, and that have influenced regulatory legislation. There is discussion of the 'social chapter' of the Maastricht Treaty and related EC directives; and the entry of the countries of the former Soviet Union into the world market economy is acknowledged, as are controversies about privatization and 'green' issues.

There are ten chapters, divided into three parts. The book opens with a discussion of different sources of business ethics, and with the limitations of some of these sources, as well as with suggestions about how the limitations might be overcome. It then proposes a division of business ethics into 'narrow' and 'broad' varieties. Narrow business ethics deals with all the groups financially connected with typical businesses. Broad business ethics deals with relations other than the financial ones – relations of business to the state, to public institutions and even regions of the planet. Chapters 3 to 6 take up narrow business ethics in detail; Chapters 7–10 turn to the broader issues.

This is a jointly authored book in the sense that we have each contributed to all the chapters, and have discussed and agreed all revisions at all stages. The opinions expressed are those we each hold or a compromise that is close to what we think individually. The book is not, however, jointly authored in the sense that equal amounts were written by each of us. In this sense Tom Sorell is the principal author, having produced the first draft of most of the book and done various kinds of legwork; John Hendry amended that draft and added significant amounts of his own material.

One section from Chapter 3 was previously published by Tom Sorell in *Business Ethics: A European Review*. Passages in Chapters 1 and 2 have been drawn with permission from course material by Tom Sorell for the MSc in Public Relations at the University of Stirling.

The authors wish to acknowledge the assistance of the following individuals and organizations in the preparation of the book: Peter Webster, Ethical Investment Research Service; Dr M Howe, Director, Competition Policy Division, UK Office of Fair Trading; Terry Larkin, Office of Fair Trading Press Office; Sean Hamil, New Consumer; Publications Dept., the UK Trades Union Congress; The School of Management, University of Stirling; Helen Pyke, London Borough of Tower Hamlets; Patrick White, Tower Hamlets Education/Business Partnership; Business in the Community; Business in the Environment; Kim Healey; *The Ethical Consumer;* the National Rivers Authority; John Sauvem, Greenpeace; and Heather Draper.

Much secretarial help has been received in producing this book. Denise Powers of the Philosophy Department, The Open University, keyed in an early draft of the first six chapters; Jo Grantham and Shelley Blake of the Judge Institute, Cambridge, worked on the final draft of the whole work.

Tom Sorell
John Hendry

# Companies

The following companies are referred to in the text:

Allied Lyons, **127**; Allied Steel and Wire, **126, 127**; Apple Corporation, **204**; Architype Design Co-operative, **183**; Argyll Group, **3**; Avon Products Inc., **107**; Banco Ambrosiano, **3, 8**; Bank of Credit and Commerce International (BCCI), **4–5, 6, 8, 139**; Barclays Bank, **84, 201, 202**; Barlow Clowes, **4**; BAT Industries, **162**; BBA, **14**; Bell (Arthur) and Son, **3**; Benneton, **138–9**; Bodyshop, **163, 185**; Boots Microcheck, **183**; British Airways, **148, 176**; British Coal, **175**; British Rail, **163, 170, 171**; British Steel, **126**; British Sugar, **73**; BTR, **153, 160**; Buckmaster Fellowship Fund, **132–3**; *Business Age*, **145–7**; Cadbury-Schweppes, **16, 126–7, 146, 218**; Castle's Holdings, **84**; Central Electricity Generating Board (CEGB), **181, 186, 187**; Ciba-Geigy, **204**; Co-operative Bank, **130, 183**; Distillers Group, **3–4, 6**; Ecological Trading Company (ETC), **183–4, 204**; Ecology Building Society, **183**; Ecoschemes, **183**; EcoTrails, **184**; ENI, **6**; Fenman Training, **89**; Fiat, **5**; Friends Provident Stewardship Unit Trust, **133**; Gateway Foodmarkets, **122**; GE Capital, **84**; GKN, **126**; Grand Metropolitan, **29–30, 32, 33, 34, 38, 39, 40, 46–7, 48, 49, 159, 163**; Guinness plc, **3–4, 6, 8**; Halifax Building Society, **53**; Hydro Aluminium Metals, **182**; ICI, **180, 204**; Industrial Common Ownership Finance (ICOF), **130**; Istituto per le Opere di Religione, **3**; Johnson Mathey, **183**; Jones Bros, **19–22**; Kingfisher, **30–1, 32, 33, 34, 38, 39, 46–7, 49, 159, 163, 183**; Laing (John), **163**; Leeds Permanent Building Society, **84**; Lewis (John) Partnership, **16, 19–22, 109–10**; Leyland, **86**; Littlewoods Organization, **16, 107–8**; Lloyds Bank, **201–2**; London Scottish, **84**; Magnet, **127–8**; *Management Week*, **145–7**; Marks & Spencer, **16, 53, 108, 138**; Mercers' Company, **162**; Mercury Provident, **130, 183**; Merlin Ecology, **183**; Merlin Jupiter, **132**; Midland Bank, **201, 202**; Milland Fine Timbers, **184**; Mirror Group Newspapers, **5, 6, 8**; Money Advice Trust, **84**; National Bus Company, **106**; National Westminster Bank, **201, 202–3**; Nationwide Anglia Building Society, **171**; Nestlé, **60–1**; Network Southeast, **170, 171**; News International, **184**; Novo Industri, **183**; Olivetti group, **3, 6**; Paternoster Stores, **30**; Philips, **13**; Pilkington PLC, **16, 153, 160–1**; Pillsbury, **29, 30, 40, 48**; Pinke, Leaman and Browning, **183**; Plant Genetic Systems, **183**; Polly Peck International, **5**; Premier Brands, **127, 146, 147**; Price Waterhouse, **4–5**;

Provident Financial, **84**; Registry Trust, **84**; Rowntree, **16**; Royal Bank of Scotland, **184**; Royal Dutch/Shell, **24–6**; RTZ Corporation, **184**; Schroeder (N. M.) Conscience Fund, **133–4, 135, 183**; Scott Bader, **110**; Securicor, **17–19**; Shared Interest, **130**; Shell, Royal Dutch/Shell, **24–6**; Survival Club, **184**; Tate and Lyle, **73**; Traidcraft, **130, 204**; TSB Environmental, **132, 183**; United Biscuits (UB), **14, 15**; Virgin, **148**; Volvo, **16**; Waitrose, **20, 27**; Winter & Sohn, **16, 185**; Woolworth's, **30, 31**; World Challenge Expeditions, **184**; Worldwide Fund for Nature, **184**.

# Part One

# Starting Points in
# Business Ethics

# 1  Scandals and codes

In June 1982 the Italian banker Roberto Calvi was found dead hanging from scaffolding under Blackfriars Bridge in London. Calvi, who was the owner of Italy's largest private bank, Banco Ambrosiano, had long been suspected of membership of the notorious P-2 masonic lodge, which has been linked to a variety of business scandals as well as to a terrorist bomb attack on Bologna Station, killing eighty-five people. In 1981 he had been convicted of illegal currency exports, and in January 1982 the prominent industrialist Carlo Benedetti (creator of the Olivetti group) had resigned after only two months as deputy chairman of the bank, claiming that he had been refused any access to bank information, had received blackmail threats, and had been totally unable to discharge his duties.

The discovery of Calvi's body followed an agreement by the Banco Ambrosiano board, acting against his recommendations, to reveal details of a mysterious £0.8 billion loan. The loan had been made by the bank's Caribbean and Latin American affiliates with no security other than 'notes of comfort' from the Istituto per le Opere di Religione, the Vatican bank. This loan proved irrecoverable, and when Banco Ambrosiano was liquidated following Calvi's death it was with liabilities of over £1 billion. In the years that followed Benedetti and thirty-two others were found guilty of fraud for not revealing what they had known of the bank's affairs.

In the spring of 1986 two companies were locked in fierce battle to take over the largest UK spirits manufacturer, Distillers. One was James Gulliver's Argyll Group, a large supermarket chain. The other was the long-established Irish brewing company Guinness, then led by Ernest Saunders, which had recently taken over the whisky manufacturer Arthur Bell and Son and was seeking to establish itself as a major player in the international drinks industry

The two bids were closely matched, and because each was expressed in the form of an offer of a number of the acquiring company's shares for each share in Distillers, the outcome depended critically on the relative share prices of Argyll and Guinness. Each company sought to raise the value of its own shares by persuading friendly investors to buy them. But while Argyll stayed within the law, Guinness did not. The law stated clearly that it was illegal to assist in the purchase of one's own shares, but Guinness effectively paid a network of supporters to buy its shares, promising to reimburse them against any losses and offering a 'success fee' in the event that the bid was successful. In short, it cheated. Between October 1987 and the end of 1988 Saunders and many of his associates were arrested. Some, such as Gerald Ronson, founder and chairman of the Heron property empire, ended up in jail. But Guinness won its takeover battle and successfully acquired Distillers.

By the time the fraudulent dealings of the Barlow Clowes investment group were finally exposed in 1988, some £130 million of investors' money had gone missing. The company, run by Peter Clowes, had advertised itself as an investment adviser in gilt-edged securities. It claimed that the money it took from its 18,000 investors, many of them pensioners, was being invested in the safest of all securities, government bonds. In fact most of it was being lent out, without proper records, to a range of private companies with which Peter Clowes was associated. The investors' losses were eventually made good by the UK government, as it emerged that there had been suspicions for several years that the company was trading illegally; but repayment of the cash could not repair the emotional damage suffered by people who thought that they had lost their lives' savings.

In July 1991 the Bank of Credit and Commerce International (BCCI) was closed down by regulators after it became clear that top executives had been systematically defrauding the bank for years. The extent of the fraud was massive, amounting to about £6 billion – nearly half the total bank assets. Bank executives had been using clients' names to trade on their own account, and taking money out of the bank under the guise of non-existent loans and loans to people who could not repay them. This was covered up by shuttling money between subsidiaries, by taking out loans on the security of the money lent, and by some £0.4 billion of non-recorded deposits.

Most of BCCI's business was with small firms in Asia, Africa and Latin America, and with Asian businesses in the developed countries. The collapse hit something like one million customers worldwide, who either lost their deposits (often their working capital or client accounts) or had their loans called in by the administrators. Public concern focused not just on the losses suffered by BCCI customers, but also on the apparent reluctance of the regulators to act. The situation was complicated by the fact that the bank, whose principal shareholder was the ruler of Abu Dhabi, had its headquarters divided between London, Munich and other financial centres. But bank executives had already been found guilty several years before of supporting the Noriega regime in Panama, of the illegal ownership of an American bank, and of the laundering of drug money in Florida. In 1990 the auditors, Price Waterhouse, had conveyed their suspicions to the Bank of England and had insisted on the removal of two top executives, but had still passed the accounts. The Bank of England, which led a college of seven regulatory authorities in overseeing BCCI's activities, had decided to let it continue operating in the hope that it could be restructured and set on a proper footing – but this decision was, to say the least, controversial.

On 5 November 1991 the body of the publishing tycoon Robert Maxwell was recovered from the Atlantic Ocean after he had fallen, jumped or been pushed from his private yacht in the early hours of the morning. Maxwell had ruled over a complex interlocking empire of privately and publicly owned companies, including Mirror Group Newspapers and an international network of publishing and printing interests, and enquiries after his death revealed fraud on a massive scale. In the late 1980s Maxwell had run up enormous debts in order to finance the growth of the private part of his empire. In an increasingly desperate attempt to service these debts as recession bit at the turn of the decade he had then syphoned off a total of about £750 million from the public to the private companies, including about £450 million from the public company pension funds. As the fraud was revealed, questions were asked not only about Maxwell himself, and the two sons who had helped run the business, but also about the many 'respectable' City figures who had been his friends and supporters. Earlier in his career, after a previous business disaster, Maxwell had been deemed by the British regulatory authorities unfit to hold office in a public company. Yet as he had constructed his empire and perpetrated his fraud, influential businessmen and financiers had been prepared to trust him to a remarkable extent, giving him their backing and turning a blind eye to his chronic refusal to divulge information which they should have insisted on having.

In August 1990 the Turkish Cypriot businessman Asil Nadir offered to buy up all the publicly owned shares of Polly Peck International, the company he had built up into a £2 billion conglomerate. A few days later he withdrew the offer. By October the company had collapsed, with debts of £1.1 billion, and Nadir was under investigation by the Serious Fraud Office in London for improper share dealings. By January 1991 he had been charged with false accounting and theft. When Nadir left the UK, illegally, in May 1993 he had been due to stand trial on charges of theft totalling £135 million.

In the spring of 1993 several hundred Italian businessmen were arrested on charges of bribery, corruption and the illegal financing of political parties. Many of Italy's most prominent business figures were among the accused, including Francesco Paulo Mattioli, Finance Director of the giant Fiat motor company; Gabriele

*Cagliari, Chairman of the massive state-owned energy group, ENI; and the heads of ENI's turbine, petroleum, exploration and gas distribution subsidiaries. The scale of the corruption was staggering: an estimated £25 billion to £30 billion in kickbacks on public works contracts over a ten-year period. Typical of these were the bribes of several million pounds that Cagliari admitted paying to the Socialist Party in order to win a £150 million turbine contract, or the £6 million that the Olivetti company admitted paying between 1988 and 1991, to secure contracts with the Ministry of Posts worth £300 million.*

## The scandalous and the unethical

The prevalence of business scandals in the last few years has helped fuel a growing public interest in business ethics. For the majority of people, whose knowledge of business issues and practices is derived largely from what they see on television or read in the papers, the issues raised by these scandals *are* the issues of business ethics; and even for those with deeper or more extensive knowledge, they are perceived as the main issues. Scandals, then, shape our perceptions of the ethical issues confronting business. Moreover, the process of turning events into scandals – of publicity, comment and debate – constitutes our primary response as a society to these issues.

It is partly through scandal and exposure that we seek to identify what is criminal and to prevent its recurrence, and scandal does sometimes bring about moral improvement. When a piece of wrongdoing catches the headlines or is so widely gossiped about that it is common knowledge, the publicity itself can disable the wrongdoer, and others who fear exposure can be put off and change their ways. More generally, the publicity can concentrate attention on what makes a given activity wrong and can alert people who think it is wrong to other people – sometimes hordes of other people – who think as they do. In this way a moral climate can be changed, at any rate for a time. Perhaps recent scandals have served to change the moral climate in the USA surrounding the sexual harassment of women at work, or the seriousness of taking women at their word when they say no to sex on a date. Perhaps recent scandals in the UK and on the Continent have caused people to think twice about the influence exerted in private firms and public bodies by secret societies such as the Masons, or about that exerted on politicians by commercial interest groups. Will the scandals caused by the collapse of the Bank of Credit and Commerce International or by the misuse of pension funds in the Maxwell publishing organizations, or by stock-market manipulation in the take-over of Distillers by Guinness, have a similar moralizing effect on the business community? Will they alter the wider moral climate?

It is possible. It took scandals in the financial markets to inspire moralizing films such as Oliver Stone's *Wall Street*, and moralizing plays such as Caryl Churchill's *Serious Money*. Perhaps the existence of works like these is already evidence that the scandals have had an effect. The same scandals that inspired the film and the play are sometimes before the minds of business leaders who speak about the importance of business ethics to their firms or to business generally. However, though they have no doubt done something to make ethical issues topical, we would like to deny that scandals in general, and especially the lavishly publicized financial scandals of the 1980s, are a good guide to the ethical issues that confront business. We would like to deny, too, that they provide the right sort of stimulus for a change in the moral climate surrounding business.

To begin with the scandals that inspired *Wall Street*, there is the obvious point that activity on the financial markets is unrepresentative of business or commercial activity in general. The moral risks of being entrusted with other people's investments and some kinds of inside information are not the same as the moral risks of trying to manufacture motor cars at the least cost. The moral risks of making a ship's load as big as possible and its journey times as short as possible are not the same as the moral risks of producing cheap beef or cheap eggs. In short, if justice is to be done to the breadth of the moral challenges in business, then one had better not get transfixed by shady practice among the stockbrokers or bankers.

A second drawback of the well-publicized scandals is their tendency to focus on big business and big deals, as if business ethics was only a matter, or primarily a matter, for firms with huge turnovers or corporations with employees by the thousand. In the UK, where firms employing nine people or fewer made up 90.1 per cent of all businesses in 1990, and where 78 per cent of businesses had turnovers of under £100,000 per annum, an ethics for big business would be an ethics for an extremely small sector of business.[1] Moreover, and to return to the question of moral risks, it is clear that some are more urgent for small than for big business. A one- or two-man building firm that exists from contract to contract probably runs a greater risk of overstretching its workforce and failing to carry out its commitments to customers than one with the scale to reallocate employees when necessary. A restaurant with big debts and a clientele reduced by an economic recession may run a greater risk of overcharging than a big fast food chain. A small business may be in competition with sectors of a black or underground economy and therefore feel pressure to keep some of its transactions out of its official books. These are moral risks, but they are far removed from those of financial trading floors and large corporate boardrooms.

Leaving aside the details of the best-publicized scandals in business, there is the point that scandals in general may not be a good starting point for ethics in general. Scandals are occasions when a public sensibility is offended, and for a public sensibility to be offended is not *necessarily* for anything unethical to be done. When black civil-rights protesters first sat down in whites-only cafeterias in the American south, it scandalized local whites, but the fact that it scandalized them does not mean that it was wrong for blacks to sit down in whites-only cafeterias. On the contrary, it is more defensible to say that the wrong lay in what was not scandalous, in what was accepted as natural: namely, the existence of cafeterias that barred people who were black. There is another way in which the scandalous and the unethical can come apart: what starts out as scandalous wrongdoing may, with repetition and the passage of time, come to seem commonplace and unscandalous. Perhaps some forms of drug dealing are cases in point. These observations show that scandalous behaviour need not include wrongdoing and that wrongdoing need not scandalize. Or, in other words, scandal is an uncertain indicator of what is unethical.

The conclusion is not that the Maxwell case or the BCCI case or the Banco Ambrosiano case or the Guinness case are of no relevance to a book on business ethics: they are highly relevant. But what makes them relevant is not their causing public outrage, their creating scandal, but the fact that they are cases of stealing and deception and conspiracy, and the fact that some kinds of business dealing create significant risks of the same or similar types of wrongdoing. In what follows scandals will sometimes be referred to; but so will cases of wrongdoing that have received little publicity. Hypothetical cases of wrongdoing, as well as cases, real and hypothetical, of actions that morally are on the borderline will also come into the discussion. The aim is to give broad coverage of what is morally problematic in business, and also to convey a sense of how some moral risks and challenges can be met.

## Essentialist and generalist approaches to business ethics

Now there are at least two ways of securing a broad coverage of the moral territory. One is to focus on morally significant characteristics that all businesses have in common, or morally significant characteristics that are essential to the system in which business operates. For instance, if it is a defining characteristic of a business that it sets out to be profitable, and if there is something morally wrong with seeking profit, then one could say something about the morality of all business by commenting on the morality of its essential feature: pursuing profit. This *essentialist* approach, as it might be called, could be pursued with the aim of showing that business was morally suspect, as in Marxist attempts to show that profit is the theft of something from wage-labourers.[2] Or it could be pursued with the aim of showing that business was morally creditable, as when business or the market economy is represented as the embodiment of an ideal of unforced service to one's fellow human beings.[3] Although the essentialist approach will not be adopted in what follows, it cannot be ignored: it is too well entrenched in current thinking about global politics and economics to be bypassed. It is particularly prominent in thinking about economic development, and it affects issues that are central to international business ethics.

Marxist criticism of capitalism based on a certain theory of the origin of profit has already been identified as essentialist, and Marxist critiques of multinational business operations in the Third World are both numerous and influential. More recently, free market diagnoses and solutions of the problems of the newest developing world – Eastern Europe – have become commonplace, and with them have come moral prescriptions for ways of organizing society that are most in tune with the market. There are undeniable attractions in gearing business ethics to the supposed moral worth of the free market or to the supposed immorality of making profits. The essentialist approach may bring the wood into focus where before there were only trees; and the *contention* between essentialist approaches may generate a kind of insight that is not otherwise available. No one who has heard both doctrinaire free-marketeers and doctrinaire Marxists is likely to be won over to either side, but hearing both sides can improve one's understanding of capitalism in ways that the detailed examination of business case studies or national economic histories cannot.

By contrast with the essentialist approach, which conjures up moral evaluation from essential characteristics of business or the market, there is what might be called the *generalist* approach. It, too, tries to get beyond a narrow view of business, but not by latching on to moral characteristics of business in general or the market economy in general. Instead, it keeps the variety of business activity and the variety of moral risk to the fore. Both the essentialist and the generalist approach try to get beyond particular businesses, or sectors of business, to business in general, but the essentialist approach works by saying what different businesses or sectors of business have in common, while the generalist approach tries to assemble a composite picture of business ethics in general, drawn from moral characteristics that are peculiar to different branches of business. Though the characteristics are drawn from different branches of business, together they may be representative of the moral risks facing business in general. The difference between the essentialist and generalist approaches is like the difference between an aerial photograph of a town and a collection of photographs of its main landmarks taken at ground level. The collection of photographs corresponds to generalism: it leaves out a great deal and is openly selective, but it does show a few important things in life-like detail. The aerial photograph, on the other hand, while it includes everything, is unlikely to give an impression of life on the ground.

In this book a generalist approach is followed, but not with the aim of producing a composite picture of the moral risks of business everywhere.

We have not attempted to be comprehensive – to include photographs of every building in the town – and we have dealt only in passing with some of the issues that form the staple content of existing (primarily American) textbooks on business ethics, issues such as advertising, bribery or whistle blowing. What we have tried to do is to identify and discuss situations that are ethically interesting, the analysis of which has general implications for business and for society. We have also focused on issues that are of particular significance in a European or British context. In Europe the role of the state in business life is often extensive: so quite a lot of attention will be paid to state institutions, including some morally-motivated regulatory institutions, and state-owned businesses will be considered. Again, in Europe the question of the culture and politics and moral standards that should be associated with the economic union of different countries is a live one: so official attempts to articulate such a culture and politics and moral standards, e.g. in the social chapter of the Treaty on European Union will sometimes be discussed. In other words, unusually for a book written in English, we have not attempted to adopt a mid-Atlantic perspective: mid-English Channel is perhaps closer to the mark.

So much for the narrowing down of the business activity with which we shall be concerned. What about ethics? Where does a generalist approach to business ethics get its ethical content from, its sense of what is morally problematic and what is not, of what is right and wrong? As one would expect from an approach that emphasizes variety, from a range of different sources: from religion, for example, and from the law; from the rhetoric of interest groups in and out of business, from newspapers and television, from academic treatises, including, as we shall go on to suggest, works of philosophy; in short, from the whole range of influences on moral opinion in general. In addition, however, one can get one's bearings from the problems detected by specialized monitors of business activity. Among these are the morally motivated regulatory institutions mentioned earlier, institutions that exist to discourage or prosecute fraud, monopoly, threats to health and safety and so on; institutions that exist to arbitrate between producers and consumers when they are in dispute; and institutions that seek to advise individuals and businesses about their commercial dealings. Then there are the moral codes or codes of practice adopted by individual businesses or business associations themselves, sometimes on their own initiative, sometimes in response to the regulatory institutions or in anticipation of legislation, sometimes to follow fashion. Because these constitute explicit statements of business ethics and the most readily identifiable responses of businesses themselves to the ethical issues they face, these codes would seem to provide a natural starting point for our considerations.

# Moral codes in business

To see what use they can be to the identification of issues in business ethics, it is worth asking what business codes add to sets of moral precepts addressed to people generally, such as the Ten Commandments. Some codes in business undoubtedly add very little; others identify moral risks that are specific to certain kinds of business activity.

Take, for example, the Professional Charter of the UK Public Relations Consultants Association. This points out the risk of resorting to financial inducements in order to promote the interests of a client, and it prohibits the offer of these inducements when it is against the public interest. The provision dealing with these inducements also identifies the sort of people who would be the most likely beneficiaries: holders of public office and people in television, radio and newspapers. Neither the holders of public office, nor the media people, nor the occasions for offering inducements, feature in every walk of life. So the charter caters for situations that are not catered for in very general collections of moral rules.

The same is true of the revised codes of practice issued by the Association of British Travel Agents to tour operators and travel agents in May 1990. These provided for extended liability for most aspects of the package holidays that they arranged; enhanced compensation in the event of cancellations or alteration in holiday arrangements after full payment was due, and increases in the amounts that could be awarded to dissatisfied clients as a result of complaint arbitration procedures.[4] Such provisions at once give an indication of the ups and downs of the travel business, such as the need, occasionally, to alter clients' travel arrangements at the last moment, and the moral risks attending such ups and downs, e.g. the unfair refusal to allow clients to opt out of altered arrangements that they antic- ipate will be unsatisfactory. *Perhaps* some of the ABTA provisions are foreshadowed in the commandment not to bear false witness, or in the conventional moral precept that one should keep one's promises: if so, it is a pretty vague foreshadowing. The ABTA code clearly goes far beyond what a conventional morality, or a religious code for everyday life, would mention; and that is already a reason why it should exist.

The usefulness of a specialized code of ethics is enhanced when, as in the case of the Charter of the Public Relations Consultants Association, it is prefaced by an account of the typical activities of the bodies subscribing to the code, and supplemented by rules for dealing with violations of the code. In the case of the Public Relations Consultants Association there is also a code governing the application of public relations to the trading of securities, such as shares in companies quoted on the London Stock Exchange. This even more specialized code takes up questions of conflict of interest, confidentiality, and the use of privileged information that are peculiar to work in the financial services industry. Like the more general code that is intended to govern public-relations practices in general, the 'investor relations' code gives some insight into the specific moral risks of public-relations activity. As for the rules dealing with procedures for reporting and penalizing infringements of the charter, these are intended to show that the provisions of the charter do not pay mere lip-service to good practice but are actually backed by a kind of enforcement mechanism.

With this much to be said in favour of a code of ethics such as the one adopted by the Public Relations Consultants Association, are there really any significant objections to it? At least one objection may already have been suggested by a provision in the Charter already mentioned, the one dealing with inducements. The objection is that a great deal is left to the judgement of the public relations practitioner. For example, one might ask why the Charter does not come out and flatly *prohibit* the offer of inducements. Why does it make the prohibition conditional on the inducement's being against the public interest? And what, come to that, does it mean when it says 'members should conduct professional activities with proper regard to the public interest?' (provision 2.1). What counts as the public interest, and who is to judge whether or not a given activity is in keeping with the public interest?

It might be thought that some of the criticism implied by these questions is unfair, for there is bound to be some vagueness in any code, and therefore a need to use one's judgement in applying it. This may be so even in the case of inducements. Is it an inducement to a politician, for example, to buy him a coffee or even a whisky in the course of trying to make him see a client's point of view? If it is an inducement, is it one that a code of ethics ought to outlaw? Or should the code really cater primarily for such things as gifts of cars and free holidays? Granted that there can be cases where it is unclear whether a code has been infringed or whether the infringement is more than minor, it is not the existence of this sort of grey area that is being pointed out by the questions raised earlier. What is at issue is not whether a code leaves anything to the judgement of the practitioner, but whether it leaves too much. What is at issue, in other words, is whether a code is over-permissive morally. Further questions arise about the consistency of some of the provisions in the Public Relations Charter. For example, provision 3.1 calls for safeguarding the confidence of present and past clients, and in some cases honouring this provision would call for a breach of provision 2.1, which insists on the importance of the public interest. In general, the Charter is much more insistent on confidentiality than on openness, which makes it objectionable to public-relations people who insist on openness. The emphasis on confidentiality may be objectionable from another angle, too, for there are documented cases in the UK of public-relations firms refusing to disclose payments to politicians enlisted as lobbyists for a certain cause, which perhaps creates conditions for the application of improper influence on Parliament. No doubt similar risks are run by legislators and public relations people throughout the world.

The upshot of these objections is not that the Public Relations Charter is of no use, but that it needs to be supplemented or changed in certain ways. Yet the changes that would make it less permissive, or that would get it to call for more openness are the sort of changes that would probably reduce its following among practitioners: the less that a code demands, the easier it is for practitioners to agree to be bound by it; the more it demands, the harder it is for people to abide by it voluntarily, at least in sufficient numbers.

Let us turn now from codes of ethics for professional and business associations to codes of ethics adopted by companies. In the USA and Europe these codes have been the subject of several recent studies. A report of one such study carried out by Edgar Wille mainly on UK and European company codes gives a useful summary of their typical concerns.[5] Foremost among them was a concern with employees. Very nearly as prominent was a concern with making a contribution to the community or with behaving as a good corporate citizen. The three next most prominent concerns were striking a balance between the interests of stakeholders, serving the customer, and maintaining the free market.

Though the phrases 'behaving as a good corporate citizen' and 'making a contribution to the community' might naturally be taken as interchangeable, Wille found that in some cases they meant different things. Occasionally, 'contributions to the community' were taken to consist of actual cash grants or sponsorships; 'good corporate citizenship', on the other hand, sometimes came to nothing more than carrying out normal business activities without breaking the law. In yet other cases the value of good corporate citizenship was connected in company formulations of their codes with the value of the free market or with the value of character traits like resourcefulness and showing enterprise. Wille quotes a statement from the Dutch electronics multinational, Philips, in which these various elements are interwoven:

> The industrial enterprise fulfils an important economic and social role in society. Its primary function consists in the production of goods and the provision of services. It thereby creates employment and income and opportunity for people in or outside the enterprise… Private enterprise, essentially characterized by initiative, adaptability and the willingness to take risks, must have sufficient freedom of action if it is to be able to adjust to constantly changing circumstances. In turn private enterprise is expected to understand its position and role in society.

The variety of different understandings of what are often called the same values is a reason for being uneasy about codes of ethics. One suspects that so long as the phrase 'good corporate citizen' features in the codes of ethics of different companies, the moral differences between the companies will be disguised, and the company that puts special effort and money into creating good community relations may get no more recognition than one that only talks about corporate citizenship. Perhaps the same danger attends the publication of codes of ethics in general: issuing a code is a way of appearing to be upright even if the fine print of it is uninspiring or if it is ignored in practice.

## The limitations of codes

Recent studies of codes of ethics reveal a certain amount of uniformity in the presentation of ethical 'do's and 'don'ts', and also enlarge on the typical shortcomings of ethical codes. Edgar Wille's 'The Value of Codes of Ethics to the Individual Manager' is very guarded in its approval of company codes.[6] Wille concedes that it is sometimes useful to have written guidelines, and also specific guidelines in areas like safety, or, differently, corruption or bribery. He sees the value of lively or inspiring declarations of what a company expects of its employees or what it stands for; but, on the other side, he confesses to the suspicion that 'a lot of the statements made by companies in codes of ethics and mission statements belong to the "apple pie and motherhood" type of declaration. No one would greatly disagree, but neither would anyone be greatly motivated by the obvious'.[7] Moreover, Wille has doubts about the value of even a stimulating code that exists primarily on paper and that is only really effective when it is applied. Finally, he is not sure that everything put into ethical codes deserves to be there: polemics in favour of free enterprise, for example, have no place in ethical codes, in his opinion.

Not all codes suffer from banality of expression. The mission statement of the North of England industrial firm BBA begins, 'Grit and gumption are preferable to inertia and intellect'. Not all codes suffer, either, from the problem of preaching 'apple pie and motherhood'. For example, the code of the UK confectionery firm, United Biscuits, forbids arrangements to buy from suppliers that are conditional on suppliers buying from United Biscuits. It also declares a 'pay on time' policy rarely adhered to by even major British companies. Again, the code disapproves of the disparagement of competitors, even by implication. These are unusual provisions, and, in the case of 'pay on time', provisions that can cost money, and they give an impression of ethical rigour. On the other hand, the provision for financial dealings in UB shares on the basis of inside information are unusual in appearing to be rather lax. Trading of UB shares on the basis of inside information is permitted so long as it is conducted openly and with the company's knowledge. A more exacting requirement would disallow these dealings, in the interest of maintaining equality between all shareholders.

Two of the limitations of ethical codes pointed out by Wille – their tendency to promote values that are so uncontroversial as to be banal, and their tendency to have more of a life on paper than in the activities of managers – are really limitations in their power to motivate people. These limitations are made worse when ethical codes seem to the people who have to follow them to be composed according to a formula; or when the force behind their introduction is not some defect in the ethical culture of a company, but the fact that ethical codes are in fashion. Things are perhaps worse still when the fashion is not home-grown but imported – in the case of ethical codes mostly from the USA.

These limitations in respect of motivation are important, but they are not the only ones. Undue permissiveness is another common limitation, as we saw in the case of the Public Relations Charter, and as we suspected in the case of the financial-dealing provisions of the United Biscuits code. Avoidable conflicts between the precepts of a code are a further limitation. There was a hint of an avoidable conflict in the Public Relations Charter when the value of promoting the public interest clashed with what may have been the over-emphasized value of confidentiality. At times values do not so much conflict as tend to be obscurely weighted. Failure to reflect sensitively enough the moral risks of a particular business or profession is another common limitation. It comes to light when a widely available but highly general code, like the Ten Commandments, is considered as a basis for criticizing the conduct of public relations, or when a general code of ethics for public relations has to do duty for public relations activity involving trade in securities. In the remainder of this chapter we shall explore the limitations identified above: limitations in respect of motivation, avoidable conflicts, and undue permissiveness.

A final limitation of codes of ethics counterbalances the strength of being specific about moral risks. It consists of being very narrow in its view of what can go wrong morally in a given variety of business activity. For example, it would be a mistake to suppose that the moral risks of tourism were confined to the risks of cancelled or altered travel arrangements covered by the ABTA code of practice. There are other considerations, such as the effects of tourism on a local culture or landscape. The problem of inattention to these broader ramifications of business activity can be called the problem of narrowness, and we shall say more about narrowness in Chapter 2.

## Beyond moral codes

The limitations of moral codes do not show that they are of no use in identifying important issues in business ethics. On the contrary, for the purpose of identifying issues, codes seem to have fewer drawbacks than, for example, the simple lists of stakeholder interests that directors and managers resolve to keep in mind. Where codes fall down, at least as a rule, is in failing to inspire people to implement them and in failing to prepare people for the cases where they do not apply straightforwardly. In this book only a small burden will be placed on codes of ethics and codes of practice: we shall look to them to set out some of the problems in business ethics, and no more. We shall look outside the codes for solutions to the problem of motivation, and also outside the codes for solutions to problems about conflicts of precepts, questionable weighting of values, permissiveness and sensitivity. We shall also look outside the codes for a source of a solution to the problem of narrowness.

Some of the limitations of codes can be overcome when there are exemplary people and exemplary businesses to give a lead and set a standard in applying them. Other solutions depend on applying the codes with the help of analytical skills, or on locating the precepts of codes in more substantial moral frameworks. To an extent that is perhaps surprising, the skills and frameworks required to do this can be provided by philosophy. Other ways of overcoming the limitations of codes – the limitation of narrowness, for example – depend on taking into account values, such as the value of sustainable economic growth or the value of living in greater harmony with other cultures and with nature, that are perhaps more vigorously discussed outside philosophy, e.g. in political movements such as 'the greens'. But philosophy goes a long way.

## Problems of motivation

Consider, to begin with, problems of motivation. This was where the banality of codes of practice came in, where their existence merely on paper came in, and where their tendency to be adopted to follow a fashion, and a foreign fashion at that, was mentioned. We may begin with the problem of foreignness, or, to be blunt about it, the rather blatant Yankee stamp of many codes of ethics, which makes some people in Europe, at any rate those not working for American multinationals, sense a kind of encroachment on their moral culture. Such people may feel that what is distinctive about Europe needs to be protected and also that there are valuable business and ethical traditions that have grown up on this side of the Atlantic and that need to be developed in their own way. What would encourage such development? Part of the answer would be to draw upon business history so as to publicize morally instructive practices from the ethical culture of European business. In Britain there are a number of companies whose pioneering work in the development of an ethical culture deserves to be studied: the John Lewis Partnership, Pilkington, Rowntree, Cadbury, Marks & Spencer and Littlewoods are examples. In the rest of Europe there are no doubt many other comparable cases, including, for example, Volvo in Sweden and Winter & Sohn in Germany. Cases such as these might help to identify a moral business culture that is distinctively

European; though no doubt the description of that culture would have to draw upon an awareness of what is believed and done elsewhere, and especially through local branches of US and Japanese multinationals.

Besides being able to refer to exemplary companies, it is important, if the motivating power of codes of ethics is to be increased, to be able to refer to exemplary people – people who in a certain sense personify a business and whose values rub off on others in a business not only through codes of practice but through their personality and through the mythology that grows up around them. There is perhaps no better spur to the observance of codes of ethics than the existence in particular businesses of very senior managers who are powerful enough and visible enough to exercise a wide influence, and whose behaviour brings a code of ethics or a mission statement to life. Yet important as these exemplary figures are, they do not live forever, or stay in a business forever, and their values may be hard to adapt to new situations. Worse, their powers of articulating their values, as opposed to living their values, may be limited. This is why it may be necessary, for maximizing the good influence of these people, to have the means of articulating the values clearly, recording them, and adapting them to changing situations. Among the skills needed for making what is benign in the influence of exemplary figures last are philosophical skills, perhaps skills that are acquired by the business people themselves, perhaps skills that are bought in at the stage when missions and ethics are being defined.

## Keith Erskine and Securicor

The need for these skills may be illustrated by the case of Keith Erskine, who, from 1960 to 1973, masterminded a very dramatic improvement in the fortunes of what was at first a small British security services firm, one that became a multinational, diversified business well known under the name of Securicor.[8] Like other individuals who have become well-known for imbuing their businesses with a sense of mission, Keith Erskine entered Securicor at a time when it was at a low ebb, and dedicated himself so completely to turning it around that other people working for him were inspired to follow his example.

Securicor started out as a professional neighbourhood watch scheme in London in 1935. Its Hampstead branch broke away to become the core of a security-guard business that lapsed during the Second World War and revived after it as a source of employment for ex-servicemen. This was how Securicor began. By 1956 the company was on the verge of failure. It was bought by one of its clients, the Allied Hotels–Kensington Palace Hotel Group, which was controlled by the Erskine family. At the time of its purchase it was marginally profitable, but later it began to lose money, and Keith Erskine, who had persuaded his brother to buy Securicor through the hotel business in the first place, decided to take it in hand. He applied himself to the task very singlemindedly, working eighteen-hour days and sleeping at Securicor headquarters five days a week. In the early 1960s Erskine began to see the opportunities there would be for security firms to make money by protecting cash deliveries, and he foresaw the need for security services on a national scale when motorway-building in the UK began to make provincial cities accessible to organized crime in London. A branch network was built up, often with branch offices set up before business for them had been arranged. Erskine's company had major investments in property suitable for branch offices, and large amounts were spent on communications systems. Over the fourteen years that Erskine was associated with the company – he died in a car accident in 1974 – profits multiplied forty-five times to about £38 million on a turnover that was eighty-five times as large as when Erskine took over.

Erskine the man was no small ingredient in the company's success. His highly disciplined working day, starting with its 5.00 am swim in the Serpentine, often in the company of other staff; his insistence on the senior management keeping up at first hand with security operations in the field; his willingness to undertake some of the jobs of ordinary staff himself; his distaste for any of the outward distinctions between management and workers, and so on – all these things created a very high degree of staff loyalty and raised morale among men whose jobs as nightwatchmen were often very boring.

Reading about Keith Erskine, we were impressed by what he achieved, but disappointed by the few sayings and written statements of his beliefs that he left behind, and that in some sense are all that now remain of him to sustain the company. For example, one of the Securicor mottos credited to Erskine runs, rather uninspiringly, 'Get down to the nitty gritty, never mind the airy fairy, the talkie talkie must lead to the doey doey'. Again, a statement of Securicor values, apparently dating to 1974, mixed potted company history and quotations from Pope and Emerson with financial results and a tour through Securicor euphemisms for managerial titles – 'helper' for manager and 'Good Housekeeping Team' for management team.

The statement of values bears the stamp of Keith Erskine, and perhaps it struck the right note while he was alive and at the centre of the business putting it into practice. Read in isolation from the man, however, it sometimes seems to be over the top. For instance, it ends up by saying that 'in Securicor we have ceased to follow the false gods of doubt and division. We try in all modesty to follow the gods of brotherhood and service'. Elsewhere, in a nine-point elucidation of 'Securicor cares', point number 2 reads, 'We respect the dignity of man'. This seems too general and grandiloquent for an explanation of an advertising slogan. Another excerpt: 'They say it is love that makes the world go round. Certainly we could not take hate or fear as recipes for Securicor'. This, too, seems inappropriately general and sentimental. The statement as a whole could never be fairly accused of sounding banal, and it is too heartfelt to be of the mere apple pie and motherhood variety complained of by Wille, but it lacks the system and sobriety that might have made it serviceable in a Securicor without Erskine, or in another company anxious to learn from Securicor. For eliminating its tendency to miscellany and sentimentality without necessarily taking the life out of it, philosophy might have been of some use.

## More applications of philosophy

Problems of motivation were not the only ones thrown up by the examination of codes of ethics in business. There were also problems to do with conflicts of precepts, questionable weighting of values, and permissiveness. We want to suggest that philosophy can help to counteract some of these problems as well, and to indicate how it can do so. Philosophy can help in two ways. First, it contains moral theories that may be used to justify and criticize various claims about what businesses should and shouldn't do. Second, it supplies techniques of argument and analysis that can help people, when it's necessary, to respond to rhetoric, including moral rhetoric. Moral theories and their implications will be discussed in Chapter 2. What we shall do now is to illustrate how philosophical techniques of argument and analysis may be brought to bear.

## Weighting principles: the Jones Bros. case

Let us start with avoidable conflicts between values and a controversy about the retailing firm of the John Lewis Partnership. This controversy arose from John Lewis's decision in 1990 to close two moderately profitable department stores in North and South London. Before discussing the decision, something had better be said about John Lewis. The business was started in 1864 as a draper's shop in central London. Its founder, John Lewis, who lends his name to the present Partnership, was a scrupulously honest businessman who saw early the value of offering for sale a very large range of clothing items at low prices. His policy of not advertising, which is still in force in the Partnership today, did not prevent his shop from prospering, and he was able to take his two sons into the business and give them shares in it when they were in their early twenties. One of the sons, Spedan, was responsible in the 1920s for establishing the business as a partnership of all of its employees, a partnership dedicated to certain commercial and ethical principles, foremost among which are profit-sharing and democracy in relations between managers and managed. The

Partnership trades in England and Scotland through around twenty department stores; it also operates a Waitrose supermarket chain, mainly concentrated in London and the south of England. In 1990 turnover was just over £2 billion. Profit after partnership bonus distribution but before tax was £69 million.

So much for the Partnership. Let us now turn to the department store closures in 1990, and in particular to the case of the North London store, Jones Bros. which ceased trading on 21 July 1990. The decision to close Jones Bros. was announced in January 1990, but apparently it had been under consideration for decades. Jones Bros. was located in the North London neighbourhood of Holloway, in turn-of-the-century premises that were expensive to heat and light and too cramped to permit extensive storage. A further problem with the premises was that they were not properly designed for efficient deliveries of stock. According to the local manageress, there was also a shortage of staff accommodation and a poor telephone switchboard. In the statement issued when the closure of Jones Bros. was announced, John Lewis said that the building was 'no longer in keeping with the environment of a modern department store, nor with the efficient goods handling required for profitable retailing'. The company was making it a policy to open large, purpose-built department stores outside town centres, and people who were used to shopping at Jones Bros. were invited to use other, fairly distant, London branches of John Lewis instead.

About the same time that the closure of the store was announced, a 'Save Jones Bros.' campaign was started in North London. The campaigners pointed out that Jones Bros. was the only quality department store in the Holloway area, and that it had been trading profitably for about 50 years under John Lewis ownership. In the opinion of the campaigners, a slightly dowdy and unpretentious building was far more attractive than a brand new and anonymous glass box on the outskirts of London. The campaigners collected 11,000 signatures on a petition asking John Lewis to reconsider its decision. They mounted a very extensive leafleting campaign until the last moment, and they organized a picket at the John Lewis board meeting on 13 June 1990. In a letter to the local management the campaigners wrote, 'By closing Jones Bros., not only will the local community suffer bitterly, but we, as loyal customers, will have no alternative but to think of John Lewis as a company interested solely in maximizing profit, with no concern for inner cities or our loyalty'.

John Lewis consistently chose not to respond to the moral rhetoric of the Save Jones Bros. campaigners, and replied to letters of protest and adverse press comment by explaining the commercial reasoning behind its plans for department stores and indicating how the Jones Bros. closure fitted into those plans. In a way the avoidance of moral issues was out of character, for the company is very much concerned with the ethics of its business dealings, and it makes its concerns explicit in the written Constitution of the John Lewis Partnership. Indeed the constitution lays down rules not only for activity within the firm, but also for relations with suppliers, customers, and the community in general.

Is there anything in the Constitution with a bearing on the Jones Bros. case? To the extent that the Jones Bros. case raised the question of the responsibility of the Partnership to the community, the answer is 'Yes'. The Constitution says that 'The Partnership shall endeavour constantly to keep on the highest level of good citizenship its behaviour as a group within the general community'. An official company document entitled 'About the John Lewis Partnership' also contains relevant comments. An opening section about the Partnership's 'basic principles' says in part that 'To the community at large from which it makes its money it offers a participation in community life appropriate to its resources of money and people'. It goes on:

> The Partnership... very firmly believes that each of its branches owes the duties of a good neighbour to the particular community in which it operates. In taking over establishments, whether production units or shops, the Partnership has been careful not to interfere unnecessarily with their local character or traditions. Such department stores all trade under their own name. The Partnership recognizes that the vitality of a shop, as of a plant or any other organism, often depends upon a number of small and apparently insignificant adaptations to a particular environment, and these it is careful not to check [i.e. interfere with].

Though these comments have a clear bearing on the issues raised by the moral rhetoric of the Jones Bros. campaigners, it is perhaps not very surprising that John Lewis passed up the opportunity to quote them in their response; for pretty obviously they lend themselves to an interpretation that supports the Jones Bros. campaigners. These comments seem to make a virtue of being sensitive to the needs and characteristics of local communities, and yet the decision to close local department stores that were not even trading at a loss seems to be notably insensitive. The refusal to reconsider the decision even after local feeling was demonstrated to be outraged seems to aggravate the insensitivity.

Let us confront the issue directly and ask whether John Lewis did indeed go against its stated principles in deciding to close Jones Bros. The short answer, we would argue, is that they did not go against their stated principles; for even if one takes it that the decision to close Jones Bros. violates John Lewis's principle about being sensitive to the community, the principle is only one principle among others, and some of the other principles override it. The Constitution says that 'the Partnership's ultimate aim shall be the happiness in every way of all of its members'. Because this principle states an ultimate aim or goal, it overrides the principle of sensitivity to the community where the two conflict, and in the case of Jones

Bros. the two perhaps did conflict. For one thing, from the point of view of all John Lewis's members nationwide, the limited profitability of old fashioned department stores like Jones Bros. in urban areas was more likely to keep down the level of bonuses generally, and therefore keep down the level of members' happiness, while the policy of relocating to newer shops, rather than reducing the number of shops, avoided redundancies, which kept members' happiness from falling lower still.

Now to say that John Lewis did not go against its stated principles in closing down Jones Bros. is not to say that its principles are morally good ones, or that its priorities among principles are morally good. It is perfectly possible for a company to make a decision in keeping with its principles, and for its decision to be morally wrong. Is this so in the case of John Lewis? Are its principles, and its order of priority among principles, wrong? There would be some reason to think so if it subscribed to a principle of increasing profit at all cost, and if it used this as the sole reason for closing Jones Bros. But it is clear from John Lewis's decision not to make a single one of the 400 Jones Bros. employees redundant that policies on staffing levels were not rigidly determined by profit considerations. As the 400 were given jobs in other John Lewis branches that were not previously understaffed, it appears that John Lewis was prepared to close Jones Bros. at the cost to its profits in the short term of overmanning. What about the principle that puts members' happiness first? Is this morally questionable, for example because it does not give sufficient weight to the interests of the local community or customers in cases like that of the Jones Bros. closure? The answer, we think, is that there is nothing wrong with the principle as a principle of a commercial firm, but that in the case of Jones Bros. the suddenness of the announcement of the closure and the unwillingness of the firm to solicit the views of the local community were not given sufficient weight, and, worse, were probably not publicly given any weight.

If there is any moral wrongness in the decision to close Jones Bros., it would seem to lie in the one-sidedness of the thinking behind it, rather than in a mistake of principle. It is not that a morally wrong principle was used to justify the decision, but that a morally harmless principle was the only principle to be used, or the only principle to be given much weight.[9]

## Morality and constraint: meta-ethics and Royal Dutch/Shell

In discussing the Jones Bros. case we tried to bring to bear the kinds of question and argument that philosophy might make available. We have been concerned with questions of consistency, with conflicts of principle, real and apparent, and with how to give weight to different principles.

These are very routine concerns in philosophy, but they are not particularly distinctive of moral philosophy. We would now like to turn to moral philosophy more specifically, and to questions with which it can help.

We shall be concerned here with the ways that different businesses understand their social responsibilities, and we shall be referring to mission statements and statements of business principles. Before we get to one such statement, however, we have to draw briefly upon one of the two main branches of moral philosophy, the branch that is concerned with the explanation of moral concepts, such as right, duty, obligation and so on, the branch called *meta-ethics*.

The part of meta-ethics on which we are going to rely concerns the concept of morality itself. An important feature of morality is constraint. Unlike the concept of legality, say, that of morality is not *only* concerned with constraint. But the demands of morality are very often experienced as constraints or restrictions upon one's sphere of activity. In very many cases what happens is this. Someone wants to do something that is somehow gratifying, and morality comes along and gives reason why one should not do that type of action, however gratifying it is.

The sort of reasons that morality gives for such a constraint are usually founded on very general facts of the case. For example, morality specifies that certain things that are permissible when done to rats are not allowed in the case of human beings: it implies that being a human being is by itself a reason for being spared certain types of treatment. Another very general reason for morality's prohibiting something is that it would cause pain or distress to others. Again, morality sometimes says that one course of action is worse than another, and so better avoided, because it would benefit fewer people. Though this is a different type of argument, the reason given for omitting the action is again general: one is usually told to think of the simple numbers helped, not their identities or talents, or family backgrounds. Finally, morality sometimes frowns on an action by saying that it is not the sort of action that someone with such and such a desirable character should contemplate.

In fact each of these sorts of reason corresponds to a distinctive approach to normative ethics in moral philosophy. Normative theories, inspired by the eighteenth century German philosopher Immanuel Kant, draw some of the standard moral obligations from what it is to respect persons or humanity. Utilitarian theories, usually associated with the British nineteenth century philosophers Jeremy Bentham and John Stuart Mill, try to represent moral obligations as variations on the obligation to bring about the greatest good for the greatest number. Moral obligations may also be understood as ways of developing the best sort of human character, i.e. a virtuous character: this is the approach to normative ethics sometimes called virtue theory, and associated with the Greek philosopher of the fourth century BC, Aristotle.

Now leaving aside the differences between the reasons given by these theories, the reasons have in common that they tend to act as constraints: they give people considerations against doing types of thing that they are inclined to do, e.g. acting out of lust, anger, and envy. Different attitudes toward the constraints imposed by morality are relevant to our understanding of what it is for people to be morally better or worse than one another. People who are morally upright usually wonder whether what they do or are inclined to do is all right morally, i.e. they wonder whether they are ignoring or violating constraints. People who are less upright but have moral sensitivity nonetheless, see that the existence of constraints is a reason against doing certain things, even a decisive reason, though they may not be able to rise to this realization and act accordingly. People who are completely immoral know they violate constraints but don't give the constraints much weight; and the amoral do not see what most people regard as constraints even as weak reasons against doing a thing: the constraints simply leave them cold.

Now the concept of constraint, which is so central to morality, can only be applied if there is some difference between what people are inclined to do and what they ought to do. This difference disappears either where one's natural inclinations are very elevated or, at the other extreme, where the conception of what one ought to do is very permissive. Consider the first extreme that threatens the application of the concept of constraint, the situation where people's inclinations are very elevated. This might be the situation in a community of Mother Teresas. In such a community there might never be an inclination to do a thing that, on an impartial or reasonable view, shouldn't be done: the members of the community would simply be too holy. This situation is rare, however, in normal social or business life. At the opposite extreme, where the only moral prohibition is on doing things unspontaneously or inauthentically, constraint starts to disappear because what ought to be done is defined so as to coincide pretty closely with what one feels like doing. Another, and very common, way in which the concept of constraint can disappear, or start to disappear, is where the precepts are not necessarily permissive, but where they rationalize accepted practice. And this is often how it is with statements of business principles and mission statements. They often read as if they result from a two-stage process: first, a review of the actual activities of a company; second, a formulation of objectives tailored to fit the actual activities, so that it is difficult to see how most of the activities could fail to fulfil the objectives, or, in other words, difficult to see how the objectives are genuinely demanding.

To illustrate this, let us take the objectives stated in the list of general business principles of the Royal Dutch/Shell group. These are 'to engage efficiently, responsibly and profitably in the oil, gas, chemicals, coal, metals and selected other businesses, and to play an active role in the search for and development of other sources of energy'. Do these objectives really set targets distinguishable enough from Shell's continuing activities to allow for the gap between 'is' and 'ought' or between 'what we would do anyway' and 'what we should be doing'? It might be thought that the words 'efficiently' and 'responsibly' set standards for conducting these activities that could fail to be met and hence are genuinely demanding. This impression at first appears to be borne out by what Shell goes on to say. It mentions a responsibility to society, and says that in pursuing its business activities the group undertakes to act as a responsible corporate member of society. But what in practice does this mean? According to the Shell statement itself, it primarily means business as usual. 'The most important contribution that companies can make to the social and material progress of the countries in which they operate is in performing their basic activities as efficiently as possible.'

It is true that Shell acknowledges that it is possible to go beyond business as usual in fulfilling its social responsibility, but when one looks at the annual report to find out what the additional activities falling under this heading are supposed to be, it is a remarkably mixed bag. In the 1986 annual report, for example, there is a section called 'Shell in Society', which claims credit for contributions to local communities in the form of 'payments to contractors, distributors, suppliers and financiers, remuneration to employees... as well as taxation payments to host governments'. This is exactly what we mean by raising to the level of the ethical the activities one undertakes anyway. It is rather like saying that before I make any contribution to charity or do any voluntary work, I am already doing my bit for the community because I pay taxes. An exactly parallel way of thinking would even endow many of my acts of purely self-interested consumption with a moral aspect. According to this way of thinking, when I buy my tenth Big Mac or my fourth gold watch, I am doing something morally admirable, because I keep the fast food worker in employment and help the watchmaker in Geneva see out his career until he collects his pension.

Of course some of the consequences of my purely self-interested acts do have benefits for others, but these benefits do not add to my moral credit unless the consequences were foreseen and intended *because* they benefited others. The Shell companies don't go into business in various countries so that they can pay taxes and take on employees: they go into those countries to trade profitably. The efforts of their employees contribute to this goal, and that is why they are paid. We would not deny that as a result of employing people Shell benefits them; what we are denying is that in doing so it is making a contribution from which it can claim moral credit. Other activities described in the very same section of the annual report quoted are indeed morally creditable, precisely because they are distinct enough from Shell's ordinary business activity to benefit recipients other than Shell itself. Into this category we might put their reafforestation and scholarship programmes and even their sponsorship in Australia of a foundation for helping children without the money to play tennis.

## Summary

In this chapter company codes and statements of principle have been claimed to be preferable to scandals as guides to issues in business ethics. But codes are not usually intended as *mere* guides to the issues: they are sometimes considered to be a means of *solving* moral problems thrown up by business or a means of *improving* behaviour in business. In this role they leave something to be desired. On their own they cannot be relied upon to motivate: they sometimes need to be brought to life by successful figures – Keith Erskine of Securicor may have been an example – who can make an ethical approach to business inspiring. Or they made need to be enlivened by a company culture in which ethics is second nature. And sometimes being brought to life is in its turn not enough: the codes may exhibit lack of clarity in the weighting of their principles, or they may try to give a moral gloss to activities that businesses do not deserve moral credit for. These were the problems illustrated by the discussion of the Jones Bros. closure and the Shell International statement of business principles. In identifying the problems, we have found that analytical skills routinely practised in philosophy, and applications of the branch of moral philosophy called 'normative ethics', have proved useful, and if one major theme of this chapter has been that codes have a more limited role in practical business ethics than might have been thought, then another is that philosophy also has a more extensive role than might have been thought.

But philosophy was supposed to be only one source among others for the generalist approach to business ethics endorsed at the beginning. A wide variety of sources for both the business content and ethical content of business ethics were acknowledged to be useful. Philosophy is a prominent and authoritative source of this content, but not the only one. In the next chapter normative ethics, the branch of philosophy with the most direct bearing on questions of right or wrong, will be found to have an important justificatory role in business ethics. But in subsequent chapters other sources of ethical content in business ethics, from the propaganda of interest groups to the decisions and recommendations of regulatory institutions, will also come into their own.

# References

1 Small business predominates in Germany (1,900,000 companies with fewer than 500 employees, responsible for 50 per cent of GDP), France, Italy, Spain and Holland. See C. Randlesome *et al. Business Cultures in Europe* (Oxford: Butterworth-Heinemann, 1993).
2 Karl Marx, *Capital* (1867), part 3.
3 D. Green, *The New Right* (Brighton: Wheatsheaf, 1987, pp.217ff.) Cf also W. J. Baumiol and S. Blackman, *Perfect Markets and Easy Virtue* (Oxford: Blackwell, 1991).
4 OFT Annual Report, 1990, p.24.
5 Edgar Wille, 'Ethics at the heart of business' (Ashridge Management Research Group, October 1989).
6 British Institute of Management, Professional Practice Committee, Discussion Papers, April 1991.
7 *Ibid*, p.2.
8 This discussion draws heavily on Derek F. Channon, 'Securicor', in A. Campbell and K. Tawadey, *Mission and Business Philosophy* (Oxford: Butterworth-Heinemann, 1992), pp.197–219.
9 Postscript: since the closure of Jones Bros., John Lewis has decided to build a Waitrose supermarket on the site of the old department store.

# 2 Narrow and broad business ethics

Problems with codes of ethics or statements of principle in business dominated the last chapter: we considered their lack of power to motivate, and cases were discussed in which the priorities among their precepts were unclear, and in which they set objectives too close to business as usual to be morally demanding. Another problem with moral codes in business is that of narrowness. A code of ethics for a firm is narrow when its provisions concern only those employed in the business or, in addition, only groups who are directly concerned financially, such as shareholders or current customers. By contrast, a code of ethics for a business can be said to be broad when it declares responsibilities to all those mentioned by a narrow code as well as to the community or society in general, or to the environment. Now the activities of a firm or industry can be in keeping with a broad or narrow code, whether a code is explicitly adopted or not, and business ethics in general can be said to be broad or narrow according as the code it is in keeping with is broad or narrow.

On paper, breadth in business ethics is not at all rare: as Wille's study showed, many codes of ethics acknowledge a responsibility to society or the community. Often, however, this responsibility is constrained by responsibilities to shareholders, employees and so on; and where there is a conflict between being broad or narrow, narrowness often wins as a matter of policy. Indeed there is probably a presumption in favour of extreme narrowness when, as is not uncommon, the interests of even those closest to a firm conflict. In such cases the interests of shareholders, in particular their interest in seeing high returns or dividends, are often considered to outweigh the interests of employees, suppliers and customers.

Perhaps the deepest questions in business ethics concern the justification of narrowness or breadth. If it is always wrong for some firms to ignore the interests of society but permissible for other firms to do so, what makes it right or permissible? Which of the wider interests is most urgently in need of being met? Where the interests of those most directly involved with a firm are given great weight, how far should a firm go in catering for those interests? Like some of the questions raised in the last chapter, the answers to these cannot be expected to come from codes of ethics, or business practice, or the law, or regulators' demands alone: the answers need to be arrived at with the help of theory, in particular the body of theory recognized in normative ethics in philosophy, and, further afield, in politics and ecology. Unlike the questions raised in the last chapter, however, the questions raised here will in one way or another sustain the whole book. The problem of narrowness in ethical codes, the possibility of distinguishing between the concerns of a narrow and a broad business ethics, and the conflict between the two are perhaps the central problems of business ethics.

## The justification of breadth

As a starting point for the justification of breadth in business ethics let us consider two initiatives described at a meeting in 1991 of the Marketing Forum of the UK Confederation of British Industry. The theme of the meeting was 'Corporate conscience goes to work'. Representatives of two large public companies, Grand Metropolitan and Kingfisher, gave accounts of their own ventures in social responsibility and predicted that similar activities would increasingly be included in the plans of other firms like theirs.

Grand Metropolitan is a UK-based multinational with interests in food and drinks production and retailing. In 1989 pre-tax profit was £732 million on a turnover of about £9.2 billion.[1] In his account of the Grand Metropolitan's attitude toward corporate social responsibility, Howard Chandler, Group External Relations Director, began with the acquisition of the American foods group Pillsbury, toward the end of 1988. During the period leading up to the take-over, Grand Metropolitan had given assurances that it would continue Pillsbury's philanthropic activities in its headquarters city of Minneapolis. Chandler explained that:

> Minneapolis, even by American standards, is something of an epicentre for philanthropic causes. So there was considerable apprehension in the city about Grand Met's intentions to maintain Pillsbury's record for charitable giving. It was very important to affirm our wholehearted commitment to these causes, by placing our own individual stamp on the community programmes that we wanted to support. One community leader told us in private that if we had not chosen to do this, but had just continued to make charitable contributions in perpetuity, to the same beneficiaries, it would have looked to the community as though we were doing it out of obligation, rather than by choice.[2]

The need to honour assurances made during the take-over was not the primary reason given by Chandler for committing Grand Metropolitan to charitable giving. On the contrary, local conditions in Minneapolis seemed to matter less than general attitudes toward business in America as a whole. In America, as Chandler saw things, employees and consumers expected more of business than in the UK: if businesses did not make conspicuous efforts, e.g. to demonstrate concern for the environment, or to benefit the communities from which they drew skilled labour, they would lose out in the competition for both customers and employees.[3] It was in order to satisfy general expectations, then, that companies had to associate themselves with corporate social responsibility; but companies might themselves benefit, Chandler suggested, by the economic development attending business-like philanthropy, particularly philanthropy intended to provide training. Training would improve the local workforce for the firm at the same time as it attracted public recognition.[4]

To put its own stamp on Pillsbury's charitable giving in Minneapolis, Grand Metropolitan concentrated on creating opportunities for young disadvantaged people. These activities were in line with those carried on by the firm in the UK. In 1988-9 Grand Metropolitan provided charitable support to the National Association of Boys' Clubs, the British Sports Association for the Disabled and the Civic Trust.[5] It is a member of the Per Cent Club, an association of big UK businesses pledged to donate 0.05 per cent of profit to charity, and its chairman has served as head of Business in the Community, an association of private firms and public sector bodies in Britain that, since 1981, has co-ordinated public-private partnership schemes to encourage enterprise and economic revitalization, notably in inner cities. Grand Metropolitan has also participated in certain 'green' initiatives. In the US and the UK alike it has been active in the recycling of bottles and barrels and the elimination of unnecessary packaging – significant measures for a major food and drinks manufacturer and retailer.

Kingfisher, the other major company to be represented at the CBI forum, is, like Grand Metropolitan, a member of Business in the Community. It is a retailing group, operating DIY, electrical goods, and pharmacy chains, in addition to the remaining outlets of Woolworth's in Britain. (It bought these last from the US parent company in 1982, under a previous trading name, Paternoster Stores.) In the year ending 3 February 1990 Kingfisher earned profit before tax of £295 million on turnover of nearly £3 billion.

Nigel Whittaker, the company's Corporate Affairs Director, told the CBI forum that Kingfisher's concern with social responsibility grew in the course of efforts to establish a trading identity and corporate culture for what was otherwise a miscellaneous assortment of retailing and property companies. Market research indicated that it mattered to high-street consumers whether retailers made a contribution to society or took measures to protect the environment. This finding inspired a strategy for securing commercial advantage:[6]

From Kingfisher's point of view... we can no longer rely on our financial and professional management reputation built up by our record of comparative success over the last eight years. We can no longer regard the excellent record for community involvement and enlightened employment policies of our major competitors like Marks & Spencer, Boots, W.H. Smith and Sainsbury as a luxury too expensive for companies who are fighting for survival, as we were at Woolworth's recently. So we have felt the need to pull together our own activities in this area into a consistent and unified approach which would meet the new criteria which are progressively being applied by consumers.

A first step in Kingfisher's programme of sorting out and strengthening its own commitment to social responsibility was the sponsorship of a book for companies promoting the conclusions that Kingfisher had arrived at in its own case. Summing up what would happen if other firms acted on the message of the book, Whittaker said:[7]

[C]ompanies will seek competitive advantage by being seen by consumers and others to be innovative in environmental and employee welfare, fair trading, ethical marketing and community involvement. Real benefits in those areas could become crucial, whereas token activities will be regarded as purely peripheral.

Whittaker was not urging companies to associate themselves with just any initiative that would make a name for them as commercially responsible organizations. The idea was to focus charitable giving and employee participation in activities strictly relevant to the business. In this way a gain to the community or the public could encourage a gain to the company. Grand Met, as we saw earlier, took a similar approach.
Neither company, then, promoted ventures in social responsibility for their own sake or only because morality demanded them. As the chairman of the CBI Forum session concluded, 'the discussion ... has really centred on enlightened self-interest rather than on responsibility without any return'.[8]

## Is corporate social responsibility in the corporate interest?

Two questions arise about the justification of corporate social responsibility by reference to self-interest. One is whether, all things considered, it is in the interest of business to take on these responsibilities. Another is whether, if it is in the interest of business, and if it is done primarily because it pays, it can really be described as morally creditable – as good in an ethical sense.
Two reasons for thinking that it may not be in the interest of companies to acknowledge corporate social responsibility are that it may hamper the efficiency of the market, or detract from the company's performance in the

market. These objections to programmes of corporate social responsibility are now widely shrugged off, both in the business ethics literature and in business, and it is notable that the two leading statements of the objections date from the late 1950s and early 1960s.[9] It is clear that directors of companies like Grand Metropolitan and Kingfisher do not believe that their competitive position will be harmed by their initiatives, and, in the case of Kingfisher at least, it is actually market research that has led it in the direction of doing more for the community.[10] So it is hard to believe the claim that healthy competitive trading does or must discourage corporate social responsibility. If the claim that corporate social responsibility is bad for business is to carry conviction, it cannot be a claim about just any form of business activity that benefits the community.

When the economist Milton Friedman wrote in the most widely quoted article on the subject that it was not for business to take on responsibilities other than making money, he took the case that perhaps tells most force-fully in his favour: price restraint. There does seem to be quite a lot of empirical evidence to support his claim that at times when there is upward pressure on prices, attempts at engineering price-restraint and wage restraint result in product shortages, labour shortages, grey markets and black markets: Eastern Europe provides many recent cases in point.[11] Prices do play an important part in signalling to everyone in the economy the relative scarcity of resources and the level of demand, and interference with these messages can have many unwanted economic effects for business and for the public at large. So price restraint, however well-motivated, may not be a good way of demonstrating social responsibility.

Other measures, however, may be unobjectionable. Besides the measures considered to be commercially justified by Grand Metropolitan and Kingfisher – straight charitable contributions – one can give the examples of joint public–private financing of public housing and public transport, the inclusion on boards of directors of representatives of consumer, ethnic or employee interests; the marketing of aerosols not containing CFCs, and the introduction of improved labelling and dietary information by food retailers. Not all these things are expensive, and some are profitable or attract investors.[12] All have a public relations value to companies.

Whether or not these cheap or relatively cost-free measures are more characteristic of ventures in social responsibility than price restraint, they suggest that corporate social responsibility from self-interest can take a wide enough variety of forms to require a *variety* of arguments against it. It is not enough to do as Friedman does and say that social responsibility has economic costs that bring in their train central government intervention and the replacement of the free market by a command economy.

An argument that is on its face more persuasive than Friedman's and yet also general is that it is not in the interest of business to take on social responsibilities because by doing so it interferes with the creative and pluralistic contention of interests – the interests of business, labour and government – on which a healthy society and a prosperous business sector within it depend. According to this argument, put forward by Theodore Levitt, social responsibility is not in the interest of business, because it interferes with pluralism, which is in the interest of business. As Levitt puts it:[13]

> Welfare and society are not the corporation's business. Its business is making money, not sweet music. The same goes for unions. Their business is 'bread and butter' and job rights. In a free enterprise system, welfare is supposed to be automatic; and where it is not, it becomes government's job. This is the concept of pluralism. Government's job is not business, and business's job is not government's. And unless these functions are resolutely separated in all respects, they are eventually combined in every respect.

This passage confuses pluralism, the idea that variety in society is a good thing, with the idea that specialization of function or competition is a good thing. That Levitt connects pluralism with competition comes out more clearly a paragraph or so after the passage just quoted. Levitt says in part, 'The only political function of business, labour and agriculture is to fight each other so that none remains dominant for long'.[14] But there can be pluralism in a setting in which the different groups co-operate; pluralism has no particular connection with competition. Again, there is no reason to think that every ingredient of welfare is the government's responsibility; and it does not follow, if some companies provide some services that government could be expected to provide, that companies in general or business in general will coalesce with government in general. Levitt's argument has no force against a society in which only this or that company takes on some of the responsibilities of government, or in which a wide variety of companies take on a wide variety of small-scale responsibilities, some of which the government has sometimes taken on and some of which it has not. Yet societies like these seem to be more typical of actual Western societies than ones in which business *en bloc* becomes indistinguishable from government *en bloc*. In particular, Levitt's argument does not seem to have much force against the societies in which Kingfisher or Grand Metropolitan operate. Still less does it have force in countries, such as Germany, in which the concept of a social market, a market within a significant welfare state, is the dominant conception of the market.[15]

The implication of the preceding discussion is that if corporate social responsibility is against the interest of business at all, that has to be demonstrated, type of measure by type of measure. It may be that there are good arguments from self-interest for not engaging in price restraint; it may be that there are only bad arguments from self-interest for refusing charitable giving where a business is clearly profitable. Whether the arguments are good or bad depends on the form that corporate social responsibility takes.

It is plausible to hold that it also depends on the size of the company and on trading conditions. On the face of it, it does not seem reasonable to expect the example set by Kingfisher and Grand Metropolitan to be followed even vaguely by a corner grocery or a local hairdresser's, even if they are prosperous. Businesses on so small a scale can only hope to serve a small section of society. In their case, not only the 'corporate' but also the 'social' in 'corporate social responsibility' seems to be pompously out of place. But this doesn't mean that corporate social responsibilities have no analogues at the level of small business. Local demands can identify would-be responsibilities.

Thus a small business can be asked to display a collection box for a charity, and it may lose some small sales because customers decide to put their change in it. A small business can also choose to contribute significantly to a project that is local and small-scale, deciding not to plough the money back into repairs or expansion. Each sort of venture attracts the *prima facie* objections that its counterpart in the corporate world attracts; but it is unclear that, any more than in the corporate case, self-interest lies on the side of doing nothing or giving nothing. Whether it does depends on the business and the good cause, and what the business is being asked to do for the good cause. In this sense there do not seem to be wholesale exemptions of scale, where the small, for their own sake, are let off the responsibilities that the big have to shoulder.

## Self-interest and morality: the need for moral theory

Benefiting the community, we have been suggesting, can be in the interest of businesses – small or big. But when it is in the interest of business, and when the community benefits *because* it is in the interest of business, does the benefit have moral worth? To answer this question in full generality, it is not enough to consult intuition. The resources of moral theory need to be brought to bear.

Moral theory is at its most developed in philosophy, and in philosophy different moral theories answer the question of the relation between morality and self-interest in different ways. At least one theory says that, in order to count as morally good, an act has to be performed without regard to self-interest. Other theories say that morality and self-interest are often compatible, but that, where the two conflict, self-interest must give way to morality. Still other theories say that the demands of morality promote the sort of goal – namely, happiness or well-being – that it is always in one's self-interest to promote, so that the demands of morality are always in one's interest to satisfy as well.

# Kant and Kantian theories

The theory that divorces morality from self-interest most strictly is Immanuel Kant's. Kant wrote that it was not happiness but worthiness to be happy that mattered in morality, and he denied that one could be motivated to do a thing if one expected gratification for doing it, or if one did it because that is where one took one's happiness to lie. For Kant, the demands of morality do not have an authority or a power to move people on the basis of prospects of pleasure or happiness, or, more broadly, self-interest. The demands of morality are not merely hypothetical or conditional, to be fulfilled only if the agent sees something for himself in complying with them. They are categorical. They have to be fulfilled no matter what. Kant held further that we always have a reason for fulfilling them. This is because demands must be addressed to something in the agent that cannot fail to be present if the demands of morality apply at all, and this is the agent's rationality. Kant counted as categorical demands or imperatives those that forbade lying or murder, and he would have treated in the same way most if not all of the prohibitions included in the Ten Commandments.

With its emphasis on the rigidity of moral demands and on the purity of moral motivation in an appeal to reason, Kant's moral philosophy has sometimes been accused of making morality look unattractively cold and harsh. Partly this charge has been prompted by over-attention to a book that was only supposed to clear the ground for Kant's moral philosophy, the so-called 'Groundwork' or *Foundations of the Metaphysics of Morals*.[16] In fact Kant recognizes a very large area of morality – associated with virtuous behaviour – where morality does not bind agents rigidly or determine what they are to do. For example, the requirement that one love one's neighbour does not determine which neighbour is to benefit when there is a choice between neighbours one can benefit, and in these circumstances Kant says that the agent must use his judgement. It is even morally permissible, where stricter duties do not rule it out, for the agent's attachments to other people to influence his judgement, so that he chooses to help his friends rather than perfect strangers. Similarly, the agent has leeway to decide how much of a sacrifice in the name of loving one's neighbour is too much of a sacrifice. Kant spells this out in the *Metaphysics of Morals*, the book he intended to carry the main burden of his moral theory and in which he undertook the exposition of the specific duties people were under.[17] This work does much to undo the impression of rigidity and impersonality sometimes given by Kant's ethics.

What about the idea that Kant is too much of a purist in moral theory? There is some basis for the impression, for not only does Kant refuse to count as morally good those actions which are in keeping with morality but which are done from fear, or for appearance's sake, or from a desire for financial gain; he even refuses to count as morally good those actions which are required by morality, but which are done on account of a warm and sympathetic temperament rather than the rational recognition of duty. This is a very uncompromising position but it isn't explained by a simple taste for moral purism. Rather, it has to do with a line of thought about responsibility.

According to Kant, it is one thing for agents who are warm and sympathetic to have made themselves warm and sympathetic. In that case moral credit of some kind does attach to the actions they do out of warmth or sympathy: the warmth and sympathy are things the agents are responsible for. But if, by the same token, the warmth and sympathy are simply part of the agent's make-up as a matter of natural good luck, and are nothing that the agent is responsible for, then the actions that they facilitate should not attract specifically moral credit. Moral credit or discredit attaches only where one is fully responsible for what one does. Kant does not deny that *some* kind of value – distinct from moral value – attaches to what warm and sympathetic people do. He says that their actions are 'amiable... generally useful... honourable'.[18] What he denies is that they are worth as much as the same actions done in the absence of any facilitating dispositions. That is why he sometimes uses as an example of someone who comes close to the moral ideal, the frigid figure who feels nothing for anyone else but who makes himself help someone else regardless – by sheer willpower. The frigid figure is someone who, however unfortunate in other respects, is fully responsible for his good works.

Kant associates moral worth with doing the right thing, and doing it only because it is right. In one sense this sets the standard for moral behaviour very high: most people who do right have a mixture of motives, not the pure motives that Kant requires. But in another sense the standard is low: one does not need to have a rich store of empathy or good naturedness to have moral worth in Kant's sense or to do right: one need only have rationality.

According to Kant, immorality is always irrational in some respect, and discoverably irrational at that. Indeed, by the application of some simple reflective questions, it is supposed to be possible to decide whether any contemplated course of action is moral or not. The questions one is supposed to ask can be roughly formulated like this. 'What if everyone did that?' 'Would it make sense to want everyone to do it?' By considering a policy as something universally adopted, one applies the test of *universalizability*, and many courses of action turn out not to be universalizable. Thus, if we tried to imagine a state of affairs in which everyone lied or broke their promises just as it suited them, the conditions would be lacking for lies or promises ever to be effective. Also, in willing lying to take place, one would have to be suspiciously selective about it. If one were to get anything out of lying, one would have to wish both that most others never lied, though one lied oneself, or that most others never broke their promises. But then one would and wouldn't be endorsing the policy of lying or breaking promises. One would see the drawbacks of the policy when one was on the receiving end and not want to suffer them, and yet one would be denying that they were drawbacks when someone else suffered them. But plainly the drawbacks are drawbacks whoever suffers them. In this way the irrationality of a policy of lying or breaking one's promises can be recognized, and once recognized it becomes impossible for anyone to say that, in given circumstances, there is no reason not to lie or to break a promise.

Other immoral policies are self-defeating in a different way from lying or breaking promises. They are self-defeating because they fail to reckon with inescapable facts about ourselves. Thus a policy of helping only oneself could be coherently universalized, but it would not make sense to want everyone only to help themselves, for human beings are simply not self-sufficient: when very young or very old they need help, and they need extraordinary good luck not to need help even when they are in their prime.

Kant held that, by reflecting on the ordinary concept of duty, people would come to recognize that the demands of morality were in effect policies of action that made sense for everyone to adopt and for everyone to want to adopt. That is why he recommended as a means of recognizing one's duty the so-called formula of the categorical imperative: 'Act only on those policies it is possible to will to hold as a universal law of nature'. But he held that, in addition to satisfying this formula, the demands of morality all had something to do with respecting persons, and never treating them merely as means to one's ends. And he believed that moral activity was necessarily a matter of self-rule or autonomy, where this consisted of the imposition on oneself of universal laws. So, for Kant, universalizability, respect for persons, autonomy, and duty are all concepts that give one an insight into the nature of morality.

## Kantian morality and business ethics

The difference between Kant's theory and Kantian theories in general – theories inspired by Kant but different in formulation – is usually a matter of their dropping the emphasis on purity of moral motivation and laying weight instead on the concept of respect for persons. Theories that say that certain forms of treatment are wrong because they are degrading, humiliating or manipulative, or wrong because they usurp choices that are properly the agent's, are often saying that certain forms of treatment are wrong because they violate a requirement of respect for persons. Again, moral theories that identify certain forms of treatment as violations of human rights sometimes base themselves on a conception of the treatment that humans deserve in virtue merely of what they share with all other humans. Such theories are, if not inspired by Kant's injunction to treat all human beings as ends and never merely as means to an end, at least in tune with it.

In practice, when business activities have a claim to be moral at all, they are more likely to be moral by the standards of a Kantian theory than by the standards of Kant's theory, and they are more likely to meet Kantian standards when they are activities in keeping with narrow business ethics than when they are activities in keeping with broad business ethics. To see how measures benefiting those close to a firm are sometimes in keeping with Kantian principles, consider protection for employees.

When a firm takes steps to protect its workforce from health and safety hazards, it is likely to be influenced by the thought that its employees are human beings who have a right to be spared illness, pain or danger when it is avoidable, and this thought comes close to the Kantian thought of what is required by respect for persons. Again, when a firm takes care to supply customers what they have agreed to supply, or to ask only the price agreed once a transaction has taken place, the rationale may come down to some such thought as that treatment of this kind is required by fair dealing and that people have a right to expect fair dealing, that people are misused if overcharged or if done out of goods and services that they have purchased with reasonable expectations. Perhaps it can also be understood to be out of respect for persons that businesses purport to present accounts that give current and potential investors an accurate picture of the financial position and prospects of a firm.

All these measures – minimizing health and safety hazards, not overcharging, presenting accurate accounts – belong to narrow business ethics. When it comes to broad business ethics, in particular the ventures undertaken by Grand Metropolitan and Kingfisher, it is not always so plausible that a principle of respect for persons, or indeed any recognizable moral principle, is in fact behind an activity intended to benefit society or the environment. Howard Chandler, describing Grand Metropolitan's policies, gave weight to the expectations of the public, but not because public expectations were necessarily valuable in themselves. Rather, weight was given to people's expectations because of the effects that not meeting them might have on the recruitment of workers or on consumer choices. In the case of Kingfisher also it was effects on consumer choice that mattered most. Now as we shall see, there are well worked out and substantial moral theories that enable a moral gloss to be given to the activities of Kingfisher and Grand Metropolitan, even if the rationale for them is not credibly a principle of respect for persons. But what is in question at present is whether a *Kantian* moral gloss can be given to them, and the answer seems to be 'no' twice over. From the standpoint of the theory of Kant himself the answer is 'no', because so much self-interest is mixed up with the intention to benefit the community. From the standpoint of less demanding Kantian theories the answer still appears to be 'no', because it is hard to see the measures flowing from a principle of respect for persons.

Are there any measures that a firm could implement in relation to society or the environment that are genuinely in keeping with Kantian morality? And could these activities be undertaken not only in theory but in practice, by a firm with real scale and profitability? Although the question needs more space than can be devoted to it here, it seems that the areas in which broad business ethics could prove their Kantianism would be those in which a society was seen as valuable not just because it was the source of consumption and labour, but because it had a value in itself. To bring this down to earth, one could imagine a society being valued because of a particular way of life or valuable institutions and customs. Examples of this sort of vision of society do not seem to be very numerous in business, but some accounts suggest that Body Shop International, by its willingness to learn from the cosmetic techniques of women from many different cultures, gives substance to its avowed principles of respecting foreign cultures and the past, and this may be as close as real life gets to Kantianism in broad business ethics.[19]

The fact that standard initiatives in broad business ethics are unlikely to count as fully fledged moral ones by Kantian standards may reflect badly on broad business ethics, or it may reflect badly on Kantianism. It may be that Kantianism sets its standards too high, and that the activities under-taken by Grand Metropolitan and Kingfisher do deserve to be given moral credit, or it may be that enlightened self-interest is one thing and morality another. Or again, it may be that the right way to classify most ventures in broad business ethics is as Kant classifies right actions done from natural warmth and sympathy, namely as acts that are honourable, amiable and generally useful, but acts that are, nevertheless, not all they might be, morally speaking – dutiful without being done from duty. This way of classifying acts would not necessarily undervalue partnership schemes in inner cities or training programmes for the disadvantaged; at the same time, it would acknowledge the basis there is for supposing that morality is in tension with self-interest. In this way the strengths of the Kantian framework – in particular its ability to find reasons, or a basis in reason, for complying with the demands of morality – could be preserved without supposing that just every aspect of business ethics was naturally accommo-dated by it. Such a result would seem to be satisfactory. In a sense it *ought* to be hard for a standard moral framework to accommodate every aspect of business ethics, and broad business ethics is one area where the strain is predictable.

## Utilitarianism

Earlier we distinguished between theories that say self-interest detracts from or excludes moral value and theories that allow self-interest and moral worth to co-exist. Utilitarianism is one of the latter theories. Utilitarianism does not say that an act is devoid of moral value if it serves one's interest, but neither does it say that there is a particularly close connection between morality and self-interest. What it does instead is to identify morally right action with what produces the greatest amount of well-being, whether or not the action also serves the narrow interest of the one doing it.

Applied to the case of Grand Metropolitan and its charitable activities in Minneapolis, utilitarianism would not necessarily offer the criticism that by going in for these activities Grand Metropolitan was thinking of itself, for if the benefits in aggregate to the community were big enough, that would not matter; if anything, utilitarianism might criticize Grand Metropolitan for being preoccupied with setting its own stamp on its policies of charitable giving. If more people benefited by a simple continuation of the Pillsbury schemes for charitable giving, then, according to utilitarianism, those are the schemes that should have been continued, notwithstanding any failure of Grand Metropolitan to establish itself as a philanthropic firm in its own right in Minneapolis. In the case of Kingfisher utilitarianism might imply that, morally, the relevance of a programme of charity to a firm's activities is less important than how many people benefit, or how great the benefit is if it is only enjoyed by the few.

Utilitarianism is sometimes summed up in the precept that one should try to achieve the greatest good for the greatest number. Some of the difficulties with the theory emerge by asking for elucidation of the term 'good' and the phrase 'greatest good'. Depending on the particular version of utilitarianism being expounded, 'good' can cover a variety of things. It can cover currently experienced pleasures, bodily and intellectual; it can cover desirable states like health; if can be restricted to things that it makes sense to desire if one is under no illusions or if one is being rational; it can refer to the things close to the top of an order of preferences. Not all these candidates for the role of 'goods' are compatible with all others. For instance, it is clear that some experienced pleasures can cause damage to one's organs or big risks of disease, and so the policy of producing as much of these pleasures as possible would conflict with that of satisfying rational preferences or desires, which would allow the damage or the risk to counterbalance the good of experiencing pleasure.

So much for questions arising from different utilitarian ideas of the good to be maximized. Next comes the idea of the greatest good. This presupposes that goods can be added up, and therefore measured or quantified, and that different goods can be compared. But there are difficulties in measuring goods, for people's preferences differ in many different ways, more than one of which may be relevant to a utilitarian calculation. Suppose that someone is positively obsessive, so that he has a strong preference over practically everything else for seeing a particular movie star. So strong is the preference that he spends each day for a year camped on the star's doorstep. How is the good of satisfying this admittedly strong preference to be compared with the satisfaction of a weaker desire for something that may be urgently necessary for survival, like a course of unpleasant medical treatment? A way of ranking preferences by urgency, strength, and perhaps the importance or necessity of what they are preferences *for*, is indispensable to utilitarianism if it is to guide decisions between doing one thing and doing another on the basis of the good produced.

Some critics of utilitarianism have doubted that any such ranking is possible even in theory, since they have doubted that there is any one scale in which, for example, a momentary desire to scratch one's nose could be compared with, say, a desire felt over a lifetime to be the first to prove some mathematical theorem. But even if this problem – sometimes called the problem of incommensurability – can be met, and even if a method is devised that arrives by uncontroversial steps at a conclusion about the benefit produced by satisfying the strong desire for seeing the movie star as opposed to the weaker desire for the unpleasant medical treatment, utilitarianism may still be criticized for permitting, and sometimes requiring, the satisfaction of immoral preferences. That is, utilitarianism permits and can even require, the satisfaction of what are, intuitively, evil or unjust preferences if they are widely enough shared. A common illustration is the mob's strong desire for an arrest after a horrible crime. Because so many want an arrest so badly, utilitarianism may require an arrest even of someone who is innocent; or utilitarianism may be criticized for needing restrictions that shield it from this sort of implication. If utilitarianism says that the desires or preferences it is going to bring into its calculations exclude the unjust or immoral ones, then it is not letting the calculation itself determine what is just or moral, as it is supposed to.

There is more than one version of utilitarianism. A common way of distinguishing between different versions is according to whether utility is attached to individual acts or to rules. Act utilitarianism assesses each act for the good it produces, and says that one ought to perform the act that in one's circumstances produces the most good. Rule utilitarianism is where individual acts are assessed as either being consistent with, or violating, rules for promoting the greatest good. 'Don't lie' would be an example of one of those rules; 'Keep promises' would be another. These rules are not merely breakable rules of thumb, summarizing what usually promotes the general welfare on the basis of past experience, but are guides to practice put forward on the understanding that binding rules contribute more to the general welfare than non-binding rules or no rules. So the onus in rule utilitarianism is on anyone who wanted to break the rule to show that this produced more good than not breaking it.

How do these versions of utilitarianism apply to business? Beauchamp and Bowie give an example of Italian taxation practice where act utilitarianism seems to work better than rule utilitarianism.[20] They describe how, by convention, firms in Italy under-declare their liabilities to tax, and negotiations that result in firms agreeing to pay more tax then take place. A multinational firm that was new to Italy, and that calculated its tax liabilities correctly and honestly the first time, fell foul of this arrangement, as it was taken to be under-declaring, and it was required to pay a tax bill higher than it should have. Act utilitarianism might have recommended compliance with accepted Italian practice rather than with the rule of telling the truth. But rule utilitarianism comes into its own when what is in question is the claim of utilitarianism to be a morality.

The matter is perhaps clearest where two courses of action are available, where the benefits produced by one are agreed to be only marginally greater than the benefits produced by the other, but where the action with only marginally greater benefit calls for lying, say, and the other does not. To illustrate, suppose that news of a big order being placed with a firm raises the value of shares in that firm held by charities, but that the value would be a little higher for a while if a lie is told about the timing of the order. Let us stipulate that the lie has no further effects. Both courses of action, then, produce money for the charities, but the course of action requiring the lie produces a little more. Here act utilitarianism demands that one tell the lie, because the benefits of doing so outweigh the ill-effects of the lie in the circumstances. The problem, however, is that too little seems to be accomplished by lying in the case under discussion. One's stubborn intuition is that if only a little less benefit would be produced by not lying at all, then it is morally better to refrain from lying. This intuition, natural as it is, is strongly opposed to act utilitarianism.

Not unnaturally, a number of philosophers have tried to formulate a version of utilitarianism that exploits the strengths of both rule and act utilitarianism. One formulation along these lines has been put forward by R.M. Hare,[21] who describes an ideal utilitarianism that would result if the rules of rule utilitarianism were able to be subjected to critical reflection that took into account and gave due weight to the peculiarities of the situations of agents deciding what to do.

## Aristotelianism

Utilitarian theories do not say that there must be a tension between morality and self-interest; but neither do they hold that the demands of morality and self-interest are usually in harmony. Other theories do imply that morality and self-interest harmonize. These are associated with Plato and Aristotle, two philosophers who lived and taught in ancient Greece. We shall be concerned with Aristotle's theory, which defines, and gives a rationale for the practice of, some central virtues. Because of its association with Aristotle, the theory of virtues in general is sometimes called 'Aristotelianism' in ethics; and because problems with the theory have led to various departures from Aristotle, sometimes 'neo-Aristotelian' theories will be in question.

Both the original and the revised Aristotelian theories hold that morality or virtue is beneficial to us and in our interest, and that we should be moral or virtuous because it is beneficial to be moral or virtuous. It is in our interest to be so. According to an Aristotelian theory, virtue is the path to true happiness or flourishing, and it is for the sake of true happiness or flourishing that it makes sense to be courageous, to be just, or to be temperate, i.e. to exercise the cardinal moral virtues. Flourishing or true happiness is the highest good, the good that does not itself need anything to justify pursuing it, and that itself is a solid justification for pursuing anything else that secures it for one. On this much all Aristotelian theories seem to be agreed. Where they disagree is over the way of life that best exemplifies flourishing or true happiness, the attributes one has to have in order to pursue this way of life with any chance of success, and the exact classification of the virtues and vices apart from the cardinal ones.

For Aristotle, the best example of a virtuous person, and therefore of a person who has a good chance of flourishing, is a figure who is responsible for great deeds and is worthy of great honour, someone with a keen (but not distorted) sense of his own worth and of the relative worth of other people. Aristotle seems to have had in mind a sort of heroic figure – a great statesman, say, or an exceptional military leader. In such a person the cardinal virtues of courage, justice and temperance are exercised not in everyday acts but in response to really formidable tests of character. Aristotle calls the sort of figure we have partially described *megalopsychos*, sometimes translated as 'great-souled' or 'magnanimous'. 'Magnificent' might be a better term: in any case, what Aristotle's choice of this figure suggests is that there is a connection between flourishing or true happiness in the fullest sense and grandeur. Or, in other words, in order really to flourish it is important not only to be virtuous but to exercise the virtues to exceptional effect, so that one stands apart from and above the generality of people. It is a conception that we take to be remote from that of most people in the West today, for it implies that only a select few have it in them to be fully moral.

A more familiar view is that everyone has it in them to be moral, but that a minority – saints and heroes, let's say – have it in them to be more than that. Saintliness not only implies doing nothing wrong, it requires a person to do a great deal of good, and in ways that go far beyond what is required by social duty. Saints are not merely morally upright but holy. Holiness may be an ideal of the moral life, but it is not necessarily typical of the moral life, and may not even be the best example of a moral life in the sense of being an example of the moral life that others feel they can and want to follow. Better examples of the moral life in this sense may be the lives of people who are not saintly but decent, who respond as they should to routine moral demands as they arise, but who do not necessarily dedicate their lives to doing good.

The difference between taking the morally decent man as morally exemplary and taking, with Aristotle, the heroic or magnificent man as morally exemplary goes deep. Aristotle believed that there was an intimate connection between morality and politics. Someone who was fully virtuous and who led the best sort of human life would not only exercise his courage, justice and temperance for the benefit of his friends and family; he would put his virtue at the service of his city by acting as law-maker and magistrate. Aristotle did not believe that such public service was for everyone: he believed in aristocracy rather than democracy. Aristocracy meant rule by the best, not rule by those who were merely wealthy or who were born with titles. Democracy meant rule by the many or by the crowd, not rule by parliament.

In its ideal form aristocracy would consist of rule by those who were morally best – those who were most virtuous. Now Aristotle believed that the wealth, high birth, and good upbringing associated with aristocracy in the ordinary sense were necessary for virtue, so that in practice rule by the morally best – moral aristocracy – would probably have been for him rule by the best of the ordinary aristocracy. However, this does not seem to have been an essential ingredient of his moral theory. What matters more, and what matters specially to finding the source of the difference between Aristotle's view and a more modern one, is the idea that virtue at its fullest is virtue affecting public life, and that public life should be the sphere exclusively of the best: this is what seems to produce his choice of the heroic or great figure as the exemplary moral figure. The heroic or great figure has the stature required for public life as Aristotle conceives it. For us, on the other hand, the morally exemplary figure can apparently be apolitical, can apparently lack a public or political life altogether. This allowance for a moral life that is private or personal rather than public, may make it easier for us to conceive the decent rather than the great as morally exemplary.

## Neo-aristotelianism

Revisions of Aristotle in our own day usually keep the idea that virtue contributes to true happiness, but they drop Aristotle's conception of the sort of character that best exemplifies virtue. For example, Phillipa Foot, one of the main exponents in our day of a revised Aristotelian theory, pictures the truly virtuous person as someone who is spontaneously and unhesitatingly benevolent. She quotes a description of such a figure from a novel by John Hersey. The character has just rescued someone from a swift, flowing river:[22]

> It was the head tracker's marvellous swift response that captured my admiration at first, his split second solicitousness when he heard a cry of pain, his finding in mid-air, as it were, the only way to save the injured boy. But there was more to it than that. His action, which could not have been mulled over in his mind, showed a deep, instinctive love of life, a compassion, an optimism, which made me feel very good...

Evidently Foot's choice of exemplary figure associates virtue in the fullest sense with decency rather than grandeur. Though the act of jumping in to save the drowning person is courageous, even heroic in the ordinary sense of 'heroic', the person who does the act is not a hero in the sense of a hero of an epic poem – someone who gets the better of countless foes against tremendous odds without ever doing anything underhand. There is no hint in Foot's account that true virtue attaches only to grand gestures performed by great men; on the contrary, for her, it is within the capacities of most or all adults to acquire the virtues, and, along with other twentieth century commentators, she thinks that the virtues are beneficial to those who lead relatively ordinary lives. Thus courage may be necessary for riding a bicycle in central London or for undergoing a course of medical treatment, and not only for the great ordeals of war, say. Justice is useful not only when it comes to formulating legislation or passing sentence, but also, for example, in confronting the recurrent and everyday problem of how to divide one's time and energy between one's career and one's family, where competing but legitimate demands need to be given different weight at different times.

Though revised Aristotelian accounts such as Foot's diverge from Aristotle's, they are nevertheless virtue theories and concerned with the cultivation of a few selected traits of character. Aristotle thought of the moral virtues as character traits that corrected some typical excesses and deficiencies of human beings. Courage was supposed to correct the defects of, on the one hand, cowardice, and, on the other hand, recklessness. Temperance introduced a measured attitude to pleasure and corrected the defects of, on the one hand, over-indulgence, and, on the other, excessive austerity. It is harder to give a neat pair of the defects that justice corrects. Meanness and profligacy would be one pair in the sphere of just distribution, lenience and severity would be another pair, appropriate to penal justice. But these three – courage, temperance, and justice – were taken to be the chief virtues.

They are a reasonable selection to make if one denies that flourishing is primarily to do with pleasure, primarily to do with wealth, or primarily to do with power or honour. Aristotle's theory was developed with an awareness of these different conceptions of flourishing, and up to a point in opposition to them. What Aristotle's account denies is that pleasure, wealth, power and so on can really be things for whose sake all activity is conducted. They cannot individually be what flourishing consists of, for we can think of lives dedicated to the pursuit of them that would not be desirable. Not that power, wealth, honour and pleasure are worthless, or that they cannot contribute to flourishing. They can contribute to flourishing, but only when the pursuit of them is kept under control by the virtues – the pursuit of wealth and power by justice; the pursuit of honour by courage, and the pursuit of pleasure by temperance. In neo-Aristotelian accounts the list of virtues associated with flourishing is longer than Aristotle's list of three. Generosity, honesty, friendship, conscientiousness, prudence and many other virtues might be added to those emphasized by Aristotle. Indeed the richness of the vocabulary for describing character is one reason why some modern exponents of virtue theory have found it more attractive than its rivals.

## Applications of virtue theory in business

Virtue theory, or at least the vocabulary that might be used to talk about virtue, has its uses in business ethics as well as in public relations that are designed to bring into prominence the ethics of a business. Not only might a firm want to be known for having employees with a certain character that the language of the virtues might be used to describe, but the challenges of business in general are commonly written about in academic, journalistic and practitioners' publications in ways that make them resemble testing military and diplomatic situations, precisely the situations to which the early theorists of the virtues paid particular attention.

To focus the question of whether virtue theory has application to business, let us return to the activities of Kingfisher and Grand Metropolitan and ask whether virtue theory provides a framework in which their ventures in social responsibility can be regarded as morally valuable and self-interested at the same time. The answer would be 'yes' if the goal being promoted by these ventures was that of flourishing or well-being, either the flourishing of individuals in the two firms, or the firms themselves, and if the ventures themselves were cases of practising charity or justice. It is unclear, however, whether the conditions for either charity or justice are met. It is unclear that conditions for justice are met because it is not assumed that the beneficiaries of, for example, the two firms' cash contributions are owed what they receive; and justice is the virtue of giving

NARROW AND BROAD BUSINESS ETHICS 47

people what is due to them, as opposed to what they might enjoy or benefit from. In the case of charity the welfare of the beneficiary has to be paramount for the giver, or, where charity is theologically understood, the love of God has to be paramount for the one who is being charitable: neither of these conditions is met if we are to go by what we have quoted from Messrs Chandler and Whittaker. The welfare of the beneficiaries matters to the two firms, of course, but it is not the crucial thing in the activities undertaken by Grand Metropolitan or Kingfisher. So we have not found in virtue theory a way of representing those activities as moral and self-interested at the same time.

## Ethical egoism

An ethical theory that coheres better than virtue theory with what Grand Metropolitan and Kingfisher thought they were doing is ethical egoism, which says that people ought to do whatever it is in their best interest to do, and allows people to do things for others if that would prevent something damaging to their interest, or if the benefits to others end up producing a net benefit to themselves. Ethical egoism outlaws pure altruism, where one acts to benefit others and there is no benefit to oneself, and it tells against courses of action where, though one gets something out of what one does for others, one does not recoup one's costs. On the other hand, ethical egoism also tells against pure selfishness and pure self-centredness, which may prove counter-productive or go against one's interests in the long run. Ethical egoism thus proves a basis for some of the same precepts as other-regarding moralities such as Kantianism or utilitarianism, but the basis for the precepts turns out to be incompatible with that given by the other-regarding moralities.

The theorist most closely associated with ethical egoism is the seventeenth century English philosopher Thomas Hobbes, who wrote some important treatises on morals and politics in the 1640s and 1650s. Hobbes believed that if people were left free to pursue their interests without the hindrances of a coercive system of law, there would be nothing to prevent everyone resorting to the extremes of violence and deception to get what they wanted. In other words, in the absence of coercive law, there might be all-out war. What is more, this war would not necessarily be conditional on each person's violently pursuing greedy policies. It could just as well be conditional on the fearful and modest reluctantly taking preventive action against the greedy. Since this possibility of war was itself a threat to anyone's getting what they wanted or keeping it, however, everyone had an interest, whatever their particular goals were, in submitting to a sovereign authority that would secure individual lives and well-being. In general, according to Hobbes, everyone had a reason for keeping to certain patterns of behaviour that prevented conflict – patterns of behaviour in any case prescribed by morality. The means by which submission to a sovereign authority was to be declared was a promise of each agent to every other – a social contract – that each would let a sovereign determine what was required by peace and security if everyone else did.

The concept of a social contract is an important one in moral theory, with natural applications to business ethics. In many countries businesses are afforded privileges, most notably that of limited liability, and they may be readily viewed as operating within a social contract entailing a range of responsibilities to society. In a similar vein, the considerable power of large multinational companies, which often exceeds that of nation states, may be argued to carry with it proportionately large responsibilities.[23] Though Hobbes's original version of the social contract was derived from an assumption of ethical egoism, the concept does not rest on that assumption. It is quite possible to argue for a social contract without being an ethical egoist.

However, the device of a social contract based on self-interest does seem particularly appropriate as a justification for some forms of business help to the community. For instance, in a period in which the differences in income between rich and poor are particularly marked, and company profits or directors' salaries are particularly high and receive publicity because they are high, increases in amounts of charitable giving may be in order if firms are to relieve possible pressure for higher corporation tax or lower prices. In the same circumstances business may press for increased spending on welfare measures by the government in order to pre-empt violent action by, or on behalf of, the most disadvantaged. In other words, individual businesses or the business community may take steps to see to it that those who benefit least by remaining peaceable and law-abiding are given an incentive to keep on being law-abiding or to maintain the social contract. More specifically, the social contract idea allows the choice of certain forms of help to be justified by what people in society expect – since it might be one of the background conditions for the maintenance of the contract that the behaviour of each of the parties to the contract be easy to predict. So the egoistic social contract would accommodate the thinking behind Grand Metropolitan's decision to continue activities that people in Minneapolis had become accustomed to Pillsbury conducting, for example.

Ethical egoism has a certain naturalness as a framework for justifying corporate social responsibility and is the framework that seems to be implicit in the thinking of real firms engaged in real ventures in social responsibility. It is also perhaps a natural moral counterpart to the prevailing political philosophy of free-market capitalism, in which the economic pursuit of self-interest by competing businesses is supposed to be for the benefit of all. But even with the addition of a social contract, ethical egoism as generally interpreted is not very convincing as a general moral framework. In particular, it has no room for any actions beyond those implied by the social contract. Certain acts that call for a great deal of self-sacrifice, and that might therefore ordinarily be regarded as close to ideal morally, should not be done at all. It is even possible to interpret ethical egoism to be saying that it is morally wrong to perform acts that are heroic or saintly.[24]

## Moral theory and the presumption against self-interest

According to the preceding discussion, ventures in corporate social responsibility that are in a firm's self-interest can also have moral worth. This is not only how it is according to ethical egoism: utilitarianism allows self-interested acts to be morally right, and so does virtue theory. Kantianism allows self-interested acts to have significant value, even if not moral value. On the other hand, it is hard to find a convincing moral theory that both allows self-interested acts to have moral value and does not demand acts that go *beyond* self-interest. A convincing moral theory might well imply that the initiatives of Grand Metropolitan and Kingfisher had moral worth, but it would probably also imply that Grand Metropolitan and Kingfisher had obligations to do further things that they might *not* regard as in their self-interest, and that they might refuse to do. As a large-scale retailer of meat and meat products, Grand Metropolitan might be affected by utilitarian arguments implying that certain common animal-rearing practices are wrong: perhaps the balance of utility would recommend purchases of meat from suppliers that shunned the practices but that were more expensive. Kingfisher, with its DIY outlets, might be affected by utilitarian arguments about the need to reduce the sale of certain increasingly rare timbers, or by arguments from utilitarianism and other moral theories for special promotion of energy-efficient home appliances in its electrical goods shops. These arguments would have more than their usual force if it was on a utilitarian basis that the *charitable giving* of these firms was supposed to have moral value. If it takes a utilitarian framework to endow certain acts of corporate giving with moral worth, and if moral credit is going to be claimed for those acts, moral *dis*credit has to be admitted for other acts shown in a *bad* light by utilitarianism.

Leaving aside Kingfisher and Grand Metropolitan, moral theories are likely to make particularly big demands of firms that establish themselves in a community where they constitute a major concentration of money and skill, and where there is a big background need for money and skill. This would be so in many Third World countries, for example. Again, moral theories are likely to make big demands where firms have useful resources in a time of emergency, even where the emergency takes place in a rich country. At the uncontroversial end of a spectrum of different cases a merchant fleet operator might have its ships commandeered for war duty, or the communications facilities of a mining firm with operations in the wilderness might be enlisted in a search for missing persons. At the other end of the spectrum the disused but habitable houses of a property speculator might be taken over to relieve homelessness. In such cases the demands of morality may introduce forms of corporate social responsibility that are very far from being justified by self-interest. Nor need the emergencies that justify measures against the self-interest of business be short-lived or sudden, like those we associate with hurricanes or earthquakes. The indebtedness of Third World countries might constitute a long-term emergency that justified banks taking big losses. And the large imbalances between incomes in Northern economies and incomes in Southern economies might contribute to a moral argument for allowing, for example, the manufacture of textiles and other goods to be transferred without economic penalties to Southern economies from Northern ones. The transfer might be required even if it meant that Northern textile manufacturers had to try to adapt to the production of other goods or a narrower range of textile goods.

Emergencies and crises apart, moral theory would demand that certain firms whose activities caused pollution or reduced the stock of valuable animal and vegetable life paid for cleaning up the pollution or for replacing, where possible, the stock it had taken away. These measures would be identified by moral theories as requirements of justice, whether that was understood in terms of virtue theory or a social contract, or as a Kantian categorical imperative. Such requirements would have to be met whether or not it was in the interest of a firm to do so. In the same way a business might have to publicize and undertake to correct a manufacturing fault at great expense to itself in money and bad publicity; or it might have to accept the disproportionate imposition of duty or tax on its products and a reduction in demand for them in the interest of public health. This is how the treatment of cigarettes in many Western countries might be morally justified. In all these cases the demands of self-interest would be overridden.

Self-interest is no more guaranteed to harmonize with the demands of narrow business ethics than with the demands of broad business ethics. For instance, it may be in the interest of businesses to be free to discontinue the employment of women who need to take maternity leave; and yet this policy leaves women employees who want to be parents at a disadvantage in relation to men in the same jobs who want to be parents. It is thus arguable that justice demands the provision of maternity leave. Again, it may be in the interest of a business to present accounts over a period of several years in such a way that profits are shown to increase steadily over those years; yet the demands of truth-telling may argue for the presentation of figures that show the firm to be erratically in profit and loss over the period.

# Broadness, narrowness and moral priorities

We have seen that moral theory sometimes makes demands in keeping with self-interest and sometimes makes demands that conflict with self-interest. Only ethical egoism rules out the possibility of conflict between morality and self-interest altogether, and it is not a very plausible theory. Virtue theory allows for a conflict, since some kinds of things that are in one's narrow self-interest do not promote flourishing, which is more fundamentally in one's self-interest and which is what morality promotes. As for Kantianism and utilitarianism, they explicitly allow for a conflict, and they say that the demands of morality override those of self-interest when there is a clash. A moment ago we gave some examples of the sort of measure that might be called for where morality demanded one thing and self-interest another in the sphere of narrow business ethics; and, before that examples of what morality might require in the area of broad business ethics were given. It would not be hard to think of cases where these demands conflicted with the demands of self-interest in broad business ethics. For example, the money required to clean up pollution might simply exhaust the funds that a company had set aside for help of all kinds to the community, including help to the community that would enhance its image as a corporate philanthropist.

So much, then, for conflicts between morality and self-interest. But what about conflicts within the sphere of morality itself? For may it not happen, in the sphere of narrow business ethics, that, for example, moral duties to employees and moral duties to creditors recommend incompatible courses of action? And may it not happen, in the sphere of broad business ethics, that duties to a local community and duties to care for the environment cannot be discharged simultaneously if a firm is to stay solvent? Finally, is it not equally possible for there to be a conflict between the moral demands of narrow business ethics and the moral demands of broad business ethics, as when a labour-intensive but highly polluting manufacturing process could be replaced by something much cleaner, but at great financial cost and at the cost of significant unemployment?

Conflicts of this kind are not merely conceivable; they are typical of ethics generally, and of business ethics in particular. Unlike an individual person, a business is an essentially economic entity, and can act in the moral sphere only through the actions of its employees and agents, which actions it must pay for. Any moral act, in this situation, is likely to carry an economic cost, which must be met by depriving some other party (often the shareholders) of something they would otherwise receive.

Apart from the utilitarian precept of maximizing the total good, moral theory presents us with no simple method of resolving this type of problem. We can only respond by making practical judgements as to what is the appropriate balance of behaviour in any particular case, and while these judgements may be informed by moral argument, that argument will often not lead to a definitive conclusion. Sometimes the conflicts of responsibility may be avoidable or preventable, and there are good moral reasons for arranging a firm's or a society's affairs so that the probability of facing the conflicts is minimized. Up to a point the law in Western industrial countries works to assist this process, though there is no neat legal formula for dealing with the situation, any more than there is a philosophical one. Philosophy can lead us to the relevant considerations. It can get us to ask how many people are affected on each side of the conflict, and how much of a difference to any one of those the conflicting courses would make. It can get us to ask which rights would be affected by doing one thing rather than another. But the relevant considerations may not favour one resolution of the conflict over another. In short, there are limits to what moral theory can accomplish even on what we might regard as its home ground.

## Summary

In most of this chapter moral philosophy has been plundered as a source of justifications for broad business ethics. Different theories from moral philosophy have been consulted in an attempt to say what makes it right for a firm to give money to charities or to start inner city skills training, or to offer other sorts of help to the community. Along the way the same theories have sometimes been brought to bear in the justification of policies in narrow business ethics. Thus, a principle of respect for persons might justify certain ways of safeguarding the health of employees or of keeping faith with investors. Theories from moral philosophy offer a wide array of justifications, often convincing ones, for narrow and broad business ethics alike. But theories do not prevent conflicts of moral demands from arising, and they provide no simple method for resolving these conflicts. We should add that there are certain issues which, predictably, the theories do not engage in what are intuitively the appropriate terms. Issues surrounding the treatment of animals are probably not even addressed, let alone satisfactorily resolved, by the Kantian super-principle of respect for persons; and issues concerning the treatment of the environment tend to be discussed as if the environment had no claim of its own to considerate treatment, as if it mattered only because certain treatments of it had bad consequences for humans or other animals. It is in considering these issues that we may have to look at times outside moral philosophy, or at least traditional moral philosophy, for a suitable theoretical apparatus. Questions about the ethics of dealings with animals and the environment will be raised toward the end of this book, when we return to specific issues in broad business ethics. Before that we shall consider in very much more detail the demands of narrow business ethics.

# References

1  R. Adams, J. Carruthers and Sean Hamil (eds), *Changing Corporate Values: A guide to social practice and environmental policy and practice in Britain's top companies* (London: Kogan Page, 1990), p.232.

2  *Business Ethics: A European Review,* 1 (1991), p.33.

3  *Ibid.,* p.32.

4  *Ibid.,* pp.33–34.

5  Adams *et al, op.cit.,* p.284.

6  *Business Ethics: A European Review,* 1 (1991), p.39.

7  *Ibid.,* pp.39–40.

8  *Ibid.,* p.40.

9  T. Beauchamp and N. Bowie, *Ethical Theory and Business* (Englewood Cliffs, NJ: Prentice-Hall, 1983), articles by Milton Friedman and Theodore Levitt.

10 Marks & Spencer and the Halifax Building Society are active in schemes involving secondments of their staff to the housing charity Shelter in the UK. The secondments aid staff development, particularly in the form of exposure to different organizational cultures.

11 Beauchamp and Bowie, *op.cit.,* p.82.

12 A study published in June 1992 by the British National Children's Homes disclosed that while only 7 per cent of businesses believe new shareholders are likely to invest in a firm that works with charities, 78 per cent of shareholders say they would rather buy shares in such a company themselves.

13 Beauchamp and Bowie, *op.cit.,* p.84.

14 Ibid., p.85.

15 C. Randlesome, W. Brierley, K. Bruton, C. Gordon and P. King, *Business Cultures in Europe* (Oxford: Butterworth-Heinemann, 1993), p.3.

16 Immanuel Kant, *Foundations of the Metaphysics of Morals* (original edition, 1785). There are many editions and translations, a standard one being by L.W. Beck (Indianapolis: Bobbs-Merrill, 1959).

17 Immanuel Kant, *Metaphysics of Morals* (original edition, 1797). Part 1 has been translated by John Ladd, *The Metaphysical Elements of Justice* (Indianapolis: Bobbs-Merrill, 1965), and part 2 by Mary J. Gregor as *The Doctrine of Virtue* (Philadelphia: University of Pennsylvania Press, 1964 and 1971).

18 Kant, *Foundations.* The pasage quoted is from *Kants gesammelte Schriften* (Berlin: Walter de Gruyter), volume VI, p.399.

19 Sally Yeung, 'The Body Shop International – The most honest cosmetic company in the world', Ashridge Strategic Management Centre Case Study, 1991, p. 3.

20 Beauchamp and Bowie, *op. cit.,* pp. 276–79.

21 R. M. Hare, *Moral Thinking* (Oxford: Oxford University Press, 1981).

22  Phillipa Foot, *Virtues and Vices* (Oxford: Blackwell, 1978), pp.4–5.
23  See Tom Donaldson, *The Ethics of International Business* (Oxford: Oxford University Press, 1989).
24  An ethical egoism that was defined in terms of 'enlightened' self-interest would not be subject to these criticisms, but to develop such a theory we should first have to define 'enlightened', and this would lead us back to one of the other moral theories as a foundation. In a Christian context, for example, enlightened self-interest would judge an act by how it would affect one's prospect of going to heaven. An enlightened recognition of the benefits of being virtuous or dutiful might lead us back to Aristotelian or Kantian ethics, and so on.

# Part Two

# Narrow Business Ethics

# 3 Consumers

Businesses acknowledge responsibilities to a number of groups that are financially connected with them, and of these the largest is made up of consumers. Indeed, when people talk of the responsibilities of large consumer goods manufacturers, they often equate consumers with the public at large. It is true that nearly every member of the public is a consumer. Nevertheless, a firm's responsibilities to consumers are not the same as its responsibilities to the public. Even a monopoly supplier of things that practically everyone in the developed world uses, such as telephones or electricity, has duties to those who pay for telephones and electricity that it does not owe to other members of the public. The position is clearer in the case of a supplier of products and services with a very limited clientele: the supplier has responsibilities to its own consumers that are not responsibilities to consumers in general, let alone society or the public in general. To the extent that these responsibilities are moral, they belong to narrow, not broad, business ethics.

Obvious as these points may seem, they do not go without saying. In many societies, notably the UK in the 1990s, 'consumer' is often used as a synonym for 'citizen', and consumer rights are often run together with citizens' rights. This very inclusive sense of the term is misleading. Yet it is not easy to find a better word than 'consumer' for what is under discussion. 'Customer', which is less misleading, is too narrow. It does not cover those cases where the consumer of a company's product, e.g. a food product, is not a customer of that company but of an intermediary, e.g. a supermarket. Nor will 'customer' do when it comes to talking about consumer magazines, consumer groups or consumerism. For the most part, this chapter concerns consumers in the sense of buyers of a firm's products who are individual members of the public.[1] But occasionally – the context will make it clear when – 'consumer' needs to be stretched so that it applies to any potential buyer or any potential user of a service or product.

## Consumers as kings, consumers as victims

Rhetoric about consumers provides two conflicting images of the people who buy things. In one image consumers are discerning, demanding and need to be deferred to. Thus the slogan, 'The consumer is king' or 'The customer is always right'. At other times consumers are potential victims who need to be defended by the law, by individual firms' consumer charters, consumer protection schemes, and by consumer journalism and television. The rhetoric that conjures up the first image is usually to do with the economic dependence of firms on consumers. Firms that want to stay in business have to sell things that people want to buy, on terms that will make the buying easy and pleasant. If a willingness to take trouble to accommodate the consumer – a willingness to treat the customer as king – is expressed by the style of selling, then that, too, is justified by the dependence of seller on buyer. A business is after all at the mercy of the economic power of its customers and consumers, who are always being enticed to buy from competitors; so it pays to do what it takes to keep one's customers loyal, including treating them as kings.[2]

On the surface the rhetoric associated with the image of the consumer as potential victim has a very different thrust. It emphasizes the financial sophistication of business people in comparison with the typical customer, and it usually takes the point of view of the individual consumer whose economic power may be small, rather than the combined economic power of the many. The message of this second sort of rhetoric is that, since consumers are weak and the firms that they buy from are strong, consumers need protection, and need it on the moral grounds there always are for protecting the weak from the strong.

Although the images we have before us are not very similar, the rhetoric in both cases is decidedly pro-consumer, and fussy customers who also know how to exploit the protections extended to the unwary or the ill-informed benefit twice over by making firms treat them now as kings and now as victims. In what follows we shall first consider whether there are sometimes moral or other grounds for *not* deferring to a customer, even if it is economically advantageous to do so; and, symmetrically, whether there are sometimes cases where firms have commercial grounds for being excused from the duties attending consumer protection. The suggestion toward which we will be led is that the pro-consumer drift of the familiar types of rhetoric is sometimes overdone. There are occasions when consumers are over-deferred to for the sake of more business or overprotected at the expense of business. To recognize this is not to repudiate the bulk of the protections to consumers that are either voluntarily complied with or legally enforced: most of these are in any case morally justified by the need to protect human beings from avoidable harm. It does, however, mean thinking twice about how much is justified by the bare fact that a lot of consumers want something, or by the fact that someone who asks for something has the status of a consumer.

## Consumer demands with moral costs

It can sometimes be morally expensive to give the customer what he wants. At one extreme of a spectrum of cases there is significant demand worldwide for films and photographs of women and children who are being sexually assaulted. These films and photographs would be bad enough if the assaults were simply faked for the camera; but usually what is photographed in hard pornography in the present day is real assault, which is flatly impermissible morally.

Hard pornography may be agreed to provide a clear case where it is morally wrong to meet consumer demand, but it might be thought that this case is too far from the range of normal business activity to have a widely applicable lesson. For one thing, the sale of hard pornography is illegal in many countries, and for another, the cruelty involved in making it is not typical of what is involved in making other products for which there is a big demand. These differences are undeniable, but to call attention to them is to miss the point of the case of hard pornography. The point is that there are certain things that no amount of consumer demand can justify. In the case of hard pornography the weight of consumer demand is overridden by the impermissibility of the things done to satisfy it, namely violence and sexual assault.

Where consumer demand can be met legally and there is less agreement about the harm caused, things are perhaps not so clear. Written pornography that describes extremes of violence, such as *American Psycho* or De Sade's *Justine*, has been sold in Britain and elsewhere in Europe in mainstream bookshops, and many would agree that its sale is morally as well as legally permissible. It is, however, possible to make out a moral case against this.[3] Similarly with soft pornography on film, almost universally legal in Western Europe. This could be held to demean the women it depicts, and could be held to make its audience more tolerant of hard pornography. These points amount to a moral argument against meeting a demand for soft pornography. But the argument is controversial. Some people deny that women who take part voluntarily in pornographic films and who say they are happy to do so are really demeaned. Some people doubt whether a taste for hard pornography is in fact aroused by indulging a taste for soft pornography.

Another controversial moral argument against the satisfaction of demand can be mounted in the case of cigarettes. The worldwide demand for cigarettes is massive, and any attempt to prevent that demand from being met could be greeted by a correspondingly massive public outcry. Indeed any failure to satisfy consumer demand in this case would almost certainly be treated by the consumers themselves as a morally impermissible restriction of freedom: their freedom to smoke if they choose. But there are also strong moral arguments in the other direction. First, smoking significantly reduces life expectancy. In providing consumers with cigarettes, tobacco companies are causing them actual and identifiable harm. The justification given for this is that the nature of this harm is quite explicit and is of the consumers' choosing, but from most philosophical perspectives what is morally good is not to be equated with what people want – that indeed is the whole point of ethics; and within most ethical systems inflicting injury on oneself, hastening of death in the cause of pleasure, and assisting others in these acts are morally wrong. The argument from consent may also be challenged in the case of cigarettes on more specific grounds. In the first place, smoking is addictive, so that there is a sense in which the very act of consuming cigarettes deprives consumers of their freedom of choice over whether or not to consume. In the second place, consumption is encouraged by massive advertising campaigns, the nature and extent of which are themselves morally controversial.

For other products and in other circumstances, a case against satisfying consumer demand can also be made. In non-Islamic countries the sale of alcoholic products is not generally seen as raising moral issues. If used responsibly by responsible adults, such products are not a risk to health. However, they are not always used responsibly, and in many cases excessive consumption leads not only to the death or injury of the consumer (most notably in road accidents) but to the death or injury of other members of society as well as to social disorders and damage to property. Here the broader moral responsibilities of business to society at large need to be taken account of, and we need also to address the question of how far a business may be responsible not only for its product but for how that product may be used by its consumers. Alcoholic drinks manufacturers, like armaments manufacturers, will generally disclaim such responsibilities on practical grounds if no others. But it would clearly be morally wrong to provide alcohol to someone in the expectation that they would cause a road accident or armaments to someone in the expectation that they would initiate an unjust war. If these consequences were so unlikely as to be quite abnormal, the moral problem would disappear: there is nothing wrong in supplying a kitchen knife, even though it might conceivably be used for murder. But it is less easy to provide an ethical justification for meeting the consumers' wishes when the chances of misuse, though relatively small, are nevertheless significant. Ignorance in this case is not necessarily an excuse.

Of course misuse of a product is not always intentional, and there may also be grounds for not satisfying consumer demand when accidental misuse can result in harm. In the normal run of things a company will not intentionally supply such a product, for commercial as well as for moral reasons, but an over-eager satisfaction of consumer demand can still lead to difficulties. In the late 1960s and 1970s a number of multinational companies, including the Swiss company Nestlé, sought to expand their activities by aggressively marketing powdered baby milk in Third World countries.[4] We know now that bottle-feeding is a poor substitute for breast-feeding in this context. Besides the additional health risks introduced by the need for a bottle and for frequently contaminated locally available water, breast-feeding has a natural contraceptive effect and often provides the only effective means of population control. This was not clear in the past, however, and while companies were criticized by some doctors for their marketing, which portrayed bottle feeding as better than breast-feeding, they could find others to support their decisions. For the consumers, these claims were probably not critical anyway, as they needed little persuasion to buy the product. There was a natural presumption in favour of any product from the developed world, and in situations of poverty the freedom it afforded from the constraints of breast-feeding – constraints above all on the women's ability to work – were eagerly welcomed.

Unfortunately, these eager consumers were also poor and uneducated. They were often unable to read the preparation instructions or to appreciate their import if they could. Typically, and understandably, they stretched the milk powder as far as they could. All too often the result was severe malnutrition, leading to sickness and death. As these consequences became apparent, and a matter for public debate, or as in Nestlé's case, boycott, the companies concerned modified their marketing strategies. But they did so only gradually – and grudgingly – over a period of 15 years, and without accepting moral blame. From the point of view of their critics, however, the companies were not only wrong to sell their products in the knowledge that they could be harmfully misused, but also had a moral obligation to monitor product use, check this use for safety, and to withdraw from supply if this process led to any expectation of harmful misuse.

This last argument, like those against the supply of tobacco, arms and alcohol, may not be conclusive. But the fact that in these cases the arguments for and against are inconclusive is less important than the fact that there are arguments for and against – that it is not obvious that the satisfaction of the demand for soft pornography, cigarettes, alcohol, arms or baby milk, is right, even though it may be perfectly legal. Moreover, the range of cases in which it can at least be asked whether accommodating the consumer is morally permissible extends well beyond the cases where meeting the demand poses a threat to safety or health or where it leads to extreme cruelty or injustice.

Consider the example, based on fact, of a driving school in a racially mixed section of London. Intending customers of the school are asked whether they are willing to be taught by instructors of a different race. Whites are asked whether they feel comfortable being taught by oriental or black people, blacks whether they mind having white instructors, and so on. The question is put because customers in the past have sometimes asked to change instructors on racial grounds, and settling the matter in advance is thought by the management to save embarrassment all round and to have the effect of retaining customers who might otherwise leave. Is it morally right for customers to have a veto over instructors on racial grounds? It is certainly wrong if it is done to indulge racialists. On the other hand, what if the demand for instructors of the same race generally comes from members of races who suffer the discrimination, and who, because of that discrimination, would feel even more uncomfortable with a white instructor than they feel already at the thought of driving in London traffic? In that case the status of a request for an instructor of the same race might resemble a defensible request by women for female driving instructors. In general a customer's refusal to deal with a firm's staff on sex or race grounds would appear to be sexist or racialist and, morally speaking, it should probably not be accommodated unless it is shown not to be racialist or sexist after all. But whether it is racialist or sexist depends on the background to the refusal.

So far our discussion has focused on cases where meeting the demands of the consumer is of clear benefit to the business. However, there may also be cases where accommodating the customer is unfair to the one doing the accommodating. In a British newspaper article on the pros and cons of having one's house enlarged the writer quotes a London architect who finds the task of designing two stations for the London Underground far less arduous than adding a couple of rooms to an existing house:[5]

> It's a world I hope never to return to… We've done it in the past and it's a nightmare. It almost always ended in tears. The wife hated it, or the husband hated it. You should not embroil the architect as a therapist in your own domestic problems with endless meetings over gin and tonic. I'd rather open a restaurant on a Greek island.

In the same article, a builder complains of clients who take advantage:

> 'I know there are cowboy builders – but there are also cowboy clients.' Mr Barrett, who runs Hayling Builders near Portsmouth, was referring to rogue householders who ask him for advice and then go on to commission a cheaper firm to carry out his ideas, or even do it themselves. 'You talk to people and if you are not careful they bleed you of your time and brains.'

Here is a case where a provider of a service feels (with some justification) that the line has been crossed between what can reasonably be given to potential customers in order to get business, and what needs to be paid for.

There are other cases where the impression that the consumer is within his rights to make special demands is strong from one perspective but less strong from another. Take the example (once again drawn from real life) of a chef and restaurateur who caters for gourmet tastes, and who is considered by most of his customers and most other leading chefs and restaurant critics to be a master cook. One day a customer who comes to the restaurant because of the chef's reputation sends back a dish that is cooked by the chef and asks that it be altered to his (the customer's) specification. The chef refuses and the meal ends in some acrimony, though the customer is not charged. Who is in the right?

It might be thought that the customer is. After all, his meal was very expensive, and it is he who had to eat it. Surely he should have had the dish prepared to please him. In a more run-of-the-mill restaurant, with a different chef, this way of reading the case would be plainly correct. What makes the reading controversial here is that the chef is out of the ordinary and that the customer came partly because of the chef's reputation. This fact makes the customer's situation comparable to that of someone who commissions an artist to paint a portrait. The one who commissions the painter may also be paying a great deal of money, and he may dislike the portrait, but it is not obvious that the artist is obliged to repaint the portrait to please him, even if the one who commissions it is the only one who will ever see it. In the case of the portrait commission one buys not only the artist's ability but also his freedom to exercise it in a way that he judges appropriate. It may be the same with the master chef. Of course even the painter and the chef can be careless and unscrupulous in painting or cooking, not bothering to exercise their ability: in that case the customer is wronged; he is not getting what he pays for. Nevertheless, it is possible for the customer to get what he pays for and still not be pleased.

## The commercial expense of consumer protection

In the cases surveyed in the last section there are generally commercial reasons for accommodating the customer but moral reasons either for not doing so or for not *having* to do so. Might there also be cases in which there are moral reasons for accommodating the customer but stronger commercial reasons for not doing so? Because moral reasons are normally overriding, such cases are rare. The ones we are going to discuss depend on a mix of reasons, including commercial ones, for not doing what it would be at least morally desirable to do.

Consider first the situation, well-known to travellers, where an airline has overbooked the seats on a flight. Customers arrive expecting to travel after having booked, and a minority are disappointed, sometimes at great inconvenience. The overbooking is deliberate: a certain number of passengers book a variety of flights to the same destination at approximately the same time, and choose the most convenient, informing the disappointed airlines too late or not at all. As a result, airlines lose fares. Overbooking is meant to compensate for these no-shows. Is it justified? A reasonable answer to this question is that overbooking is a case of bad business ethics in response to bad business ethics. Customers are irresponsible if they make bookings they intend not to honour, and airlines are irresponsible if they do the same thing, even if, in a sense, customer irresponsibility provokes them to be irresponsible. This answer becomes less compelling, however, the greater the loss to the airline through negligent booking on the part of customers. If a firm faces bankruptcy or take-over because its loads are too small, if no-shows are largely to blame and if market conditions prevent it from taking specific action against no-showers, e.g. by charging a significant cancellation fee, then one might hold that, in self-defence, they are entitled to overbook, so long as they fully compensate those who are disappointed when a flight is full.

A rather different but ethically similar situation might arise in the case of an exaggerated health scare concerning a food product, such as occurred in Britain at the end of 1988. A widely publicized statement by a junior Minister of Health in the UK government suggested that British egg production was a prime source of salmonella infection. The publicity caused sales of eggs to plummet and more than 700,000 chickens in flocks suspected of infection were slaughtered by government order. Up to a year after the initial statement, egg sales were still down by 10 per cent on levels before the scare. In the period from December 1988 to August 1989 egg producers are estimated to have lost £70 million. Long-term investment in new chicken flocks also dropped markedly, with an increase in the risk of flocks failing health tests. A detailed review of the evidence by a British Member of Parliament and a specialist in cooking hygiene who advises the United Kingdom egg producers' association throws doubt on the finding that salmonella in eggs was a significant threat to human health.[6] Salmonella poisoning did increase in the UK in the period leading to the egg scare, and some of the cases appear to have been linked to eggs, but the poisoning continued to increase markedly when the egg scare had reduced egg consumption by a quarter, and at the temperatures eggs are normally broken out for cooking, the levels of contamination present are too low to make anyone ill.[7]

Although the health scare associated with eggs seems to have been exaggerated, the decision to issue warnings was explicable. The UK Ministry of Health had been embarrassed by cases of food poisoning in hospitals for which it was responsible, it was advised by one of its own laboratories that salmonella could be spread in laying flocks, and it recognized that consumers would wish it to take action in these circumstances. Had the Ministry merely conveyed its concerns to the egg producers, however, and left the decision to them, and had the egg producers continued to regard the evidence of a health hazard as negligible, issuing no health warning, would they have been acting immorally? So long as they were genuinely convinced that there was no health hazard and so long as they took steps to test the contrary evidence, it can be argued that the egg producers would have done nothing wrong in conducting business as usual. This reading of the case is of a piece with the impression, strong in retrospect, that egg producers were unfairly disadvantaged by publicity that was not entirely well-grounded scientifically, and that seemed flimsy not only to the egg producers but also the Ministry of Agriculture in 1988. So far as the evidence went, consumers were in no real danger, and the cost of taking precautions was very great.

In these last two cases, and in others where a product carries an identifiable but remote risk of only moderate harm to the consumer, the moral reasons for accommodating the customer may not be sufficient to warrant the commercial collapse of, or serious commercial damage to, a business.

## The case of consumer credit and indebtedness

The message of the preceding sections is not that deference to the consumer is always inappropriate, or that consumer protection is always overdone. It is that deference to the consumer is sometimes inappropriate and protection sometimes overdone. To put it another way, it doesn't follow from the fact that someone is a consumer that he or she needs to be deferred to by a business or protected by legislation. The deference or the protection has to be justified by further facts about the person who buys things or further facts about trading conditions. Modest as this conclusion is, it will almost certainly meet resistance; for all readers of this book are consumers, probably quite sophisticated ones, who can hold their own in disputes about goods and services, and who may feel that if they succeed in these disputes they deserve to. Consumerism – the belief that consumers' interests are more weighty than those of producers or sellers – is second nature to us, and the source of perhaps the most authoritative-seeming hunches about what is right and wrong in business ethics.

A way of counterbalancing consumerism without being driven to its opposite extreme is by considering a case where both consumers and businesses have responsibility for things going wrong. Of the range of commercial difficulties that have arisen in the 1980s and 1990s the problem of indebtedness is perhaps the most natural illustration. The Annual Report of the Office of Fair Trading for 1990 summarized the preliminary findings of a survey on indebtedness in the UK that had been carried out the preceding year. The survey disclosed that in 1989 21 million households in Britain made use of consumer credit. Of these, nearly a fifth were classified as 'heavy' credit users, i.e. people with four or more different credit commitments. More than two million households experienced difficulty paying a debt in 1989 and 560,000 households passed the test of serious indebtedness adopted in the survey: they were in arrears to at least three creditors.[8] More recent statistics given by the Money Advice Support Unit of the UK National Association of Citizen's Advice Bureaux record that in the first half of 1991 a very large number of debts in the UK were associated with housing: cases of arrears of between 6 and 12 months on mortgages totalled 162,000; and there were 37,000 repossessions. Further evidence of difficulties with repayment comes from the area of proxy-debt (debt consisting of payment in arrears) incurred for electricity, gas and water supply, where people with a very large accumulation of debt suffer disconnection, or have to switch from proxy-credit to prepayment arrangements. In a 1986 paper given to a conference on the topic of consumers in debt, Gillian Parker estimated that 1.5 million electricity users were in difficulty with repayments.[9] There were over 78,000 disconnections for non-payment of electricity bills in Britain in 1988-9.

In considering the moral issues associated with these figures, it is important to ask whether there is something wrong with going into debt full stop, or with lending for profit full-stop; or whether it is only over-indebtedness or casual lending for profit or lending on extortionate terms that is wrong. It might be thought that when people take out a loan – any loan – they are living beyond their means, and that they are impatient or greedy for things that they ought to – morally ought to – forgo, until they can afford to buy them without a loan. It might be thought that lenders are accomplices in immorality when they allow, and even encourage, people to enjoy now what they may not be able to pay for later. These views are intelligible, but they seem to beg the question of whether a loan is ever affordable, and they do not give weight to the economic advantages there may be to society of commercial credit arrangements, or the advantage to individuals when they purchase at any rate *some* goods on credit.

If purchasers are able to meet loan repayments from income without having to go into debt to meet normal expenses for food, transport, clothes and other necessities, then a loan – even a loan for something that is not a necessity – would seem to be affordable in just the way that a thing bought with cash is affordable. To take out a loan, then, is not necessarily to live beyond one's means. As for the social utility of lending and borrowing, the following considerations have been put forward in a recent article by Andrew Howe Browne of the British Bankers' Association:[10]

> Saving is the counterpart of lending. Savers could not benefit from interest without borrowers to pay it. Indeed, the lending of deposits is one of the principal mechanisms by which the old are supported by the young in our society. About 70 per cent of personal debt is for house purchase and serviced by those of working age. It is financed in large part by the deposits of the older generation for whom the interest payments of the younger generation provide income.
>
> Loans to consumers cannot be dismissed as unproductive and so contrasted with loans to industry. Loans to consumers enable industries to sell their goods. Consumer expenditure, facilitated by credit, was the engine of

post-recessionary growth in the 1980s. Furthermore, domestic labour-saving devices enable people to be more productive in other ways, for example, by going out to work or creating wealth at home. Finance enables a free society to choose the kind of wealth it wishes to create and whether it wishes to do so at home or 'at work'.

Though the first of these two points does not quite show that saving depends on loans, only that saving with interest depends on loans, Howe Browne does call attention here to the way that saving and lending for interest can be beneficial to savers and lenders. Howe Browne's second point shows that the general economic benefits of the purchasing power released by loans may justify loans.

Views sharply opposed to Howe Browne's were presented by Michael Schluter at a conference held in September 1989 by the Institute of Business Ethics.[11] Schluter is the director of the Jubilee Centre, a small policy studies research group with a Judeo-Christian perspective. Schluter claimed that in a culture in which people have large debts the economy suffers in the long term, as more and more money goes into debt-servicing and less and less goes into the purchase of goods and services. Commenting at a time when the British economy was still buoyant, he also called attention to the effects on the banking system if, as the result of a major economic downturn and unemployment, borrowers were simply unable to repay loans or overdrafts. This would add, he predicted, to the already serious problems of default in bank lending to governments. And these large-scale effects were in addition to loss of productivity caused by anxiety about debts among employees, as well as non-economic side-effects, such as strains on marriages and families. Schluter estimated that 4-6 million people in Britain suffered from overindebtedness, and that there was a danger that those who were borrowing small amounts, or who were succeeding in servicing their debts, would be enticed into taking on unmanageable further amounts of debt.

Schluter makes clear how, in circumstances in which credit is easy to obtain, and in which people are encouraged to use it, often without adequate knowledge of the consequences, things can go badly wrong. But he is mainly concerned with methods of controlling high levels of debt; he does not argue that all purchases should be financed out of current savings. He differs from Howe Browne in pointing out how a culture of credit can have high economic costs that are not easy to see, and in pointing out how a culture that permits sensible levels of borrowing can also encourage over-borrowing.

Even on Schluter's showing, it is not credit full stop that is morally questionable: it is the culture of credit, and of course overindebtedness itself. Let us turn, then, to overindebtedness and the atmosphere that encourages it. People who know the problem at first hand acknowledge that there are some borrowers who take out loans never intending to repay them, and who are deceitful and cynical in their dealings with financial institutions; but though such people exist, they appear to form a small minority.[12] More typical is the case of someone who intends to pay, but either suffers a drop in income or an increase in interest rates, and who, once he is in difficulty, does little to alert the lenders to his problems, so that they get worse and worse. Relative to the borrower's resources at the time it was first incurred, a debt might have been manageable, only to become less manageable later. These are not the only examples of understandable debt, honestly entered into. Many debts arise as part of a process of trying to increase income. Women who after being out of the job market return to paid work, or the self-employed often need to take out loans for things required by their job or business or to save them time. Debts incurred for this purpose are quite different from running up a credit card bill for designer track suits.

Even those who go into serious debt to finance questionable consumption are not always solely responsible for their excesses. They may be tricked or pressured into agreeing to loans on extortionate terms, they may be enticed into loans by firms who do little or nothing to investigate their ability to repay, or they may be made the beneficiaries of unsolicited increases in credit. Sir Gordon Borrie cites the case of a student who had incurred a considerable debt on her bank credit card.[13] The student's mother reluctantly paid off the debt, only to learn that, in response, the bank had notified the daughter of an increase in her credit limit. A newspaper man who made the rounds of some large London shops one afternoon in 1990 managed to obtain thousands of pounds of credit without having to provide any solid proof of credit-worthiness.[14] Examples like these show that indebtedness is sometimes made easy by businesses that provide credit.

Is the problem of overindebtedness the result, then, of over-casual lending to the young, the inexperienced, or the easily tempted? Elizabeth Stanton,[15] Director of the Retail Credit Group, denies that, in general, the lending is casual:

> The retailers whom I represent, the major high street stores who offer credit to their customers to purchase goods in their stores, have been among the pioneers of the innovative technology which enables them to make thorough credit vetting checks very quickly. If you are in the store and the application is processed while you wait the checks are as thorough as when an application is posted in.

Stanton goes on to describe just how thorough the checks are, by the use of credit reference agencies with their access to electoral rolls and records of county court judgements and bankruptcies, and how applications are credit-scored. It is possible that these checking procedures were relaxed during the recent period of sharp decline in retail sales in Britain, or that they were never made use of by some of the less sophisticated or less scrupulous retailers. But the provision of credit was not, as a rule, casual, at least on the part of retailers. On the other hand, the National Consumer Council has complained, in its 1990 report, *Credit and Debt*, that credit-referencing techniques are oversensitive to evidence of ability to repay and not sensitive enough to the burden of debt on any one borrower.[16] This means that an individual who was keeping up repayments with difficulty would score well in credit reference checks, permitting the release of credit that would finally make repayment of all debts impossible.

Not that the person who usually experiences repayment difficulties is necessarily a heavy user of credit or a heavy borrower. *Credit and Debt* tends to suggest that heavy borrowers and those who are over their heads in debt are not usually the same groups of people. The report indicates that debt in Britain in 1980s grew with the increase in the availability of credit but that, perhaps surprisingly, the growth in the number of those using credit was not in line with growth in debt. In other words, people who were already using credit decided to use more.[17] In addition, the use of credit, and the number of sources of credit used, tended to increase with income: the more people earned, the more they borrowed. These trends were noted in a period when home-ownership in Britain, and loans for home purchases, increased markedly. The typical heavy borrower that emerges is a relatively high earning person with a significant past record of using credit, not someone who is inexperienced and of modest means.[18] On the other hand, the young and inexperienced, the unemployed and those on low incomes, are disproportionately represented among borrowers who have difficulty repaying loans, particularly home loans. Students, households with young children, and households in which a marriage or relationship has ended are also particularly vulnerable to overindebtedness. Elderly people know least about credit, and also use it least.

There is compelling evidence in the NCC report that the growth in indebtedness in the 1980s was associated with the growth in the supply of credit for housing combined with a lowering of the requirements for lending from established sources of credit, such as building societies. There was a marked growth in the number of loans covering all or more than the purchase price of a first home. In 1986 and 1987, for example, over half the loans to first-time buyers were for mortgages amounting to between 95 per cent and 100 per cent of purchase price. Amounts loaned – calculated as multiples of the annual income of borrowers – also increased. Again during the 1980s, the quality of mortgaged property, measured in number of rooms and the age of the property, declined markedly. First-time buyers in the 1980s were relatively young – by 1988 20 per cent of all buyers were under 25 and over 60 per cent were under 35 – and had relatively low incomes. The NCC report[19] summarizes:

At a time when there was an increase in the supply of credit available from both the retail and wholesale lending markets, mortgagers were forced to lower their lending margins. They took on higher risks – in the borrowers they recruited and on the types of property on which their loans were secured.

It is possible that, by comparison with building societies, banks were more prudent. Andrew Howe Brown, in the article already quoted, points to a much lower rate of repossessions for banks than for building societies: 'One bank, for example, reckons that its repossessions in 1990 were only 15 per cent of that experienced by building societies generally'.[20] But the performance of what the NCC calls 'the monetary sector' – banks, building societies and other deposit-takers – bordered in many cases on the irresponsible.

Borrowers did not behave impeccably either. To begin with, they saved much less in the 1980s than they had previously. In 1989 only around 5 per cent of disposable income was not taken up with consumption, compared to 13.8 per cent in 1980.[21] By 1990 the figure was still under 8 per cent .[22] At the same time attitudes to the use of credit changed in ways that increased the risk of overcommitment. Consumer attitudes to the use of credit were surveyed in Britain in 1979 and 1987. In 1979 only 6 per cent of respondents agreed with the statement that credit was a 'sensible' way of buying goods and services; by 1987 credit was 'no longer viewed as an emergency measure, to be used for the necessities of life. For many people, it is a way of acquiring discretionary goods, to underwrite immediate consumption'.[23]

Although people became more willing to use credit to finance consumption, they did not become noticeably more adept at interpreting the costs of credit, and there is evidence that many people used credit without really being able to compare the cost of different forms of credit. Between 1980, when the NCC reported on public understanding of the annual percentage rate (APR) as a measure of the price of credit, and 1987, when another British survey returned to the question, the level of understanding had risen very little. In 1980 virtually none of those surveyed could say what 'APR' stood for; in 1987 20 per cent of those surveyed could decipher the acronym, but only a fraction of those could see how APR bore on decisions between different forms of credit. This was despite the publication of APRs by lenders in order to simplify the comparison of costs. Calculations of the cost of loans often tended to ignore the possibility or probability of increases in interest rates. As a result, in the mortgage market, many who borrowed at levels that they knew would place them under financial strain were unable to keep up repayments. High risk loans became more popular: there was a growing tendency for borrowers to make use of loans for consumption secured against their homes.

It appears, then, that blame for the levels of indebtedness reached in Britain in the 1980s must be shared by lenders *and* borrowers. Lenders have sometimes extended credit casually or on terms that were imprudent, but borrowers who have suffered have not always been the victims of malpractice on the part of those offering credit. On the other hand, borrowers whose problems were already serious have sometimes been preyed upon by the unscrupulous, and some consumers who are both too poor to be offered credit and yet who, being poor, need credit, appear to be in a particularly difficult position. Consumer protection is clearly in order in these latter cases; and consumer education, itself a form of consumer protection, is in order where there is a risk of overcommitment.

One form of consumer protection in the UK consists of the powers of the Office of Fair Trading to withhold or revoke licences to offer credit. These powers have been exercised mainly in the motor dealer and finance company sectors, but the total number of businesses affected adversely by OFT decisions annually is not large: just over 100 nationwide in 1990 in the two sectors just mentioned. The National Consumer Council has recommended significant increases in the undeniably very modest current charges for credit licences, the proceeds of which could be channelled into money advice for consumers.[24] The NCC[25] also recommends:

- Far greater use of risk-assessment techniques, and far greater sharing of the resulting information by the associations of major lenders in the UK, and the credit-reference agencies.
- The use by credit-reference agencies of information that better reflects the scale of a borrower's overall commitments, rather than the borrower's success to date in servicing particular loans.
- Ceilings on loans secured against property.
- Half-yearly statements from credit card companies indicating running totals of expenditure and accumulated debt.

All these measures appear to be useful in preventing overcommitment among creditworthy borrowers. To alleviate the debt problems of the very poor, the NCC recommends the formation of credit unions,[26] and the extension of the use of a friendlier 'social fund' administered by the UK Department of Health and Social Security.

Credit insurance is another measure routinely recommended to prevent debt problems: borrowers pay a premium for insurance that guarantees repayment of a loan in the event of unemployment, illness or death. In the past, UK lenders have sometimes made it incumbent on borrowers to opt out of paying for credit insurance, and many who failed to do so, or who were unaware that they would be insured unless they opted out, paid for it unwittingly, and had to go to considerable expense to withdraw after having failed to opt out initially. This so-called 'inertia selling' – selling that takes place unless the buyer actively rejects it – is frowned upon by the Office of Fair Trading wherever it takes place, whether in the insurance market or outside it. The NCC is also against inertia selling, while urging borrowers to persuade lenders to opt for credit insurance.[27]

But there may be special reasons why inertia selling is justified in the case of credit insurance. To begin with, there is the scale of the problem of overindebtedness itself, and the pervasiveness of its ill effects, the point stressed by Schluter. Second, there is the apparent irrational contrariness of people specifically advised to take out the insurance: the NCC report notes research that shows that the advice itself appears to prompt people to discount the risks, whether there is any statistical basis for discounting the risks or not.[28] If objectively the risks are high, as they have been proven to be, the obstacles in the way of ignoring them should be greater rather than smaller. This consideration counts in favour of credit insurance one has to opt out of. Third, there is the fact that a relatively small number of people who unwittingly pay for credit insurance decide to withdraw from it when given the opportunity. This suggests that, on a considered view, borrowers may be in favour of it after all. Finally, the inertia selling of credit insurance gets over the objections there may be to credit insurance being made mandatory.

## Uncontroversial protections

The fact that consumers are partly to blame for the problem of indebtedness, and that they are sometimes unreasonable in other commercial dealings, does not show that their misfortunes are always the result of greed or negligence. To locate the area where the consumer undoubtedly *does* require protection and where the consumer cannot be expected to fend for himself, we may be helped by getting a glimpse of a range of relevant legislation, and by seeing what regulatory authorities think is either not catered for by the law or not easy to enforce.

### Competition and consumer protection

In the UK the range of consumer-protection legislation is very wide, and some of it, notably competition legislation, is intended to benefit all participants in the market, not consumers exclusively. Thus the Competition Act works against impediments to the growth of markets and the entrance of new competitors into markets. The Resale Prices Act outlaws the fixing of minimum retail prices by manufacturers. The Restrictive Trade Practices Act makes it illegal for businesses to reach agreement on market share, or to divide among themselves different geographical areas as the special territories of one or another. Apparent violations of this Act are referred to the Restrictive Practices Court. Among references to the Court in 1991 was one dealing with two major British sugar producers, Tate and Lyle and British Sugar, to maintain market share at 1986 levels and to refrain from aggressive price competition. Another reference in 1991 concerned a cartel among manufacturers of steel roofing components, which added to the cost of a wide range of construction projects. The Fair Trading Act regulates monopoly practices. Cases of actual or potential monopoly power may be referred to the Monopolies and Mergers Commission, which may prohibit a proposed merger or acquisition or may act to curtail existing monopolistic powers that are considered to go against the public interest. In 1989, for example, it issued orders intended to increase the range of beers available to consumers in public houses, most of which were owned and controlled by a small group of major brewers.

The competition rules of the European Community are founded on Articles 85 and 86 of the Treaty of Rome. Article 85 prohibits any measure that restricts or distorts or prevents competition where it affects trade between member states of the European Community. Article 86 outlaws the abuse of a dominant position in the market.

The moral justification for legislation promoting competition or outlawing anti-competitive practices seems relatively straightforward. Where businesses portray themselves to consumers as being in open competition, or where, as in European society, there is an implicit agreement or accepted presumption that this will be the case, any secret collusion over prices amounts to dishonesty, or at least to a violation of the social agreement. This is unjust both to other firms in the market and to consumers. Consumers are put at a disadvantage, because the firms in question continue to operate as if price competition were in force: they take what are in fact artificially high prices as the lowest the market will bear. Meanwhile, other firms in the market are misled about the extent of competition in the market, and will miscalculate the effects of different legitimate strategies for increasing market share through pricing. Where businesses acquire a monopoly position, or where, as in the brewing industry, a few suppliers exercise effective control over the distribution channels for the industry, both small businesses and consumers may need protection from the potential abusers of monopoly power.

### Trading standards and consumer protection

Other pieces of legislation bear even more directly on consumer protection than do British or EC competition rules. Nearly fifty of these are enforced by the Trading Standards Service in Britain. There is the Trade Descriptions Act, which outlaws inaccurate and misleading descriptions of goods for sale; the Consumer Credit Act, which is supposed to prevent misinformation about the terms of lending agreements; the Consumer Protection Act, which lays down general safety requirements, assigns liabilities for defective products and prohibits misleading prices; safety regulations and orders under the European Communities Act; the Control of Pollution Act and the Health and Safety at Work Act; the Food Act, which regulates the sale of food and drink; the Animal Health Act; the Road Traffic Act, which contains provisions restricting overloading of vehicles and preventing damage to roads; and the Weights and Measures Act, which is intended to ensure uniformity in quantities of goods bought by consumers.

Outside the sphere of strictly enforceable legislation there are codes of practice and voluntary undertakings that businesses have agreed to be bound by, sometimes to pre-empt legislation. An example here is statements of practice in the insurance industry. These were introduced to compensate for the burden under English and Scottish law of full disclosure of material facts on the part of people applying for insurance or holding insurance policies. In a noticeable number of court cases innocent misrepresentation or failure to disclose facts was found sufficient to void contracts to pay insurance claims, although the judgements stressed the unfairness of this result. Judicial criticism and the threat of reform of the law resulted in more explicit application forms for insurance, where facts thought by the insurer to be material were clearly elicited, and the possibility of material but undisclosed facts being discovered at the time of a claim was reduced.

Non-statutory mechanisms for consumer protection in the UK are not confined to statements of practice. They also include ombudsmen schemes. These have proliferated in the financial services sector, where there are ombudsmen for the banks, the building societies, the unit trusts, and the insurance industry. Other sources of consumer protection, sometimes set up by statute, include 'consumer watchdog' bodies, which have been established in the UK to monitor the policies, particularly in regard to pricing, of the recently privatized telephone, electricity, gas and water companies.

At the level of the European Community, consumer protection usually takes the form of legally binding 'directives', which set out in broad terms the sort of protection being sought. The terms of the directives are arrived at after consultation between member states and interested parties within member states. Member states then arrive at legislation to ensure that the directive is implemented in individual jurisdictions. Occasionally the national legislation both predates and goes beyond the scope of the directive, as in the case of the UK Consumer Credit Act, which was in place 12 years before the corresponding directive came into force in 1986. Existing European Community directives govern package travel, misleading advertising, consumer credit, and product liability. There are also a number of directives on safety. Possible directives currently under discussion concern unfair contract terms and timeshare property sales.

One rationale for so extensive a range of directives, codes and legislation, and for a service in the UK specially charged with enforcement, is given in a brochure published by the Institute of Trading Standards Administration:

Consumers in less sophisticated times could rely on their own skill and judgement when buying goods. In this technological society, however, where man-made fabrics can look like traditional ones and additives can enhance the flavour of poor quality food, the buyer may be at a disadvantage. Most of the Trading Standards Laws are designed to restore the balance of knowledge and information which existed when everyone was their own expert.

This is more clearly a rationale for trade-description legislation than for consumer credit law or even regulations governing food hygiene, but it suggests the general principle that protection is in order wherever buying goods or services calls for more knowledge than the average consumer can be expected to possess. This principle is morally defensible in a number of different ways. It would receive support from the Kantian prohibition on treating other agents merely as means, if the knowledge that the consumers lacked was typically exploited by sellers of goods and services. It would get backing from utilitarianism if it were often true that consumer ignorance harmed consumers or made them displeased with what they bought – regardless of whether traders took advantage. And it would get support from any morality requiring beneficence, such as Christian morality.

Some specific pieces of legislation in the list given earlier might have narrower moral justifications in addition to the one concerning consumer knowledge. The wrongness of lying might justify some of the provisions of the Trade Descriptions Act. The wrongness of putting people into danger through negligence might justify some of the provisions of the Food Act, the Animal Health Act or the Consumer Protection Act. The wrongness of usury might justify some of the provisions of the Consumer Credit Act. And so on.

A rather different justification for the legislative and regulatory mechanisms in place to protect UK consumers is given in the Annual Report for 1990 of the Office of Fair Trading, the body that oversees the Trading Standards Service and Consumer Advice Bureaux, among other things. In the introduction to the report, Sir Gordon Borrie, the then Director General of Fair Trading, appears to be sympathetic to the theory that the rational self-interest of consumers and businesses, properly pursued, removes unfairness and inefficiency, but he thinks that certain facts of life, both about consumers and about trading conditions, require the operation of self-interest to be assisted:

Even the best-informed cannot be expected to find out that a company is about to collapse. Relatively sophisticated consumers can suffer information overload with more information thrust before them than they can handle. Those who are less sophisticated – but not necessarily gullible – are even more exposed to detriment. People can be genuinely bewildered at some of the commitments they have taken on. Some high-pressure marketing and selling practices have now become so skilled and expertly honed that the average and even above-average consumer may have little prospect of mounting a satisfactory defence against those who would part them with their money. The sales manual and the vigorous training will enable every consumer objection to be overcome. The population at large may not show the attributes of typical policy-makers and text-book writers. As much as it is important to raise the skills and critical awareness of consumers, we must be alert to the everyday realities and, in particular, take care to be mindful of the norms of consumer behaviour. Such norms may well fall short of 'rational' behaviour. At least one in ten adults have had such significant difficulties with reading and writing as to affect seriously almost every aspect of their lives. Many people completely fail to understand percentages, let alone interest rates... People do have great difficulties in understanding (let alone comparing) competing deals with banking, insurance, credit, financial services and so on ... Ironically, the situation may become worse as regulatory initiatives require more and more information to be provided for consumers.[29]

In practice, Borrie believes, official urgings to consumers to exercise a duty of care on their own behalf – to be energetic in safeguarding their interests – have to be combined with regulatory, educational and policy initiatives.[30] All of these, legislation included, take up the slack left when self-interest operates imperfectly.

On the business side, too, rational self-interest 'should jolt any company out of behaviour which is inefficient or indifferent to its customers',[31] but in practice it is not strongly enough developed or not quick enough in producing results to prevent businesses from being 'dishonest, unscrupulous, cavalier, inefficient, or indifferent'.[32] The OFT Annual Report for 1990 describes a range of objectionable business practices. The most complained about were high pressure selling techniques in the timeshare market, which is also associated with problems over the security of deposits and over misleading descriptions of timeshare resorts. Misleading information or unduly limited information also presented problems in the area of consumer credit. In the funeral market a failure to itemize charges was found to be commonplace. Broken agreements between builders and their customers was a cause of dissatisfaction in the home-improvements market, and carpet and furniture retailers and manufacturers admitted to serious consumer dissatisfaction with promptness of deliveries, the availability of information on which to base decisions to purchase goods, quality of goods and security of deposits. In the used car market the practice of falsifying mileage by turning back the odometers of automobiles was widespread. And consumers complained of receiving increasing quantities of junk mail. Finally, the OFT report noted problems of indebtedness, sometimes aggravated by questionable lending policy. According to Borrie, legislation and systematic  enforcement are required where, as in these cases, the effective pursuit of self-interest by business gives out.

It is striking how much faith Borrie places in rational self-interest. While recognizing its practical limitations, he evidently thinks that in theory it is enough to determine the scope of business and consumer responsibilities alike. But that it may be an inadequate basis even in theory is revealed when one asks whether rational self-interest rules out the consumer excesses that Borrie himself[33] complains of:

> I have no doubt that some consumer complaints are unjustified. The customer is not always right. I have in mind here situations where the grievance is imagined or exaggerated or whether expectations are wholly unrealistic. I can also have no sympathy for consumers who are themselves dishonest or reckless.

It is far from obvious that the behaviour complained of here is not prompted by self-interest, even rational self-interest.

A more satisfactory basis than self-interest alone for responsible consumer behaviour would be self-interest constrained by the precepts of conventional morality – the morality systematized in normative ethics. Whatever makes it wrong to lie makes it wrong to press dishonest consumer complaints against a business; whatever makes it wrong to break one's agreements makes it wrong, for example, to fail to keep up payments arranged in good faith and openly and on well understood terms between a consumer and a business. Morality is needed over and above self-interest not only to determine the scope of consumer responsibilities but also to determine the scope of business responsibilities for consumer protection. The proper limits of deference to customers – the proper area in which it is right to accommodate customers who make special demands – this may be determined by the self-interest of a firm; but the proper limits of consumer protection do not seem to be.

An illustration of this point may be provided by the erosion in English law of the principle of *caveat emptor* – buyer beware. In the nineteenth century judges began to rule that buyers had to be able to rely on sellers to provide goods that were reasonably fit for their advertised purpose. Yet even after the obligation to sell goods of merchantable quality was enshrined in the Sale of Goods Act, 1893, contracts between individual buyers and sellers might contain escape clauses which shielded sellers from liability, and which were upheld by courts. Clearly these clauses were in the interest of the sellers; equally clearly they were not in the interest of, and often were unfair to, buyers. Unreasonable exemption clauses were not outlawed until the Unfair Contract Terms Act of 1977.[34] The 1977 legislation, as its name implies, was justified by considerations of fairness. Was the legislation also justified by the enlightened self-interest of sellers – on the grounds that a market will generate more profit if buyers can trust sellers? Though it may be true that a business will lose out in the long run if it does things prohibited by morality, so that it is in its interest not to do those things, opportunistic departures from this policy now and then, doing no harm to its reputation, may be in its self interest. When they are, consumers are harmed. It follows that self-interest can be as little relied upon to minimize harm to consumers from business as it can harm to business from consumers.

## 'New' or 'ethical' consumers?

In an earlier section some of the responsibility for overindebtedness was seen to lie with consumers whose rates of saving and ways of deciding which forms of credit to use left a lot to be desired. Some of the debt problems of consumers could have been prevented if people had delayed some purchases and calculated the true costs of others. Another way of putting it is by saying that consumers had responsibilities to do their sums and put off some of their buying, just as, in other circumstances, they have responsibilities not to lie in pressing complaints and not to break agreements. These latter responsibilities flow from the general moral responsibilities to be truthful and to observe the requirements of justice, responsibilities that often override the responsibility to look after one's own interests.

How far do the responsibilities of consumers extend? There are pressure groups who argue that the responsibilities go far beyond not lying and not breaking agreements. They argue that, especially in the rich countries, people should worry about the cost to the environment in the manufacture of some goods, and the use of others. They argue that consumers should worry about the economic benefits to immoral governments of certain purchases. They argue that consumers should give weight to facts about the wages and conditions of the people who make the goods they buy. They argue that the cost in suffering to animals of different products needs to be taken into account. They argue that decisions to purchase goods ought to be influenced by information about the political affiliations of companies, and the extent of their charitable contributions. They even argue that consumers should ask themselves whether they really need to buy or use certain goods, or certain quantities of goods.

The approach of the new consumer groups may be contrasted with that of, for example, the long-established Consumers' Association in the UK. At least as its concerns are reflected in the pages of its magazine, *Which?*, the Consumers' Association is more occupied with comparing and ranking goods by how well they serve their purpose than with encouraging second thoughts about whether the goods should be bought in the first place. A large part of what is reported in *Which?* consists of results of independent testing of goods and services. Such testing has clear benefits. It discloses safety problems and undesirable design features. Giving publicity to these things can have the effect of raising standards by getting the poorer manufacturers to produce to the standards of the competitors found to be best. Consumers are spared some bad purchases and the loss of a lot of time in comparing products. Can anything more reasonably be expected of a consumers' association?

In the UK two recently established publishers of consumer magazines bring to bear patterns of product evaluation that are quite different from those of the Consumers' Association. The Ethical Consumer Research Association publishes *The Ethical Consumer*, which, 'at the simplest level... takes the approach of the ethical investment movement to buying shares, and then applies it to buying everything else'.[35] Ethical investment aims at getting a return only from firms whose operations, in the broadest sense, are morally acceptable, and it considers that the moral acceptability of these operations is put in doubt if independent commentators raise questions about, for example, firms' links with oppressive political regimes, their dealings with trade unions; their use of animals in product-testing, and so on. In a similar way, ethical consumption aims at purchasing only from firms whose operations are morally responsible.

Another organization involved with publicizing the ethical character of firms in the consumer market in Britain is New Consumer. Its methods of collecting business information differ from those of the Ethical Consumer Research Association, as do some of its criteria of morally acceptable operations, but its aims appear to be similar. It publishes a magazine called *New Consumer* as well as consumer guidebooks and reference publications. In a book giving 'ethical profiles' of 128 firms operating in Britain, three members of New Consumer explain that the information is designed to help those who can afford it to go beyond green consumerism and make their purchases sensitive to a range of social issues.[36] Just as *Ethical Consumer* tries to generalize the thinking behind ethical investment, *New Consumer* tries to generalize the thinking behind green consumerism.

*Ethical Consumer* and *New Consumer* promote ethics not in the sense of ethical systems like utilitarianism and Kantianism, but in the sense of a series of stances on social issues that are reflected in one's everyday behaviour. This informal way of thinking about ethics at times reduces the persuasive power of their arguments for changing one's buying habits. Thus consumer ethics is sometimes advertised as contributing to an improved, because more coherent, lifestyle. The *New Consumer* logo is printed over a sentence-length statement of purpose for the magazine: 'to provide people with information and practical strategies for integrating their economic choices with their values and their lifestyles'. The idea that integration is desirable, that it is a problem for one's consumer choices to be at odds with one's other choices, is also taken up in the inaugural number of the Ethical Consumer:

> I observe people whose behaviour as consumers does not seem to fit in with the rest of their lives. It is as if being a consumer is somehow detached from everything else they do: the tireless trade union leader after an evening of meetings drives home in a car made by a company with a record of hostility to trade unions; the churchman, renowned for his campaigns for social justice... dines on fruit picked by people who have been forcibly removed from their land by a company who now pays them starvation wages; the nuclear disarmament campaign supporter whose favourite pastime is listening to records on a stereo manufactured by a company who makes missile guidance systems.[37]

This is a clear statement of the sort of appeal that ethical consumption can have for people whose lives are organized around one central task or cause with moral content, but it also raises the question of whether ethical consumption can be expected to move someone whose commitments to nuclear disarmament and trades unions are much weaker than his commitment to a comfortable life for himself. Whatever else is felt to be wrong in the life of the non-campaigner, it won't be that his consumer choices are strongly at odds with his other strong values, or that his life doesn't add up, for we are considering someone who doesn't necessarily have values focused enough or strong enough to make him identify with the campaigners just described, and who may not value a life dedicated to any one thing.

Plainly if a certain pattern of consumption is going to be urged upon people as ethical, then there is a more direct and powerful argument for adopting it than that it will smooth the bumps in their lifestyle, namely that it is ethical: adopting it will counteract some wrong or correct or reduce some maltreatment, or it will produce some benefit to many people. But will changing one's purchasing decisions usually have that effect? And might not consumption in any case be handled wrongly when it is simply made more sensitive to the ethical character of producers and retailers? Might not the morally urgent thing be to reduce consumption rather than to refine it?

*Ethical Consumer* takes up these questions, but does not seem to answer them in a fully satisfactory way. It concedes that, taken purchase by purchase, the effects of ethical consumption may be small, but it insists that purchases send a message to a producer in the same way that a vote, ineffectual on its own, sends a message to a party or a government.[38] This analogy between voting and purchasing is questionable, however, because votes are cast as part of a process in which politicians are expecting a message and are interested in what the message is, and in which they and voters do something to make public the issues that their message will concern. Purchases do not have this communicative power unless they are endowed with it, e.g. by being made part of a boycott or a consumer campaign, and even then the purchases belonging to the campaign may or may not have the desired effect.[39] In the absence of such a campaign the only message that can reasonably be read into a drop in sales is that a product is less popular, not that its maker or seller is.

Depending on the philosophical standpoint adopted, it could be argued that, in some cases at least, the effect of the consumer's behaviour is not critical to his moral position. If the production of something entails unethical behaviour on the part of the producer, and if this is known to the consumer, then any purchase of the product in question might constitute an abetment of that behaviour, which is itself immoral, irrespective of whether or not a message is communicated thereby, and irrespective of whether that message has any effect. On this line of argument, which would be consistent with a Kantian, Christian or rule-utilitarian (though not necessarily with an act-utilitarian) position, a focused policy of ethical consumption clearly represents a moral response. But it is debatable whether this extends to cases in which the wrong-doing of the business is not directly related to the manufacture of the product concerned, e.g. to the purchase of Australian produce from a company that mistreats its workers in Brazil. And while non-purchase may be a moral response, it can also be argued that it is doubtful if it is an adequate moral response. However limited the effects of his action may be, does the consumer not have a moral duty to do more than simply turn the other cheek?

Whether or not we take account of the effectiveness of an action, then, there are arguments to the effect that something more than purchasing decisions are required to constitute distinctively ethical consumption. Something more seems to be required, something like 'consumer campaigning', which calls for activism beyond presenting a certain collection of carefully chosen goods at a checkout counter. So it is an open question what ethical consumerism comes down to in practice and what good effects it can be expected to have.

Another issue we can address is whether the important thing is to consume with more moral sensitivity or to consume a lot less of everything. In an article on 'green consumerism' *Ethical Consumer* addresses this issue.[40] It quotes a spokeswoman for the Green Party who says in part:

> Of course it is better to use recycled paper and lead-free petrol, but it is even better to use less paper and less petrol. The logic of big business is that it must promote consumption. We suspect that however green-tinted companies become, they will find it hard to encourage people to consume less.[41]

The *Ethical Consumer* comments:

> This argument expresses one of the central concerns of environmentalists –
> that perhaps the words 'green' and 'consumerism' do not belong together at
> all... It is easy to explain why this concern is misplaced. Radical, political,
> ethical or green consumerism, whatever you choose to call it, is simply a
> method used to achieve particular goals under an existing system (free market
> consumer society). You do not necessarily condone or encourage a system
> simply by using it.[42]

However, this argument threatens to prove too much. If purchasing
something is not necessarily to endorse the consumption-promoting
behaviour of a company, why should it be seen as an endorsement of other
aspects of the company's behaviour? Yet ethical consumerism is predi-
cated, as we have seen, on the idea that to purchase a thing is to signal
approval of it and to support or at least condone the activities of its maker.

Besides threatening to undercut ethical consumerism itself, the argument
is not to the point, for what is at issue is whether someone who believes in
ethical consumerism can consistently argue for consuming less. There
seems no reason why not. But this still leaves the Green entitled to ask
whether it isn't better to get *that* message across and forget about product-
by-product or company-by-company ethical profiles. It is possible that
ethical consumerists can respond by showing that there is such a thing as
sustainable consumption, and that promoting this is compatible with
providing ethical information, but this is plainly a big task.

Nothing said so far should be taken to discredit the activities of the new
consumer organizations. On the contrary, at a time when, as we have seen,
companies trade on their reputations for good works, it is important to
have independent sources of information concerning the ethically sensitive
activities of firms. Whatever else may be said, firms should not get the
benefits of an undeserved reputation for probity: the new consumer organizations are among the forces that can prevent this. They also provide, in a
way that the Consumers' Association does not seem close to providing, a
forum for broaching the question of how much and what kind of
consumption is morally acceptable.

## References

1   The case of corporate customers will be considered briefly in Chapter 6,
'Other Businesses'.
2   In practice treating consumers as kings usually means treating the
young and able-bodied as kings. Though old consumers can have
considerable purchasing power, they are not often before the minds of

product designers. Pat Moore, a New York product designer who set up a firm catering to the needs of the elderly and handicapped, is an exception to the rule. According to an article in the *Guardian*, for 1 August 1989, she learned about attitudes to the elderly the hard way, by disguising herself as an old person and seeing how she was treated. She is responsible for designing easy to open packaging and containers for pills that register the number already taken.

3   Sue Edwards, 'A Plea for Censorship', *New Law Journal*, November 1991, pp. 1479-80, contains a description of the pornography typically prosecuted under the UK Obscene Publications Act, and considers the status of widely sold hard pornography.

4   For a fuller acount of this episode see J. E. Post, 'Ethical dilemmas of multinational enterprise: an analysis of Nestlé's traumatic experience with the Infant Formula controversy', in W. M. Hoffman *et al*, (eds), *Ethics and the Multinational Enterprise* (New York: University Presses of America, 1986).

5   *Independent on Sunday*, London, 16 February 1992.

6   T. Gorman and R. North, *Chickengate: An Independent Analysis of the Salmonella in Eggs Scare* (London: IEA Health and Welfare Unit, 1990).

7   *Ibid.*, pp.25, 35.

8   *OFT Annual Report*, 1989, p.29.

9   Gillian Parker, 'Consumers in Debt', paper given to the Consumers in Debt conference organized by the National Consumer Council, 1986. Cited in the NCC report, *Credit and Debt* (London: National Consumer Council, 1990).

10  A. Howe Browne, 'The banks and personal credit', *Banking World* (January 1991), pp. 17–19.

11  Schluter's contribution and others are published in N. Cooper *et al*, *Personal Debt: is it too much encouraged?* (London: Institute of Business Ethics, 1990).

12  'There is little or no basis for thinking that there is a sizeable section of society which does not mind being in debt and is cynically abusing the system': John Attewall, Co-ordinator for the Money Advice Support Unit, Greater London Citizens Advice Bureau, in Cooper *et al*, *op. cit.*, p. 3.

13  Sir Gordon Borrie, 'Law and Morality in the Market Place', *Trent Law Journal* Lecture, unpublished typescript (1987), p. 6.

14  Paul Crosbie, 'How I Raised £10,000 in Just One Hour', *Daily Express*, London, 20 December 1990.

15  Cooper *et al*, *op.cit.*, p.12.

16  *Credit and Debt op. cit.*

17  *Ibid.*, p.33.

18  In the UK, 'blue-collar' lending used to be a specialist commercial activity. The deregulation of the banking sector and the entry of the

building societies into the loan market was expected to change that, but three established down-market lenders, Provident Financial, Castle's Holdings and London Scottish, actually prospered in the 1980s and early 1990s. A factor was their emphasis on small loans and active debt collection.

19  *Credit and Debt*, p.23.
20  *Ibid.*, p.19.
21  *Ibid.*, p.2.
22  Howe Browne, *op.cit.*, p.17.
23  *Credit and Debt*, p.28. The volume of repayments from high earners, on which the picture of the typical 1980s borrower is based, may mask the levels of repayment difficulties among low- and middle income borrowers, according to the NCC report.
24  *Ibid.*, p.83. Independently of the NCC proposals, the UK lenders have moved to fund local credit counselling services. In the Leeds and Bradford areas, Barclays Bank, The Leeds Permanent Building Society, GE Capital and The Registry Trust set up a team of advisers in June 1993. A national Money Advice Trust was established in 1990.
25  *Ibid.*, pp.85–90.
26  *Ibid.*, p.12.
27  *Ibid.*, p.88.
28  *Ibid.*, p.87.
29  *OFT Annual Report*, 1990, pp.17–18.
30  The educational initiatives include the publication of a range of free, clearly written, widely available leaflets on buying by post, doorstep salesmen, credit agreements, methods of managing personal debt, and buying used cars.
31  OFT Annual Report, 1990, p.15.
32  *Ibid.*
33  *Ibid.*, p.16.
34  Sir Gordon Borrie, *op.cit.*, pp. 12–13.
35  *Ethical Consumer*, vol.1 no.1, March 1989, p.1.
36  R. Adams, J. Carruthers and Sean Hamil (eds), *Changing Corporate Values* (London: Kogan Page, 1990), p.4.
37  *Ethical Consumer*, vol.1, no.1, p.6.
38  *Ethical Consumer*, vol.1, no.1, p.7.
39  For a detailed discussion of different types of boycott and how they can be successful, or, short of this, effective, see N. Craig Smith, *Morality and the Market: Consumer Pressure and Corporate Accountability* (London: Routledge, 1990), Ch.9.
40  *Ethical Consumer*, vol.1, no.4, September/October 1989.
41  *The Guardian*, London, 12 September 1988.
42  *Ethical Consumer*, vol.1, no.4, p.12.

# 4  Employees

Businesses routinely acknowledge responsibilities to those they employ. Indeed the relationship of employment is one of the most important in society. Those who work for a living may spend up to half their waking hours acting as employees, while those who do not feel deprived as a consequence. Employment is often treated as a 'right' – something to which all people of working age are morally entitled. Yet the obligations of a business to its employees, and vice-versa, are often unclear, and frequently a matter of public controversy. In this chapter we shall begin by looking briefly at the nature of the contractual relationship between a business and an individual employee, and at the moral obligations of one to the other. We shall then look at the obligations of a business to its employees as a whole, and in particular at issues of employee participation and equal opportunities. These issues have recently come to the fore in public debate as a result of disagreements over the 'social chapter' of the Maastricht Treaty, and much of the chapter will be concerned with the moral dimensions of that debate. Finally we shall look at some illustrations of what might be construed as 'good practice' in this field.

## The employment contract

In principle the relations between a business and an employee are governed by a legal contract of employment. However, such contracts often leave out more than they put in, and while the terms of employment of a manual worker in a unionized company are likely to be relatively clear, those of a manager or professional employee are not. Tasks and responsibilities, hours of work, location, and travel requirements may all be unspecified. Moreover even when the terms of employment are relatively specific, there is the question whether the business and its employees have any moral responsibilities to each other beyond those of the contract. For example, the employment contract is an agreement to exchange wages or salary for work, but it is commonly held that a business has an obligation not only to pay for work done, but also to continue, if possible, to provide future work for the employee. To some extent this obligation is built into a range of legal requirements, making it difficult for a business to end an employment contract and requiring redundancy payments if it does. However, there is no legal requirement for a business to behave in such a way as to minimize the chance of redundancy.

Does a business have any moral obligation in this respect? Many employees, and a good number of businesses, would argue that it does. In Japanese business there has been a well-established tradition, only recently questioned, of life-time employment. In Europe and North America a few large firms, and many family-owned firms, have also espoused policies of continued employment. Such firms usually manage their affairs for stability rather than rapid growth, attempting to provide their employees with long-term security rather than hiring one minute and firing the next. On the face of it this seems very laudable. However, the business's obligations to its employees have to be considered alongside its obligations to other stake-holders. For example, is a policy of continued employment beneficial to the shareholders? Many business leaders would argue that, while treating their employees well and responsibly is in general in the shareholders' interests (because it leads to higher employee loyalty and productivity), an over-emphasis on job security goes against shareholder interests by restricting the options for growth and incurring unnecessary expenses in recession.

We may also need to take account of creditors. When a business goes into receivership or liquidation, the employees come right at the bottom of the pecking order of those who have a claim on its assets. This is sometimes seen as unjust. When the Anglo-Dutch lorry and truck manufacturer Leyland went into receivership in early 1993, the employees complained bitterly that they did not receive the redundancy payments to which they would have been legally entitled had the firm still been in business. But they were at least paid for the work they had done, whereas the creditors had supplied goods or services for which they had not yet been paid. In this situation it seems quite reasonable that the creditors should have, as they do in British law, priority over the employees. In a company that is still trading, however, paying employees for the next week or next month is usually treated as a higher priority than paying creditors for the past week or past month, even though the creditors have supplied their services and the employees have not. Even if the need of employees for future employment is greater than the need of creditors for payment, which may or may not be the case, this is difficult to justify morally. Only if the oblig-ation to retain employees were socially accepted as an overriding one, so that it was effectively implicit in the contracts with creditors, could a reasonably strong case be made.

Another responsibility of businesses to their employees might be to their growth and well-being while in employment. In this context we might ask to what extent a business is morally obliged to provide its employees with benefits such as education and training, or to enable them to pursue their own development through, for example, day-release arrangements. And to what extent should it take account of personal needs in the allocation of tasks or duties? Because employment can be hard to come by, a business will often be able to persuade an employee to make considerable personal sacrifices – often at the expense of spouse and children – in the interests of the business. In many companies employees are expected to treat work as their primary responsibility, and to relegate families, leisure and personal development to second place. This may be good for shareholders, but from a moral standpoint it would seem to be tantamount to the exploitation of a weaker party (the employee) by a stronger one (the business), and this would make it unacceptable within most ethical philosophies.

## Responsibilities within employment

If a business has moral responsibilities to its employees, so too do the employees have responsibilities to the businesses employing them. The extent of these responsibilities depends upon the nature of the employment. Casual hands or one-off consultants may have no obligations other than to do the jobs for which they are paid. Permanent employees, on the other hand, may reasonably be expected to display some degree of loyalty to the business, especially if it is providing them with job security, a sense of belonging in a community, support and understanding in times of personal difficulties, and so on. The question is, how far should that loyalty go? Is it reasonable to expect, as some businesses do, total loyalty from employees, or are there limits beyond which the demands of loyalty are unreasonable?

What happens, in particular, when the behaviour expected in the business is at odds with what would be morally acceptable in society at large, or to the individual concerned? This might include asking one employee to invade the privacy of another, or asking an employee to tell lies or conceal the truth when the success or reputation of the business is at stake.

There seems to be no reason in principle why moral standards within a business should be any different from those outside it, or why a person should apply different moral rules to his behaviour when in work from those applied to his behaviour the rest of the time. If a business or its employees act in a way that would be morally reprehensible in any other context, the chances are that it is morally reprehensible in a business context too. The fact is, however, that people do often behave as if there was one moral code for everyday life and another, looser one, for business. On the premise that 'all is fair in love, war and business', they leave their morals behind them when they go into work. As a result, those employees who take their morals with them can be placed in a very difficult position.

Consider, for example, a case in which a company has been in breach of a law governing toxic emissions. The breach was inadvertent, a consequence of the difficulties of co-ordination that beset any complex organization. Once it is discovered the company takes action to rectify the situation, but this requires a plant redesign that will take 12 months to put into effect. In the meantime, to admit to the breach would mean stopping production, which, combined with the effect on its reputation, would seriously damage the company. Although the high emissions might cause very serious illness, the chance of their doing so is small, and the company instructs its employees to lie about the emission levels. One of the employees believes strongly that this course of action is morally impermissible, but when he puts this view to his superiors he gets nowhere, so in the end he talks to the press. Is this 'whistle-blowing', as it is sometimes called, morally permissible, morally impermissible or an unacceptable breach of loyalty and confidentiality?

The line of argument most commonly used in such cases is to assess the likely damage to the public from keeping quiet and to the company from being honest.[1] If the risks to the public were minimal and the costs to the firm high, then, it is argued, the employee's duty of confidentiality would override any other considerations. If the risk to the public was serious, however, the whistle-blowing might be permissible and, in certain cases, obligatory. Such an analysis has two weaknesses, however. First, it excludes damage that is done by acts that establish dishonesty as a legitimate practice. The immediate effects of a lie might be beneficial, but can still be outweighed by the long-term effects of an accumulation of lies. And even if the effects appear beneficial, it can still be wrong, as in Kantian or Christian ethics, to lie. Second, it fails to address the fact that the costs and benefits cannot be objectively calculated, and that the business and the employee might genuinely differ in their judgements of the seriousness of the breach.

In practice businesses tend to place a great emphasis on both shareholder returns and employee loyalty, and their actions reflect these priorities. Even when they have a clear moral dimension, decisions are often made on commercial rather than moral grounds, and whistle-blowers are either fired or given every encouragement to leave. If asked to describe how they would respond to a hypothetical situation, however, the directors of these same companies will usually profess honesty and openness, and this suggests that they recognize that their practices fall short of society's expectations, at least.

An employee, faced with a situation of this kind, would appear to have a duty to act responsibly – not to cause damage on the basis of an unsubstantiated rumour, or without giving his employer a chance to rectify the situation. Providing this is done, however, there seems to be no sound argument to suggest he should behave any differently from a moral perspective than he would if he were not an employee. There seems to be no sound basis either on which a business can encourage or oblige its employees to behave in anything other than a morally responsible way.

Moreover, we can go further than this. Major breaches of safety standards may be relatively rare, most people have found themselves in a situation in which they knew a wrong was being committed, and felt instinctively that they should do something to stop it, but ended up turning a blind eye – either because they were scared (if witnessing a crime) or because they wished to avoid the hassle and possible risks to themselves of taking action, or because they felt pressurized by a perception that the wrongdoing was in some sense socially acceptable (cheating the tax-man, for example, or selling a second-hand car without disclosing faults). Inevitably these types of situation arise in business as well as in social life. Sexual harassment, the invasion of privacy, minor safety infringements, or cheating of customers and suppliers, are allowed to pass unnoticed. If a business has a moral obligation to prevent such things, as it surely does, then it also has an obligation to its employees to ensure that they do not feel pressurized in any way to ignore them. Fenman Training, a producer of training videos, has the following statement posted on its walls:

> We believe in honest and fair methods of doing business. Our policy is 'Active Honesty'. For example, if a colleague became aware that a supplier had mistakenly undercharged us for goods or services and clearly had not noticed the error, we would expect the colleague to point this out to the supplier. Likewise, if we had overcharged a customer.
>
> We believe in the importance of trust and mutual respect in business and we believe that a policy of Active Honesty pays for itself in the long run quite apart from the self respect that it makes possible for colleagues. *This company will never penalise anyone for being honest regardless of the cost to the company* [emphasis in original.]

This type of approach is unusual in business but it is surely morally desirable. By making it quite clear where everybody stands, the firm minimizes the possibilities for half-truths, evasion and cover-up. As a side benefit for the company, a lot of emotional energy that would otherwise go into agonizing and frustration is put instead into making the business successful.

## Fairness between employees

We have so far assumed that the responsibilities of a business towards one employee are the same as those towards another. In practice, however, firms do not behave as if they had the same obligations to all employees. Women often work on terms that are significantly inferior to those of men, and part-time staff are regularly excluded from protections enjoyed by full-time workers.[2] There are further variations, especially between one country and another. Racial minorities have legal remedies for discrimination in hiring in some jurisdictions, but not in others, and standards of health and safety can be high in one country and low in the next. In introducing employment legislation or agreeing to be bound by international agreements regulating the working environment, some governments attach greater weight to growth in employment than to an improvement in the conditions of those who already have jobs. At times they argue that improvements in working conditions are undesirable because they will cause the loss of jobs or prevent the creation of new ones. Other governments think that certain improvements are simply requirements of justice, and favour their intro-duction irrespective of their alleged economic consequences.[3] Still other governments consider the consequences of improved working conditions, but deny that they include increased unemployment or anything else that is untoward.

At the level of firms, there are also important variations of attitude and practice. Some businesses headquartered outside Europe introduce, through British or Continental subsidiaries, a pattern of industrial relations not typical of Europe. Companies operating in high-wage northern Europe often offer terms of employment different from those in low-wage southern Europe, and so on. These variations are very marked, and any attempt to harmonize practices across different countries and regions is apt to be controversial, provoking economic objections from one quarter and moral ones from another. Recent attempts by the European Economic Community to set European-wide standards in employment practice therefore provide a rich context for exploring the moral dimensions of business–employee relations. In the following sections we shall focus on the controversy surrounding the 'social chapter' of the 1991 Treaty of Maastricht, concen-trating on the moral arguments for and against the measures proposed for achieving equality in employment conditions, and the measures proposed for achieving employee consultation in the direction of a business.

## Maastricht

In December 1991 a treaty was signed at a summit of the European Economic Community held in the Dutch town of Maastricht. The purpose of the treaty was to replace the European Economic Community with the European Community, setting in train the long-term transition from a trade area spread out over twelve member countries in Western Europe to a political union of many more nations, potentially extending far into what was once the USSR. A protocol on social policy attached to the treaty, agreed in December 1989 by eleven of the twelve member countries, made the Community competent to set policy and introduce employment legis-lation over a much wider area than was provided for by the Treaty of Rome, the agreement that originally set up a six-member Community in 1957. The protocol, commonly known as the 'social chapter' of the Maastricht agreement, is associated with a 'social action programme' – a series of proposed pieces of legislation, mostly in the form of directives, intended to give effect to the social chapter. Among the matters that would be governed by these directives are part-time and temporary work, working hours and rest periods, mass redundancies, financial participation by workers in firms, and the establishment of European company councils for consulting the employees of firms operating on a pan-European basis.

If put into force, the directives would add to legislation concerning employees that is already binding on member countries. Some of the legislation is founded on articles of the Treaty of Rome or previously agreed directives. Article 119 is particularly relevant. It requires men and women to receive equal pay for equal work. The article has undergone clarification through cases brought under it against employers in different member countries and through the Equal Pay Directive and several Equal Treatment Directives. Article 118a of the Treaties constituting the Community (The Treaty on European Union and the Economic and Monetary Treaty) also has a bearing on employment issues, although its scope has been disputed. It concerns the 'working environment', interpreted at times to mean health and safety in the working environment, but interpreted at other times, especially by the European Commission (the body charged with implementing the Treaties) to cover working hours and pregnancy and maternity-leave arrangements.

The social chapter was welcomed by the British Trades Union Congress (TUC), and by its Europe-wide counterpart, the European Trade Union Confederation (ETUC). The British TUC, whose influence, membership and legal rights were all significantly reduced under a succession of Conservative governments in Britain in the 1980s, looked to the European Community as a source of legislation enabling workers, and trade unionists in particular, to regain lost influence. A TUC booklet, *Unions After Maastricht: The Challenge of Social Europe*, comments: 'The door is now open for legislation on the fundamental question of information and consultation of workers, and the portmanteau provision on "working conditions" opens new doors'.[4] This appears to be a reference to the provision in the Social Action Programme for the creation of European company councils for information and consultation, and Article 2 of the social chapter, which dedicates the EC to support member states' activities in the area of working conditions and 'the information and consultation of workers'. The TUC comment goes on:

> There are interesting elements perhaps for the longer term under unanimous decision making, for instance on co-determination. The reference to the employment rights of third-country nationals perhaps gives some leverage on the question of equal rights for workers from the ethnic minorities – although many of them are of course EC citizens.

'Co-determination' refers to a variety of methods of consulting and exchanging information between employers and workers beyond what is available in meetings of workers' councils. The TUC was also understandably interested in the status of third country nationals, citizens of non-EC countries, typically those from the Caribbean and Indian sub-continent, represented in British trade unions. In other EC countries questions of the rights of workers from third countries would bear on guest workers from southern Europe, immigrants from Northern Africa, or people from former colonial countries much further afield.[5]

The tone of the TUC comments was optimistic. Was the optimism justified, in view of the fact that the UK, alone among the twelve member countries, refused to sign the social chapter and was exempted from its provisions? The optimism may have been in order: new voting procedures introduced under the 1986 Single European Act allowed many binding decisions to be taken by qualified majority vote in the Council of Ministers, removing the veto power that the UK might have exercised over policy sympathetic to trade unions or to workers. On the other hand, the social chapter contains a number of restrictions and exclusions that employers, and governments sympathetic to employers, might have been expected to welcome, and that were indeed included in order to conciliate them. For instance, Article 1 of the social chapter, while committing the signatories to improved conditions for workers and increased influence for them in industrial relations, promises to take account of differences in practice in these areas in national jurisdictions, and to reflect the need to maintain competitiveness. Similarly, the second paragraph of Article 2 of the social chapter empowers the Council of Ministers to introduce directives concerning working conditions and industrial relations, but at the same time says, 'Such directives shall avoid imposing administrative, financial and legal constraints in a way which would hold back the creation and development of small and medium-sized undertakings'. Again, the provisions of Article 2 are explicitly curtailed. They do not apply to 'pay, the right of association, the right to strike or the right to impose lock-outs'. This presumably means that any directives inspired by it would leave intact pre-existing union legislation in the member states.

The exclusions and escape clauses scattered through the social chapter call into question claims that it favours workers rather than employers in industrial relations. Even provisions in EC Treaties and protocols that seem obviously intended to promote the interests of workers in general, or of disadvantaged workers, are not always what they seem. Thus the inclusion in the Treaty of Rome of Article 119, requiring that men and women should receive equal pay for equal work, 'was initially prompted not by any fundamental belief in the equality of women and men, but to prevent member states that employed low-priced female labour from undercutting their partners'.[6] An equal pay article of the social chapter (Article 6) does appear to acknowledge the existence of discrimination against women as an evil worth combating in its own right, and it even encourages measures for preventing, or compensating women for, disadvantages falling specifically upon females pursuing a career; but, as we have already seen, the force of what apparently are moral imperatives in the chapter is significantly dissipated by clauses allowing established national practices to go undisturbed, and by reminders of the need to promote competitiveness and economic growth.

## Moral demands and economic and political costs

Perhaps the largest issues raised by the social chapter are those that remained between the lines. Foremost among these, signalled by the escape clauses that we have mentioned, are issues concerning the economic and political costs of measures benefiting employees. The economic costs range from the price of administering compliance with the new regulations to increases in labour costs arising from proposed entitlements, e.g. to job security during pregnancy. Political costs are associated with the hostility in some member countries to mandatory changes in local practices and institutions, and resentment at the trend toward centralization. The question is, do these costs outweigh the benefits to employees where there are moral arguments for the benefits?

The short answer is, 'It depends'. Some benefits are intended to remedy or prevent unreasonable disadvantage or outright harm; the more extreme the disadvantage or harm the less likely that the economic costs of the benefits can be too high. The same is true where the source of the disadvantage is something morality forbids – such as wilful denigration or mistreatment. Other benefits make acceptable conditions better, or agreeable conditions even more agreeable. Here the moral costs of not having the improvements are much smaller, other things being equal. Not only do the moral costs vary according to pre-existing conditions; it may also matter whether morality conflicts with politics or economics. Perhaps the political costs of new employment measures are more disputable in some cases than the economic costs: that would take away from their weight as objections to the new measures. Economic considerations, on the other hand, are sometimes thought to count for more. These are among the factors that would influence a judgement as to whether, all things considered, it is best to introduce, for example, increased job protection for part-time workers or statutory maternity leave. Whether in the actual debate about the measures the political, economic and moral factors are each given appropriate weight, however, remains to be seen.

Many of the measures concerning employees contemplated in the EC Social Action Programme are straightforwardly justifiable in moral terms. This is particularly evident in the case of health and safety directives. Thus the moral requirement that one minimizes harm justifies a proposed directive on controlling levels of exposure to asbestos, the directive making it compulsory for businesses to make safety plans for construction sites, and a directive requiring the posting of safety signs. Perhaps the requirement that harm be minimized also warrants – though to what extent is controversial – a directive calling for restrictions on the number of working hours. Finally, the requirement of justice that all persons be treated as equals justifies some of the directives outlawing discrimination against women at work. Indeed the 'social dimension' of the European Community, which the social chapter and the Social Action Programme were meant to promote, is often interpreted as the area in which EC members try to meet the demands of social justice.

Can directives that are proposed in the interest of justice, or for other moral reasons, be argued down on non-moral grounds? To take up this question, let us consider the opposition to proposed EC employment measures from the EC member state least sympathetic to the Social Chapter, the UK. The UK government's views on the whole range of directives are summarized in a collection of documents entitled *The United Kingdom in Europe: People, Jobs and Progress*, issued in February 1992 by the UK Department of Employment. These documents show that the UK did not set its face against every EC proposal. One document, for example, expresses what appears to be total agreement with the European Commission on matters of health and safety. Another speaks in favour of a proposed directive for the protection of pregnant women at work, but disputes the choice of basis for the directive in the EC Treaty provisions. On the other hand, the document commenting on a directive requiring employer-employee consultation is largely hostile and dismissive, and enlarges on a general scepticism concerning the social chapter and Social Action Programme expressed in other documents from the 1992 collection.[7] We shall now turn to the disagreement over that directive.

## Informing and consulting employees

In the form in which it was put forward by the European Commission the directive required companies with at least 1000 employees, or with operations in at least two member states and at least 100 employees in each, to act on employee requests for workers' councils, the form of council either being worked out locally and specified in a written agreement, or conforming to a model set out in advance in the directive itself.[8] Is there a moral justification for these measures? The article of the social chapter that is relevant here mentions social protection and dialogue between employers and employees as aims to be promoted by member states. The aim of social protection clearly has moral content, but does the aim of dialogue, which bears on the proposal of workers' councils? If dialogue is directed at preventing conflict or confrontation, then the aim of dialogue does have moral content. The same is true if dialogue is pursued in order to satisfy a requirement of respect for persons, respect being taken to include a willingness to listen to people or to take their views seriously. The same is true again if a workers' council brings into operation a mechanism for disclosing wrongdoing: in the absence of such a mechanism the severe burdens of whistle-blowing might weigh on any employee who had something to report.

The UK objections to the directive on informing and consulting workers do not acknowledge its moral justification. They assume a different, apparently commercial, justification for workers' councils. The UK position paper suggests that what is at stake in the idea of workers' councils is not the moral requirement of respect, or something similar, but the desirability of employee participation in, and commitment to, the economic activities of their firm. Now employee participation might also be desirable for reasons related to the importance of showing respect, e.g. the importance of taking into account the points of view of as many participants of an enterprise as possible; or the importance, in a collective undertaking, of acting with the agreement and approval of as many as possible of those affected. But this is not what the UK paper implies. It implies that employee participation is desirable because of its desirable economic effects, in particular its contribution to efficiency and productivity. Again, the desirability of productivity and efficiency are not necessarily independent of moral value, since productivity and efficiency can themselves add to the general well-being, and so have moral value recognized by utilitarians. It is not obvious, however, that such a consideration enters the UK position, which seems to be that the economic value of efficiency and productivity by themselves can lend value to employee participation. In any case, since employee participation rather than the promotion of respect through dialogue is what the UK position paper regards as crucial, it does not support forums for facilitating dialogue, such as workers' councils, even though the economic rewards of industrial peace have converted employers to them in Germany.[9]

If the UK assumptions are accepted, the case for workers' councils is indeed not overwhelming. It is plausible to hold that employee participation can just as effectively be promoted by quality circles, or even by the wearing of a company uniform or company calisthenic sessions, as by discussions round a conference table. But it is not plausible that the company uniform or a daily exercise session effectively promotes respect between employees and managers. By tying the purpose of workers' councils to employee participation, by ignoring the possible moral point of these councils, the UK position paper and the EC directive miss one another. Another way of putting it is by saying that the UK position paper changes the subject when it considers the justification of workers' councils, and therefore objects irrelevantly.

## Moralizing the economic objections

This is not the end of the matter, because, as already hinted, it is possible to supply moral content – utilitarian moral content – to the UK position. One can say that economic well-being is part of the well-being that a measure promotes if it is moral, and one can say that more well-being will be created without workers' councils than with them. One can even argue that, while respect between workers and employers is an element of this well-being, it is an element that depends on the existence of businesses, and that the existence of workers' councils discourages the creation and growth of businesses. One can add – as the British employers' association, the CBI, has added – that, in the UK at any rate, the creation of workers' councils would not even remedy a felt lack of respect, since the majority of employees (63 per cent of those surveyed in CBI-member firms in 1991) feel that they are consulted enough already.[20]

Not all these considerations are compelling on close examination. Perhaps their major weakness is that they prove too much. They not only count against the formation of workers' councils that don't yet exist; they count against other institutions that do exist and are not at issue in the directives. For instance, the argument from total well-being against workers' councils could probably just as cogently be put against the existence of trade unions and a state-run health service. If trade unions did not exist, wage costs would be lower and there would be more jobs and more businesses. If so, one would have the counterpart of the point about workers' councils – that they depend on businesses and yet more businesses would exist without them than with them. A similar point could be made about the public provision of a health service. If there were no state-run health service, taxes would be lower, and perhaps average economic well-being would be higher. These considerations do not show that there should be no trade unions or health service: economic well-being is not everything, and a level of it below the maximum, even well below, is often justified for the sake of other things, including opportunities for employees to act in concert, and opportunities for everyone to have health care when they need it.

A more telling element of the argument we are considering is the finding that a majority of UK employees felt that they were consulted enough already, in the absence of workers' councils. If this feeling is shared by majorities of employees in other EC-member countries, the rationale for the directive is indeed weak. On the other hand, what if, notwithstanding the finding in Britain, there is an overwhelming majority for it elsewhere in the community? Certainly there is some evidence from the European Values Survey that in Western Europe as a whole the demand from workers for greater consultation grew markedly in the 1980s.[11] If majorities mean something when they favour employers, must they not mean something also when they go against them? And if the majority rules, must not the British minority go along?

## Political objections

Before considering the moral argument that could be constructed to bolster the UK objections against workers' councils, we noted the emphasis in the UK document on the value of employee participation rather than the value of dialogue. The UK document did not confine itself to talking about employee participation and ways of achieving it that were better than workers' councils. It also put forward arguments about economic costs, arguments that have already been touched upon: the draft directive might deter inward investment by companies put off by the red tape of workers' councils; or it might discourage growth to over 1000 employees. There were also political objections. The UK complained that the proposal of workers' councils, like previous EC proposals, 'sought to impose a limited number of specific models of consultation on the whole of Europe; these have been unacceptable not only to the UK but to other countries'.[12]

Here and elsewhere in the document on consulting workers, the EC is said to 'impose' its ideas on individual countries, to ignore or disrupt local arrangements, to prefer the rigid and universal to the flexible and particular. Similar language is used in the document criticizing EC proposals on part-time and temporary work,[13] and the general document on the social chapter.[14]

This rhetoric has a certain force, but it is also easily turned against governments who rely upon it. Thus, if it is right for the UK government to complain of measures being imposed upon it by Brussels, why is it not also right for the Scots to complain of a burden of legislation or proposed legislation from London? Why is not the proposed reform of local administration by the UK government open to the same objection made against the EC: that it is presumptuous of the centre to think it knows best. Or to take the argument further, but in a way that still has an edge when applied to the UK government position in general, why isn't it right to speak of tyrannical majorities imposing their will on minorities, so that, in the name of upholding their own freedom the minority is entitled to ignore measures that have the backing of majorities? The question would probably be received sympathetically by the UK government when thinking of itself outnumbered at Maastricht, but other cases are embarrassing. The UK government would certainly disapprove of a minority in a trade union ignoring a majority decision against a strike, or, presumably, ignoring a majority decision about anything. The rhetoric employed by the UK government against the EC is essentially individualist and anti-government, and it sits uneasily on government documents, even when it is directed against what is taken to be a potential super-government.

## Objections in the spirit of the directive

The claim that the rhetoric of the UK government can be used against the UK government does not by itself establish that there is anything wrong with the individualist message of the rhetoric. But we saw in Chapter 2 that the official morality of individualism – egoism – is objectionable, and hence that the individualist message of the rhetoric may be objectionable as well. The freedom of the individual to do what he wants is not to be defended no matter what the individual wants to do, and some ways of exercising the freedom are more valuable than others precisely because they benefit people other than the agent. By the same token, some forms of government action are defensible even when they reduce the scope for individual action – because they promote the public good.

All of that said, there may still be good objections to the EC directive on consulting workers or the EC directive on working hours. Thus, if majorities of employees throughout Europe say that they feel consulted enough, then the directive may be a solution to a non-existent problem. Again, if employees make an informed choice to work more than the number of hours proposed as the maximum in the EC directive, and doing so creates no health risk, then a provision enabling them to opt out of the provisions of the directive would seem to be defensible, notwithstanding the force of the arguments for declaring a lower maximum number of working hours. The *imposition* of a safeguard carries a moral cost that may well outweigh the moral benefit of the safeguard itself. These ways of disagreeing with the need for a directive, however, or of acknowledging legitimate exceptions to a directive, differ from the ones presented by the UK government, in that they are in the same spirit as the directives themselves. They illustrate rather than dispute or sidestep the value of respecting employee views, and they do not assume that the economic costs of a directive are decisive considerations against supporting it.

## Equal treatment

In the case of worker consultation, the social chapter and Social Action Programme take worker councils, which are widely accepted in Continental Europe, and endorse their purpose – the promotion of dialogue – in an article of a treaty protocol intended to articulate some of the social values of the European Community. The attempt to harmonize European practice by making the workers' council more widely used seems to have some moral justification, and there are member states where its adoption would raise the standard of conduct of industrial relations considerably. But harmonization can also work to lower moral standards. Thus the fears of the UK Commission for Racial Equality that legal protections for minorities enjoyed in the UK but not elsewhere in the European Community might, far from spreading to other countries, be diluted in the UK itself so as to bring its laws into line with laws elsewhere in Europe. As of 1992, race legislation in nearly all member countries of the EC was primarily concerned with incitement to racial hatred. There was little to outlaw discrimination in employment. Often protections were confined to citizens of member countries and excluded guest-workers; in the UK, on the other hand, foreign workers, and members of racial minorities holding non-British passports but resident in Britain, were covered by the law. Opportunities for civil action over discrimination were very narrowly circumscribed on the Continent, but available in Britain.

Would a harmonization downwards of race discrimination law toward the Continental norm be, consistent with what is already in the social chapter? In one sense at least it would not be, for the principles that are evidently in play in articles ensuring equality in employment conditions between men and women cannot be prevented from applying logically, even if not legally, between races and religions as well. We shall enlarge on this claim in a moment. Even if the claim is correct, however, and the social chapter is in a sense driven by its own logic to prescribe equality over a wider area than between the sexes, there is still the question whether it is likely to be by way of a revised treaty protocol that moral progress is going to be made. It would seem plausible to claim that more than a revised protocol, more even than the duplication of regulatory bodies like the British CRE in other European countries, would be necessary. Campaigning and lobbying by interest groups – the Council of Europe Minority Youth Committee is an example – no doubt have to take place as well. In the commercial world the good practice of individual firms needs to be publicized and imitated. Whether, as some ethical consumers' organizations claim, the good practice that most deserves imitation in the area of equal opportunities is that of US firms is a question we shall take up later.

## A logic of equality in EC treaties

Article 2 of the social chapter commits the Community to support member states in obtaining 'equality between men and women with regard to labour market opportunities and treatment at work'. Article 6 of the chapter requires each member state to 'ensure that the principle of equal pay for equal work is applied'. Both these provisions echo Article 119 of the Treaty of Rome. What basis in morality, if any, do these provisions have? Or, to put it another way, what makes it wrong for women to be paid less than men for the same job or to be given less favourable working conditions than their male counterparts? The answer is that where there are no differences between people relevant to the treatment that they receive, they should receive the same treatment.

Note that this principle is very general. It does not just apply to employment matters. For example, it implies that when two people have committed the same crime, they should suffer the same penalty, except where there is some relevant difference between the criminals or extenuating circumstances for one crime and not the other. Again, the principle implies that when two people are each interested in applying for a loan, and there is no difference in financial circumstances or relevant history, there should be an equal probability of each succeeding. And so on. A wrong is done when the treatment of two people is sensitive to differences that are not relevant in the circumstances, as when a judge sentences one man to five years for robbery and sentences another robber to two years because the second went to the judge's old school; or when someone who dislikes redheaded people decides, just for that reason, that he is not going to authorize a loan to a perfectly good applicant with red hair. A person's sex is like hair colour and old school in these examples: irrelevant to the treatment one is entitled to receive. It is irrelevant also in the case of the pay one receives for the work one does.

There is more to the ethics of employment than pay, however, and so there is room for dispute as to whether differences related to one's sex are all irrelevant to one's status as an employee: if pregnancy carries entitlements to paid leaves of absence and therefore extra costs, as well as the inconvenience of loss of service to an employer, then the costs of hiring or continuing to employ a woman can be higher than the costs of hiring or continuing to employ a man. In 1985 and 1990, Employment Appeals Tribunals in the UK rejected appeals on the ground of sexual discrimination against dismissal for pregnancy, holding that what mattered was length of absence from work, not the fact that pregnancy affected women uniquely.[15] The European Court of Justice, in the 1991 Dekker case, has held to the contrary that, since only women can be pregnant, to refuse to hire them because of the costs of possible pregnancy is discriminatory, and unlawful under the Equal Treatment Directive. Disagreements between these judicial bodies do not show that irrelevant differences matter to employment conditions after all, only that it is not always obvious which differences are irrelevant. A good principle to adopt in this area is that relevance must be established where it is disputed. And a test of whether something is properly taken into account is if a reason can be given for finding it relevant. In the case of pregnancy a reason can be given why women might be more expensive to hire than men, hence why a potential employee's sex is relevant to decisions about hiring. The reason given is not necessarily decisive, but it is a reason: it is very hard, however, to see why hair colour should affect one's status as a loan applicant, or why sharing a school with one's sentencer should make a difference to the length of sentence for a crime.

We have already pointed out that the principle that explains why it is wrong to pay women less than men also explains why other forms of discriminatory treatment are wrong. It is because the underlying principle has quite general application that the logic of equal pay between women and men can apply outside the sphere of sex discrimination. The logic of the response to sex discrimination has implications for other forms of discrimination, in particular racial discrimination. That is why, in a certain sense, the social chapter cannot have the provisions it has concerning men and women at work and have nothing to say about discrimination on the basis of race or religion. Even if there are no articles in the social chapter that explicitly consider racial and religious discrimination, the social chapter and, for that matter, the Treaty of Rome, through its equal pay article, have a bearing on these forms of discrimination. Indeed they must either pronounce against them or else give up the principle that treatment must be equal in the absence of relevant difference.

When the equal pay articles of the Treaty of Rome and social chapter are taken together with relevant directives and court decisions, it turns out that Community law prohibits quite a broad range of discriminatory practices, all with counterparts in the area of racial discrimination. In particular, indirect discrimination is forbidden. Indirect discrimination takes place where, even though a practice or measure does not explicitly single out a group for worse treatment, one group is disproportionately disadvantaged, and disadvantaged in a way that is not justified by the purpose of the practice or measure.

In a German court case brought under Article 119 of the Treaty of Rome an occupational pension scheme was held to discriminate against women in that it excluded part-time workers in a firm where most part-time workers were women. The fact that women fell foul of the restriction in significantly greater numbers than men meant that the exclusions from the occupational pension scheme were required by the court to be justified. An illustration in the area of race or religion is provided by a firm that requires people to clothe themselves in certain ways. Without necessarily being intended to do so, such requirements can interfere with the dress requirements of a particular religion, and so put members of that religious group at a disadvantage in what ought to be a fair competition for certain jobs. This counts as discriminatory if there is no independent reason for that clothing requirement, e.g. safety or health. Thus if a retail shop insists on male sales assistants being bareheaded, males whose religions require them to wear turbans are put at a disadvantage, even though there is no obvious reason why being bareheaded matters to the job of being a sales assistant. If indirect discrimination is recognized and outlawed in the case of women, it is hard to see how it can, in consistency, be ignored and permitted in the case of other groups.

## The logic of equality and the aim of European integration

The egalitarian spirit of such measures as the equal pay provision notwithstanding, it might be thought that the European Community is *not* committed to anti-discrimination measures across the board. This is because it is a European Community, founded on ties between cultures that until this century were nearly exclusively white, with traditions that are far from multi-cultural and multi-racial. More concretely, many of the rights enjoyed throughout the community are restricted to holders of EC citizenship, which in many countries is difficult to obtain, and is sometimes out of the reach of people who were born and brought up in EC countries as the children of foreigners. If culture and citizenship are inevitably the basis for forming one nation state as against another, or a European Community as against some other sort of community, is it not inevitable that some people of non-European origin will be at a disadvantage?

This is a large question, and one whose answer depends crucially on how 'disadvantage' is interpreted. An article that appeared in 1990 in *Interlink*, a newspaper published by the UK Commission for Racial Equality, comments on the implications for education and training of plans for an integrated Community:

> The emphasis of the Commission's own social action programme tends to reinforce this view of an integrated white Europe. In looking at education in a united Europe, the emphasis is on preparation for life in a single market economy and one component of this is the need to give greater prominence to language training and the appreciation of European cultures.[16]

The danger is that greater validity will be given to European languages, thus undermining the linguistic and cultural capital of many ethnic minorities whose mother tongue is not a European language.

If learning French or German is given much greater prestige than knowing Bengali or Urdu, even in schools in English cities where the vast majority of pupils are of Asian background, one can see how a language policy suited to European integration could appear unwelcome to British Asians, and how it could appear to make one kind of bilingualism inferior to another kind. On the other hand, one can also see how it would benefit British businesses to have employees who were fluent in the languages of Britain's main trading partners, and how it would break down distrust and misunderstanding between the majority populations of different countries in the European community if they were at home in one another's cultures.

Intellectually, the problem of reconciling Europeanism with respect for minorities is not so formidable: the rationale for a parochial Englishman's finding out about, and taking steps to feel at home with, the customs and cultures of other Europeans is comparable to the rationale for a European's finding out about the customs and cultures of countries in the wider, non-European world. The logic of the two things is the same logic; but that is not to say that each is equally easy in practice; people's identifications and prejudices will get in the way. Many whites in Europe and elsewhere do prefer living with whites to living with people of other races, even if the people of other races speak the same language as they do and have been born in the same country. So while the aim of European integration need not marginalize people of non-European origin or background, the practice of European integration may do so in fact, bringing it into tension with the egalitarian force of its anti-discrimination measures in the case of women.

## Good practice in equal opportunities

Different firms' policies toward women and ethnic or racial minorities among their employees were surveyed in 1989 and 1990 by New Consumer, one of the ethical consumers' groups mentioned in Chapter 3. New Consumer confined itself to companies operating in the UK. Of the fourteen classified as 'well above average' in respect of opportunities for women, all were subsidiaries of US companies. In the 'above average' list there were twenty-four entries, nearly half subsidiaries of American firms. There were no firms classified as 'well above average' employers in relation to opportunities for ethnic minorities, but of the twenty-one described as above average, two were British and one was a British-Dutch joint venture; the rest, once again, were American.

After discussing the grounds for these assessments and asking whether they are reasonable, we shall describe the practices of some selected firms, including one not surveyed by New Consumer. In the cases where New Consumer particularly admired policies adopted by the American parent companies of UK firms, we shall ask whether the policies sometimes owe more to cultural difference than morality.

The New Consumer survey adopts a broader perspective on equal opportunities than has been possible up to now in our discussion. For one thing, it considers the employment policies of firms with respect to women and ethnic minorities in upper echelon positions as well as jobs lower down in the business hierarchy: the cases we have mentioned so far under EC legislation concern female workers near the bottom of the job ladder. The New Consumer survey also considers equal opportunities policies for the employment of the disabled. When assessing different firms' practices in the area of sex equality, New Consumer took into account measures adopted by firms to enable women to take on both career and family responsibilities, as well as schemes providing leave for fathers of new-born children. In the area of race New Consumer did not consider UK initiatives alone, but took into account past practice in the USA. Religious discrimination, a pressing issue in Northern Ireland, was the subject of several replies to the New Consumer questionnaire, and this too entered into the rating of several firms.

## Positive discrimination: to follow the American lead?

The survey had a considerable amount to say about sexual and racial equality in employment opportunities, and in both areas, but especially in regard to race, New Consumer tended to identify best practice with American practice. Is this pro-American stance justified on moral grounds? In comparing measures taken by UK firms to alleviate inner city unemployment with those that have been implemented in the USA, New Consumer comments:

> In the USA this kind of private sector intervention is much more advanced, and many initiatives are unlikely to be replicated in the UK because they take the form of positive discrimination. Thus while many UK-based companies provided examples of training and community development programmes in areas with large disadvantaged ethnic minority communities..., a large number of US companies also cited contracts awarded to companies owned and managed by members of the ethnic minority communities as evidence of their commitment to broadening the economic base of these communities.[17]

The award of contracts to minority-run firms is not positive discrimination in the more familiar form of preferring female to male candidates, or black to white candidates, in order to raise the level of representation of women and minorities in certain firms and in certain jobs. But it is related, and far more controversial in the UK and on the Continent than in the USA, even in UK and Continental subsidiaries of US firms covered by the New Consumer survey.

At first sight, scepticism about positive discrimination appears perfectly justified, for, as in the case of hiring, how can the colour or ethnic background of people who run a business properly qualify them for favourable treatment if it could only improperly qualify them for unfavourable treatment? One simple answer is that the colour or background, though irrelevant to one case, may perhaps be relevant to the other, though indirectly. In recruitment one is always making a judgement on people's future potential (their ability to do a job they have not yet done), not on past or present performance. Past and present performance are relevant factors in making this judgement, but so are any other factors that might have influenced that performance. In recruiting students into our university courses we expect a higher level of examination performance from someone who went to a good school and came from a supportive family environment than from someone who has not had those advantages. Lower levels of examination performance does not, then, mean lower levels of ability. In giving weight to this consideration we are effectively applying positive discrimination in favour of the underprivileged, who are in many cases women, or coloured, or members of ethnic minorities. The same argument holds in respect of the recruitment of employees. A problem arises, however, when we move from a judgement based on individuals to one based on classes of individuals, such as women or ethnic groups, and when we move from allowing an element of judgement to requiring a practice that may at times conflict with that judgement, for not all members of these groups are underprivileged, and not all underprivileged people are members of these groups.

According to one American writer, Thomas Nagel, the introduction of a policy of positive discrimination in the USA has been a four-step process.[18] First, it came to be agreed that there should be no explicit barriers to the training or recruitment of women and blacks for certain professions and other high-status jobs. Next, it was recognized that even after the explicit barriers were taken down, unconscious discrimination, or deliberate but hidden discrimination, might still operate, so that it was necessary to design selection procedures that discouraged or prevented this as far as possible. Third, it was thought that even after the first two steps had been taken at the point of entry to particular jobs, professions or educational institutions, women and blacks might still be at a disadvantage in the wider society, so that their chances of reaching these points of entry were not as high as those of, say, white men. This realization justified the introduction of special training programmes for members of the disadvantaged groups. But even these training programmes were not thought to level the playing field entirely. In order to compensate for the remaining disadvantage, it was necessary to give preference at the point of entry to those whose qualifications were most likely to have been worse on account of the residual social unfairness. And with this fourth step, the policy of positive discrimination came into being. Women and members of minorities whose final qualifications were worse than white competitors, but who had had to make up for a far worse starting position in the race for those qualifications than the white men, were, so to speak, offered a nearer finishing line. There was similar positive discrimination for the women or ethnic minority managers whose firms were differentially favoured in the award of contracts by larger US companies.

Now even in the USA it is controversial whether the problem that was supposed to be solved by the fourth step could be solved without adding to injustice or, differently, reducing utility. The fact that characteristics of people that are not directly or in themselves relevant to the requirements of a job are not only taken into account but are sometimes decisive in hiring choices itself constitutes an injustice, at least at first sight. And the strains in the policy of positive discrimination do not end there. Nagel argues very convincingly that the logic of the egalitarian argument for positive discrimination in fact supports far more sweeping reform of the system of entry to the best jobs than the four steps already described. Nagel suggests that when inequalities of *opportunity* between individuals is allowed to weigh, not just inequalities between groups, one is driven toward a selection or recruitment process that randomizes success among competitors who all reach a certain agreed minimum competence.[19] More fundamentally, reflection on the grounds for preferential treatment for women and minorities eventually calls into question the justice of a system in which success is constituted by financial rewards for abilities and skills owed largely to lucky circumstances, and that confer advantages one does not really deserve.[20] Compelling as these points are, custom and expectation in the USA have overtaken them: positive discrimination is in fact practised, members of minorities and women and their spokesmen expect it to go on being practised, and this expectation is among others that inform the prevailing sense of what is just and what is not.

In the UK the fourth step of systematic positive discrimination has not yet been taken. Not only is it no part of accepted practice in society as a whole, but regulatory or campaigning bodies in this area are apparently not calling for its introduction. The current Race Relations Code of Practice issued by the Commission for Racial Equality defines equal opportunities policy so that it falls short of positive discrimination.[21] It sets out what an equal opportunities policy ought to eliminate: disadvantage in employment prospects based on racial grounds; and disadvantage that, whether or not based on racial grounds, falls disproportionately on members of a racial group and cannot be independently justified. It also sets out what equal opportunities policy can introduce: training and encouragement for members of underrepresented groups. These measures seem to be straightforwardly required by justice without having any obvious effects that are unjust. Perhaps they need to be implemented by people who have gone to some trouble to learn about the effects of discrimination on its victims and the way different methods of recruitment in fact put certain groups at a disadvantage, sometimes wilfully, sometimes not. The CRE itself publishes and distributes reports of its own investigations in this area. One study published in 1984 found that a dairy's policy of hiring on the basis of word-of-mouth recommendations of people it already employed worked against members of racial minorities.[22] Another enquiry in 1985 into the employment practices of the National Bus Company found similar effects from a system of word-of-mouth recommendations and the imposition of language tests. In a morally difficult area the CRE code of practice, taken together with training in the effects of discrimination, may perhaps give a morally more defensible specification of equal opportunities policy than the allegedly 'more advanced' American practices that New Consumer commends.

## Good practice illustrated

Leaving aside what is controversial in New Consumer's assumptions about backward and progressive equal opportunities policy, it is interesting to ask whether their survey provides any examples of good company practice that might be more widely adopted. Here is a selection of three firms whose employment policies might be regarded as morally admirable.

### Avon Products Inc.

The American-owned cosmetics multinational, perhaps best known for its army of door-to-door sales people, is highly praised in the New Consumer survey, particularly for the high proportions of women among the board members and managers of the parent company. Ethnic minorities were also found to be well represented. In Avon's UK subsidiary women were less prominent on the board and in senior management posts, and there were no members of ethnic minorities in any senior positions. Its offering of benefits in relation to family responsibilities was mixed, but very good by UK standards. Although no crèche and childcare facilities were available, job-sharing and flexi-time schemes were found to be in force, and the childcare expenses of employees at its Corby factory were met in part by the company. In 1988, the year for which New Consumer presents relevant financial information, the UK branch of Avon made pre-tax profits of just under £10 million on a turnover of £127 million. It made a number of charitable donations, including payments to the Pre-school Playgroups Association, and provided a secondee for six months to the Women's Economic Development Initiative. New Consumer's verdict: 'Avon has a particularly strong record on affirmative action in support of women and members of ethnic minorities. Its actions in reducing animal testing have been at the forefront of larger corporations, and its level of disclosure was excellent'.[23]

### The Littlewoods Organization PLC

One of the few British companies to be singled out by New Consumer for its good equal opportunities policy, the Littlewoods Organization is a Liverpool-based retailing, soccer promotions and financial services firm. It is private and family-owned, and, as in the case of some other big businesses in the UK that started out as family firms, such as the glass manufacturers Pilkington, the food company Lyons, or the confectioners Rowntrees, its ethical practices were originally introduced to reflect the personal views of some family members. In 1989 profit before tax was £64 million on turnover of £2.2 billion.

New Consumer says of Littlewoods that its 'record on equal opportunities is outstanding for the UK, providing a model of good practice for the retail sector and beyond'.[24] The record is outstanding in relation to both women and ethnic minorities. The firm has had very generous maternity-related benefits, for which there is a relatively short qualifying period of 12 months. It has a very unusual policy of offering maternity leave to women who adopt babies. Again exceptionally, maternity benefits are not confined to management level: they are available to all female employees. Men are not left out: ten days' paid paternity leave is also offered by the firm.

Littlewoods' policy on ethnic minorities is to recruit them in numbers that reflect their proportions in local communities. In 1989 the firm had plans for employing minorities at its head office at the level of 8 per cent of total workforce. These plans are backed up with a suitable training programme. It participates in schemes to reduce the inner city unemployment rate in Liverpool, and indeed funds a local employment agency as well as a local newspaper. Equal opportunities at Littlewoods extend to the disabled. Not only are they hired in considerable numbers, but there are initiatives within the firm for increasing their participation in the work of the company.

### Marks & Spencer PLC

New Consumer gave the UK clothing and food retailers Marks & Spencer high ratings in most areas covered by its ethical appraisal of firms, equal opportunities practices included. Although only one woman sat on the Board at the time the survey was being conducted, 60 per cent of store management personnel were women. There were monitoring procedures to keep track of the recruitment of ethnic minorities, and initiatives in places with high ethnic minority populations. In Bradford, which has a large concentration of people with origins in India and Pakistan, the Marks & Spencer store set up links with a local school in order partly to encourage recruitment. The M & S equal opportunity policies have to be considered against the background of exceptionally high satisfaction with the company as an employer. It has a very low rate of turnover of staff – according to the company the lowest rate of turnover in British retailing – and a high degree of staff loyalty.[25]

# Good practice in employee consultation

We came to examples of good practice in equal opportunities by way of a discussion of egalitarian principles in the treaties of the European Community. We argued that the treaty articles on equality between the sexes were grounded in ideas with implications for the question of equality between races. These ideas suggest that strong measures must be taken against racial discrimination in employment, just as strong measures must be taken against sexual discrimination. Measures that seem on balance to be of an appropriate strength are illustrated by the policies of the three firms we have just looked at.

Equal opportunities policies were not the only ones considered in this chapter however. We also considered the question of worker consultation, and the merits of an EC proposal for a certain form of worker consultation body to be established in firms of a certain size across Europe. In this connection, too, descriptions of good company practice from the New Consumer survey and other sources are worth a look.

## John Lewis Partnership

A pioneer in Britain in implementing industrial democracy, John Lewis is another example of a retailing firm run on the ethical principles of a founding family. It is comparable in this respect to Marks & Spencer and Littlewoods, and like them it has set an influential example. As will emerge, the pattern of its industrial democracy also affected that of another firm whose practice will be considered in this section, the UK celluloid manufacturer Scott Bader.

The constitution of the John Lewis Partnership, encountered already in a case study in Chapter 1, provides for the accountability of management to those who are managed. This principle is at work in the composition and powers of a 140-member Central Council in the Partnership. Four-fifths are Partner employees elected by secret ballot by other Partner employees from a total electorate of over 20,000. The remaining fifth are appointed by the Chairman of the Partnership. The Council has the power to remove the Chairman, can advise management on any aspect of the running of the business, acts as a court of appeal for allegations of mistreatment by staff, and exercises considerable financial power. In addition to the Central Council there are Branch Councils in individual John Lewis stores, and a unique system of in-house journalism, which allows a wide range of problems to be raised publicly, with appropriate responses from relevant managers. Another John Lewis institution, the post of branch registrar, also has a function in the employee consultation machinery. The registrar acts as custodian of the constitution in each branch. There is also a Partner's

Counsellor, a kind of Partnership-wide ombudsman at director level, whom the branch registrar represents locally. According to the company brochure, 'About the John Lewis Partnership', elections to places on the Central Council are vigorously contested, and other mechanisms for consultation are also heavily used. A recent first-hand account of the registrar's function indicates that it, too, is effective in promoting accountability.[26] New Consumer comments, 'The degree of employee involvement is exceptional...'.

### Scott Bader

Scott Bader is a manufacturer of synthetic chemical fibre materials used in the construction of boat and car bodies, and in the production of paints and other surface coatings among a very wide variety of other applications. It is headquartered in Wellingborough, in England, but also has branches in Ireland and France. In 1990 trading profit was just over £4 million on a turnover of about £65 million. The company employs just under 500 people.

The Scott Bader Commonwealth began in 1951 when Ernest Bader, the Quaker founder of the then 30-year-old Scott Bader Company Limited, transferred 90 per cent of his shares to a charitable trust that employees of Scott Bader could join. Through the trust the employees were supposed to be able to own and control the company. In 1963 the remaining 10 per cent of shares held by the family were transferred to the Commonwealth, and a body of trustees was created to take up the powers of directing the business associated with these shares. Membership of the Commonwealth is currently open to any employee over 18 who after a year's service agrees to accept the Preamble of the Commonwealth Constitution, to support the Constitution and abide by a Code of Practice. The structure of the Commonwealth consists of a Board of Management elected from the Commonwealth, the Scott Bader Company Limited Board, responsible for the business decisions, and the Community Council. This appears to have a role similar to the Central Council in the John Lewis Partnership. (According to an article about the commonwealth written by the son of the founder, the John Lewis Partnership was one of the models for the Scott Bader Commonwealth.)[27] Composed of representatives from the sixteen constituencies of the company in the UK and Ireland and elected by all employees, the Council approves the appointment of pay and directors, can discuss any issue it likes, can recommended action to the Board, acts as a final court of appeal in disciplinary cases, and administers funds for social and welfare purposes. The trustees protect the company constitution and mediate between the Company Board and Council in case of disagreement.

## Other issues in European employment ethics

This chapter has emphasized issues concerning worker consultation and equal opportunities in employment that are controversial in the UK and the rest of Western Europe. These are not the only areas of controversy. There is considerable disagreement between firms in EC countries over the treatment of part-time workers, over responsibilities for training, and over the support a firm should offer former workers that it has made redundant. In the UK there has been a public debate concerning the levels of pay and pay rises for those in charge of big companies, and also a controversy concerning the effect on workers, especially those employed by retail chains, of seven days a week trading. Among the issues that until recently have been considered important in the UK and some northern European countries, but that have ceased to animate debate, are the ethics of the closed shop and of strike action.

## References

1  See, for example Richard T. de George, *Business Ethics*, 2nd edition (London: Macmillan, 1986).
2  The number of part-time workers in West European countries is very large: see C. Randlesome, W. Brierley, K. Bruton, C. Gordon and P. King, *Business Cultures in Europe* (Oxford: Butterworth-Heinemann, 1993), p.138.
3  Or, as in the German case, a custom of 'social partnership'. See Randlesome *et al.*, *op. cit.*, p.36.
4  *Unions after Maastricht* (London: TUC Publications, 1992), p.12.
5  See Randlesome *et al.*, *op. cit.*, p.92, for France, and pp.92–3 for the Netherlands.
6  *Women and Europe: a Trade Union Guide* (London: TUC Publications, 1990), p. 15.
7  In June 1993 the UK refused to submit to an EC directive limiting working hours.
8  In certain countries, notably the Netherlands, workers' councils have long been established. See Randlesome *et al.*, *op. cit.*, p.298.
9  Randlesome *et al.*, *op. cit.*, p.52. See pp. 247 and 142 for the cases of Spain and Italy.
10  *Social Europe After Maastricht* (London: CBI, 1992).
11  D. Barker, *Business Ethics: a European Review*, 1, no. 2 (1992), p. 97, citing S. Harding, 'Employee Expectations and Opinions: Changes in Western European Organizations', paper presented to 1991 IPM conference.
12  *Ibid.*, p.12.

13  *Ibid.*, pp.7–8.
14  *Ibid.*, p.23.
15  See B. Hepple, 'Sex and Race Discrimination' in *Using European Equality Legislation* (London: TUC, 1992), p. 23.
16  Ansel Wong, 'An All European Underclass', *Interlink* (August 1990), pp. 4–5.
17  R. Adams, J. Carruthers and Sean Hamil (eds), *Changing Corporate Values: A guide to social practice and environmental policy and practice in Britain's top companies* (London: Kogan Page, 1990), p.20.
18  Thomas Nagel, 'The policy of preference', in Thomas Nagel, *Mortal Questions* (Cambridge: Cambridge University Press), pp.92f.
19  *Ibid.*, p.95.
20  *Ibid.*, pp.96–97.
21  London: Commission for Racial Equality, 1984; reprinted 1991.
22  Commission for Racial Equality Formal Investigation Reports: Unigate Dairies Ltd (1984).
23  Adams *et al.*, *op. cit.*, p.144.
24  *Ibid.*, p.348.
25  See A. Campbell, M. Devine, A. Young, *A Sense of Mission* (London: Hutchinson Business Books, 1990), pp.72–3.
26  Pauline Graham, 'The Registrar in the John Lewis Partnership', *Business Ethics: A European Review*, 1, no.3 (1991), p.85.
27  *Long Range Planning*, 19 no.6 (1986), pp.66–74.

# 5 Shareholders

'My primary responsibility is to the shareholders, because they are the owners of the company.' The quotation is from the chairman of one of the UK's largest companies, speaking at an informal gathering to discuss corporate responsibility; but it could easily be from any director of any large public company, in any circumstances. For the great majority of those running large businesses it is the unquestioned starting point for any discussion of business ethics. Yet it is only partly true.

The primary legal responsibility of a company director is certainly to the company's shareholders, and while this is no sanction to ride roughshod over other responsibilities, it does quite properly provide the context for all that a business does. Contrary to the common perception, however, the shareholders do not own a limited liability company: indeed no one does. The company is a legally corporate entity with its own corporate 'personality' governed by its declaration of purpose in the memorandum and articles of association. It can no more be 'owned' by shareholders than a person can. Rather, the shareholders are 'members' of the company, joining together as a company to pursue the goals for which the company was established. In return for their investment in the company, they have the right to any profits it generates, in the form of dividends, but they have neither the rights nor the responsibilities that would normally be associated with ownership. On the one hand, they cannot, for example, change the purpose of the company. On the other hand, they are not liable for any debts it might incur beyond the amount of their investment.[1]

In response to this the chairman quoted above replied that the difference was a technical one. As far as his shareholders were concerned, they were owners, and as far as he was concerned, they were owners. Once again, most senior businessmen would agree, and the political rhetoric of British governments committed to widespread share ownership has encouraged shareholders to take the same view. If we focus merely on the rights of ownership it is easy to see how this has come about. Two hundred years ago a company incorporated to trade in the East Indies, to provide marine insurance or to build and operate a canal, could do only that: the purposes of the company were clear, specific and dominant. Now, following a century of mergers, acquisitions and corporate growth, the purposes of a company are usually phrased so vaguely as to make anything possible. The effective purpose of any large company has become, simply, to engage in business for the creation of profit. While the rights of company membership are no longer restricted, however, the responsibilities are, and even if we accept that shareholders are in some, non-legal, sense owners of a company, we must ask what obligations they may have to society in return for the benefit of limited liability. Moreover, if we pursue the line of argument that affords shareholders the status they adopt for themselves, we must recognize that many shareholders see themselves neither as owners nor as members but simply as gamblers, backing a company as they would a horse, looking for profit but seeking neither rights nor responsibilities.

Whether the shareholder is understood as an owner of a company or as a member of that company, or merely as a gambler riding on the success of that company, is of critical importance for assessing the morality of shareholding. A shareholder who acts as a gambler cannot be expected to be treated as an owner. Nor should one who has been encouraged to participate on the basis of ownership then be treated as if he were a gambler. Since a business cannot know which shareholder falls into which category, however, it has to treat them all the same way. We shall argue below that, for this reason and others, there may be strong moral grounds for not using shareholding as a form of gambling, and we shall assume in this chapter that shareholders have at least the legal status of members. To what extent they should be considered not just as members but as owners of the business will depend upon the circumstances.

Whether members or owners, shareholders can, if their stakes are large enough or if they are persuasive enough, affect the affairs of a company decisively. Because shareholders usually invest in a firm in order to collect dividends that they are led by the firm to expect, a firm cannot discharge its obligations to shareholders without attempting to trade profitably. On the other hand, the measures that a firm may be tempted to adopt to cut costs and maximize profits can sometimes violate obligations to other groups, e.g. the employees. So one question about shareholders concerns the priority of the obligation to provide them with a good return, and the moral costs of putting this obligation first. To what extent is the obligation overriding? This is probably the most pressing question about shareholders for what we have been calling 'narrow' business ethics.

Another question concerns obligations that are distinguishable from that of providing a return, e.g. the obligation to present the firm's affairs and performance accurately in its communications with its investors and the wider public. In normal circumstances this obligation appears relatively straightforward. But what about in abnormal circumstances? Does it become less strict, for example, when there is keen competition for investment funds, or in a climate where investors want unrealistically quick or unrealistically big returns, or in circumstances where a firm is the target of a hostile take-over? Might not embellished results or creative accounting be necessary at times for bare survival? The questions do not stop there. Are the moral obligations of a firm to shareholders different from its obligations to other investors? To what extent are obligations to shareholders limited by the need for shareholders to exercise prudence or else bear the consequences of speculative investment when it goes wrong? How far should the directors of a company place their obligations to shareholders before their own personal interests?

In what follows we shall argue that, morally speaking, the interest of shareholders in a good return on investment does not necessarily outweigh the interests of others in a business where interests conflict. On the contrary, as opposed to some forms of investment with a fixed return, shareholding seems to require a willingness to bear with a firm and to endure some of its changing fortunes. This is reflected not only in a shareholder's accepting a variable level of dividend, dropping at times to nil, but also in the scope for shareholders having their say about the performance of the management and the composition of the board. Holding deposits in a bank requires less than shareholding, and has less scope for participation, even if the deposits are invested in turn by the bank in shares. And holding loan equity comes somewhere in between. In that case one's rate of return is supposed to be insulated from the ups and downs of the business, and the investment is secured against some asset. The upshot of all of this is not that shareholders are less justified in expecting a return than other investors, but that they are less justified in taking the return at significant expense to the business, and less justified in taking a big short-term return than other investors. Shareholding, in other words, may carry more responsibilities than other forms of investment – at least other things being equal.

If this point makes sense, then so may another: that shareholding is in theory a morally desirable form of public ownership of business. In theory – why this qualification is in order will emerge later – shareholding may even be more desirable than public ownership delegated to the state through nationalization. This point has some timeliness in both Western and Eastern Europe, where the privatization of state-owned firms has become more and more commonplace. We shall begin this chapter by looking at the obligations of shareholders to a business, and to each other. We shall then look at the obligations a business has to its shareholders, and shall finish with a discussion of the general obligations of shareholders and the issue of ethical investment.

## Obligations of shareholders

A recent description of good practice issued by the UK Institutional Shareholders' Committee (ISC) starts from the proposition that 'shareholders are the true proprietors of a company. This ownership gives rise to responsibilities which have, for many years, been acknowledged by a large number of institutional shareholders'.[2] Instead of 'responsibilities', the Committee could have spoken of 'obligations'. The obligations described include keeping up good contacts at senior executive level with businesses in which shares are held, agitating for the presence of independent directors on boards, and exercising and enlarging voting rights carried by shareholdings. Some of these responsibilities imply co-operative activity on the part of the firm in which the investment is held, co-operative activity that is hard to describe without raising moral questions. For example, in encouraging good flows of information with the firm, is there not a high risk that inside information will flow to the institutional investor, or that an atmosphere will be created in which withholding such information will look like a lapse of good faith? The ISC description of good practice acknowledges the danger, and also the costs of action to the institutional investor if inside information *is* passed on:

> Institutions do not wish to be made insiders, and [contacts with firms invested in] should not include the transmission of price-sensitive information. Where, exceptionally, there are compelling reasons for a Board to consult institutional shareholders on issues which are price-sensitive, those shareholders may have to accept that such consultation would involve the receipt of confidences which will require that they suspend their ability to deal in a company's shares.[3]

Inside information is transmissible, the ISC seems to be saying, so long as it does not lead to insider trading. But it is difficult to see how the principle that prohibits insider dealing – namely that certain holders of shares should not be put at an advantage over others by having information that is not public – can be rigorously observed at the same time as institutional investors enjoy communications with a firm not enjoyed by other investors. Either the principle is impossible to reconcile with the existence of large discrepancies in the resources of large and small shareholders, or else 'price-sensitive information' is easier to define than it at first appears to be.

Further questions may be asked about the apparently laudable aim of building up good working relationships between institutions and companies in which they have shareholdings. Do the responsibilities of institutions extend to loyalty to a company that has done its best to keep its shareholders informed and whose plans are generally approved of by institutions? The issue is broached indirectly by the ISC, under the heading of takeovers:

> Where a company has kept its shareholders informed of its long term plans, confidence and understanding will have developed between the management and shareholders, making it less likely that a hostile bid will succeed. Where

good relations have been established and shareholders understand the long term objectives of management they are more likely to support the incumbent Board in its resistance to an unwelcome bid.[4]

These remarks come close to acknowledging an obligation to stand by managements that have taken institutions into their confidence. True, the presumption in favour of loyalty may be overridden by 'a primary duty to those on whose behalf they invest',[5] but the general message seems to be that a responsible institutional shareholder will not lightly support a hostile bid for a company that has co-operated with it.

Do major shareholders have even the shadow of an obligation to retain shares in a company during a take-over? There are many who deny that shareholder responsibilities go far beyond enforcing a firm's commitment to 'maximizing long term owner value'.[6] According to this view, there may be genuine responsibilities to promote honesty and fairness and legality in the business's activities and even to make sure that the expectations of other stakeholders are in tune with the objectives of the firm.[7] But these limited obligations, so it is said, do not mean that one has to stick by a particular set of directors or that one has to be reluctant, other things being equal, to sell one's shares, or that one should buy shares only when one is prepared to wait for results. As Elaine Sternberg argues, in defence of this view:

> There is, ordinarily, no moral obligation to be, or to continue to be, a shareholder. Being a shareholder is only one of the myriad roles open to an individual or institution, and the reasons for choosing to be a shareholder are equally diverse. Although some objectives encourage long term holdings, and others do not, all are perfectly valid reasons for owning shares. And it is the shareholder's objectives for owning shares which should determine whether a particular holding is bought or kept or sold...[8]

Sternberg goes on to connect these claims with what she thinks are the proper demands of corporate loyalty:

> Loyalty does not require that shareholders stick with a company when its performance is deficient. It may sometimes be appropriate to allow a company time to recover, or to help it to do so, but the relationship of shareholder to corporation is not that of a friend, family member, social worker or doctor; shareholders do not have a Hippocratic duty to heal or preserve the corporation... The appropriate meaning of corporate loyalty is not cleaving to the corporation whatever it may do, or whatever the consequences. Real corporate loyalty is instead being true to the proper purpose of the corporation – in the case of a business, to maximizing shareholders' long term value... The right way to ensure loyalty and long term holdings is thus not to shackle investors to their investments... The proper solution is instead to make sure that shareholders' key objectives in owning shares are indeed best achieved by holding on to them.[9]

These arguments are important, because they represent a dominant strand of thinking in respect of shareholder responsibilities; but they are also flawed. The problem is that they vacillate between two quite distinct ways of assessing shareholdings, one of them having no particular authority, and the other not giving shareholders the latitude claimed, morally speaking, for disposing of shares just as they like.

Sternberg insists that shareholdings have to be assessed according to the objectives of the shareholders or their reasons for acquiring shares, but she mentions two quite different types of objectives or reasons: the personal objectives or reasons of individual shareholders and the objective or purpose of a corporation in business. When it comes to the personal objectives of shareholders, she is remarkably quick to endorse them. First, she says that they are varied, and without pausing to give examples of any, she says that 'all are perfectly valid reasons of holding shares' and that as such they should determine whether shares are held or not. This position is only as compelling as the objectives individual shareholders actually have. If someone subscribes to a share offer in a privatization simply because he likes the idea of being a shareholder, or simply because he is attracted to the advertisement promoting the offer, or even because he thinks that he can make a quick profit on the day that trading in shares begins, then it does not go without saying that all are perfectly valid reasons for buying shares. The first three reasons hardly seem to be reasons for an *investment* decision at all, and they are questionable reasons even for a more commonplace purchasing decision. After all, buying a thing simply because one likes the advertising or simply because one's friends are doing it seems to be a case of buying a thing without reference to what use it is going to be to the purchaser. As for the share purchase in expectation of a quick profit, this makes sense as an investment decision, even as a rational investment decision, but is not necessarily a case of a moral investment decision. The upshot is not that personal investment or personal decisions should be vetted or policed, but rather that they should not be considered to be beyond criticism, still less to be well-grounded no matter what reasons people have for making them.

Even people's rational investment decisions are open to critical appraisal, and from precisely the standpoint from which Sternberg thinks companies can be criticized, namely the objective of maximizing long term value. If it is on the understanding that the long-term value of their shareholding will be increased that people buy shares, then for the same reason that people cannot be blamed for deserting a company that has no interest in increasing long-term value or that is negligent in doing so, the investor can be criticized for buying shares or holding shares without being prepared to wait for their value to be increased.

More generally, we may criticize any shareholder who acts in a way that is inconsistent with a shareholding. To come back to our earlier example of the shareholder as a gambler, there is a fundamental difference between gambling on shares and gambling on horses. If someone places a bet on a horse race, his action has no adverse impact on the horse. Indeed it is only through gambling that horse-racing can take place at all. Any purchase or sale of shares, in contrast, does affect, however marginally, the fate of the business concerned. To purchase shares other than for the purpose for which they were intended is consequently to misuse the relationship of shareholding to the potential detriment of the business and so is morally questionable. The same argument can be applied to any investor who, while not necessarily gambling, is investing on a basis that is at variance with the concept of shareholding. This might include investors who are not prepared to wait for long-term value, or those who are not prepared to accept a temporary loss of value or drop in the dividend. To say this is not to assimilate the role of shareholder to that of doctor, friend or social worker: it is to draw some of the constraints on being a shareholder from the form of investment shares are. A responsible purchaser or owner of shares will accept the constraints.

Sternberg thinks that shareholders have relatively few responsibilities to the firms in which they invest, but this is because she makes some controversial assumptions about the basis of these responsibilities. Apart from the reference to personal objectives just discussed, she assumes that the responsibilities are derivable from the purpose of a corporation established to conduct business, from considerations about lines of accountability in corporations, and from legitimate expectations associated with the existence of corporations.[10] Her reasoning can be reconstructed like this: 'The purpose of a corporation is to increase its value for the owners; the owners of a corporation are the shareholders; owners call the tune; employees are accountable to the corporation, and the corporation in turn accountable to the owners; owners are accountable neither to the corporation nor to its employees; however, they may threaten the longevity of the corporation if they disappoint expectations about it, or act unjustly; so if they are wise they will act justly and predictably, but they are not obliged to do more'. Notice that even this allowance for obligations to be just and predictable is not necessarily an allowance for moral obligations: as Sternberg describes things, justice is for the sake of long corporate life. But according to some moral theories – Kant's, for instance – one either does what justice requires for the sake of being just or else one does not act morally. For Kant the idea that one can act morally for an ulterior and non-moral purpose is incoherent.

There are two further points to be made about Sternberg's argument. The first is that it ignores shareholders' responsibilities to each other. If shareholders are conceived of as owners of a company, they must be conceived of as joint-owners, with the same mutual responsibilities as in any other joint-ownership. The joint-owners of a house, say, or of a horse, each have a responsibility to look after the house or the horse for the benefit of others and not merely for themselves. Collectively they may call a tune, but as individuals they have an obligation to dance to the collective tune. In the case of a house or a home, or indeed a private company, this is generally reflected in a requirement that a part-owner may not sell his holding to somebody without the approval of the other part-owners. In a public company this technical constraint is removed, but the moral duties it represented may still have some force. If shareholders are conceived of as members of a company, then this requirement has, if anything, greater force, as the established purpose of the company provides the context for membership. In this case the shareholders could not expect, even collectively, to call the tune.

The second point is that Sternberg confuses two ideas: not being accountable within a corporation and not having a responsibility to a corporation. Even if we accept that shareholders, conceived of as owners of corporations, may not be accountable in that they are in charge (they pay the piper and so call the tune), this does not mean that they cannot be morally responsible for things done in or on behalf of corporations. This point is obvious when the roles of director and owner are occupied simultaneously: the fact that the director unfairly dismisses someone and thus acts immorally is not cancelled out by the fact that he owns the company. Ownership may bring it about that there is no official *channel* for appealing above the head of the one who unfairly dismisses someone, but it doesn't eliminate the basis in fact for an appeal, or for criticism of the decision. Being the one who pays the piper does not make just any choice of tune the right one. Running a business for immoral gains cannot be justified just because the owners or shareholders want it that way. Nor can running a business irresponsibly, without due care for the various shareholders involved.

Again, it is by no means clear that the proper purpose of a business is always to maximize long term value. This is certainly a valid purpose and, other things being equal, a morally sound one. But it is not the only one. We have already remarked that the original purpose of companies was to engage in some activity, such as trade or insurance or the operation of a utility. There was certainly an expectation of gain and shareholders would invest, then as now, on the basis of that expectation. But it was nowhere written down in the memorandum and articles that a business had to seek a profit, or to maximize shareholder value, and for many family-owned businesses and some regulated businesses (even though they are public companies) this is not in fact the primary objective. In the case of a regulated utility, for example, the primary duty may be to the consumers rather than the shareholders, while the owners of a family firm will often take a very broad view of the stakeholders, including employees and local communities among them, and be quite prepared to sacrifice their own gains for the welfare of these groups. For a public company to take a similar line would be wrong only if the shareholders had been encouraged or allowed to expect something different. Providing it was done openly, it would not be in any way improper.

In a public company many of the responsibilities of ownership or membership are delegated to the directors, but the appointment and supervision of those directors remains the direct responsibility of shareholders. Going back to our discussion of shareholder objectives, an unwillingness to exercise this responsibility, e.g. by exercising voting rights, might be seen as another characteristic that is inconsistent with shareholding. He who pays the piper must take responsibility for the piper's actions, be they the abuse of employees, the flouting of safety standards, or leading children astray.

One particular action in this respect is the choice of tune, and on this Sternberg appears to be in two minds. On the one hand, she argues that he who plays the piper calls the tune, on the other that the 'proper purpose' of any business is to maximize long-term shareholder value. Once again this is an accurate reflection of the prevailing view among senior businessmen, who are influenced by both the need for allegiance to their shareholders (who can, after all, get them dismissed or taken over) and the desire to 'get on with the job'. Most shareholders are in fact agreed on the general proposition that businesses are there primarily to add value, so the conflicts are few. However, one conflict that does arise is over the distinction between 'long term' and 'short term', with businessmen often complaining that investors are too interested in short-term profits, and too reluctant to allow businesses to build for the longer term. There is no immediate solution to this problem. It might be perfectly proper to establish a company so as to generate short-term returns only, providing that was made clear to prospective shareholders, or to pursue a strategy that rejected the maximization of expected long-term value in favour of higher potential value (but at much higher risk) or lower level of risk (but with much slower growth).

## Small versus institutional shareholders

Sternberg's general claim is that when it comes to obligations and shareholders, the direction of obligation is largely from companies to shareholders, and not so much the other way round. It is for companies to maximize owner value; it is for shareholders to hold companies to this obligation and to see to it that the necessary background conditions for success are fulfilled. There are no further obligations, and in particular no obligations to stay loyal to firms in which one holds shares. We have already tried to suggest that shareholders have further obligations just on account of what differentiates shares from other sorts of investment, and that Sternberg misses these because she takes an unduly narrow view of the source of shareholder obligations. But other positions are possible. One of these, which allows one to concede more to Sternberg than we do, holds that shareholder obligations are minimal in most cases, but substantial if one is controlling investor. This position implies that small investors, who are able to exercise no control and little influence, and whose share dealings have little if any impact on the business, can in consequence buy and sell shares *ad lib* without fear of moral censure. Controlling investors, on the other hand, including some institutional investors, are morally obliged to tread more carefully. Thus Sternberg would be right about some share-holders but wrong about shareholders in general.

One businessman who adopts a version of the position just described is Louis Sherwood, former chairman of the UK retailing group, Gateway Foodmarkets Ltd. In a contribution to a conference on the ethical considerations that bear on take-overs, Sherwood took up the question that has been dominating this section:

> What about individual shareholders? What does an individual shareholder have in the way of a human duty towards the company that he or she owns part of? Well I have thought long and hard about this issue and my conclusion is very simple. I do not believe that a shareholder has any duty at all towards the company he or she invests in. Investing in quoted securities is like backing horses. The punters owe no duty to the horses they back even though that horse, its owner, rider and trainer all owe a duty to the punters to run as hard and honestly as possible. Now by extension, and here I am sure that many of you will strongly disagree with me, even major institutional shareholders owe no particular duty to the companies they invest in. Their duty is to *their* share-holders and *their* employees. Only *controlling shareholders* in my view have a duty which arises from their potential and actual use of control and that duty is analogous to the duty of the Board of Directors.[11]

Sherwood's idea appears to be that responsibilities to a business are concentrated in those who are directly responsible for its performance – those in control. Indeed, he seems to go further, to hold that responsibilities to a business are *confined* to those who direct its activities.

This argument is difficult to sustain, for one thing because the distinction between control and influence is not always very sharp. An institutional investor may not be a controlling shareholder, but can still exercise substantial influence on the business. If, however, we recast the argument in terms of influence rather than control, then the distinction between share-holders with responsibilities and shareholders without begins to coincide with the distinction between small shareholders, usually individuals, and institutional shareholders. And that this is where the dividing line lies is very plausible. It is plausible to say that where the effects of a shareholder's buying or selling on a business are negligible, then the buying or selling is morally neutral, but that the buying or selling can be morally problematic if it is on a scale that significantly affects a firm's fortunes. It is the power significantly to affect the fortunes of firms by acquiring or disposing of a stake that the Institutional Shareholders Committee acknowledges when it acknowledges its responsibilities to a firm. It is the same power which shows that institutional shareholders cannot be compared to ordinary backers of horses.

Is the conclusion to draw that the responsibilities of shareholders are commensurate with their abilities to affect the fortunes of a company through share dealings? This conclusion would bear out Sternberg's point that the ordinary personal investor can do what he likes without acting irresponsibly, and yet also preserve something of the connection between responsibility and corporate control. The problem is that the conclusion is too permissive in regard to the very small investor. Some of the arguments we have used to highlight the responsibilities of a shareholder depend on the proposition that the purchase of shares affects a company in a way that betting on a horse does not affect the horse. But even if we accept that for individual shareholdings the impact may be negligible, and accept further that, morally, we can ignore it, we are still left with other reasons why the small shareholder may have a responsibility to act in a way that is consistent with shareholding, e.g. by waiting for a return on his investment.

To reinforce this point, we may consider another of the many defects of the analogy between the shareholder and the punter. The analogy suggests that investing, like betting, is a risky money-making venture, and that just as it should not be entered into lightly on account of the risk, so, again on account of the risk, bets should not (morally should not) be taken as a sign of long-term commitment, especially if they are small bets, or bets made by people who cannot afford to lose much. What is wrong with this way of working out the analogy is that buying shares is not only a venture in money-*making*, but also a case of participating in a public institution for money-*raising*, an institution that benefits individual firms, the economy and society in a number of easy to specify ways. Although horse-racing, too, supports a horse-breeding and betting industry, and generates considerable tax revenue, the betting analogy obscures the way in which the stock market is specially designed to bring together for the public good private sources of money and proven companies with specific plans to innovate, to save labour, and to make more efficient use of scarce materials. It is true that this function of the stock market may not be before the minds of those who buy and sell shares; but this does not mean it is not the point of the institution, or that investors should not be conscious of it and respect it – even when they have rather selfish reasons for coming into contact with the institution. And respecting the purpose of the institution means accepting the responsibilities it implies.

## The conditions of shareholder responsibility

We have been arguing that shareholders, institutional shareholders in particular, do have responsibilities to the firms in which they invest. But these responsibilities are conditional on whether the responsibilities owed by firms to shareholders are also discharged. An institutional shareholder that agrees to resist a hostile take-over bid on the basis of a firm's false or misleading report of its financial position does not *owe* the firm its loyalty even if it retains its stake. Similarly if an institutional shareholder bears with a firm that is unusually tight-lipped about its financial position or its plans: the institutional shareholder does more than is required if it gives the firm the benefit of the doubt in the absence of full information. The same is true if the institutional shareholder bears with a firm while being given less information abut its position than another institutional shareholder. It behaves generously toward the firm rather than within the limits of its duty to it, and if it had decided not to act generously, then it would not be open to the charge of behaving immorally.

In other words, a firm's duty to disclose accurately and reasonably fully its current position and prospects underpins the responsibilities of share-holders to the firm. Now there are cases where firms understandably give themselves latitude in interpreting the duty of full and accurate disclosure, namely where they are having to counter or undo misleading, false or even scurrilous information being circulated about them, say by firms that intend a take-over or have actually launched a bid. In such a case the demands of self-defence may excuse publicity that dwells only on the firm's achieve-ments or that presents the record of its directors in the best possible, rather than the clearest, light. But in the context of a take-over these rhetorical strategies can be expected to be used and are not likely to mislead anyone. That fact, and the fact that normally there are no excuses for failures to disclose fully and accurately a firm's position, make it clear that the latitude for unduly creative or self-congratulatory publicity is limited.

The latitude is even more restricted morally where the investors are individuals with relatively little sophistication in financial matters and the securities are being bought through intermediaries, such as insurance companies, commodity and futures dealers, and a range of other investment businesses. Here the requirements of full and accurate and, perhaps above all, intelligible, information apply with particular force, as investors, relatively conscientious and well-informed ones included, are unlikely to be able to see through unfair or even fraudulent trading practices. The rationale for protecting small investors from these dangers is like the rationale for the consumer protections reviewed in Chapter 3: investors lack some information and expertise that is necessary for them to make the right choices.

As in the case of consumer protection, investor protection in the UK is embodied in legislation, notably the Financial Services Act of 1986, and in self-regulation on the part of the investment industry, overseen by an industry-funded but statute-backed body called the Securities and Investment Board. The SIB regulates entry by businesses into the financial services market, and is empowered to withdraw authorization to operate from firms that violate its rules. It also regulates the self-regulatory bodies. As of April 1991, there were four of these: the Securities and Futures Authority; the Financial Intermediaries, Managers and Brokers Regulatory Association; the Investment Management Regulatory Organization; and the Life Assurance and Unit Trust Regulatory Organization, whose success in excluding the unscrupulous has not been total.

Apart from rules governing the financial controls of investment businesses over the assets they handle, the SIB imposes a wide range of requirements concerning information given by investment businesses to investors. These cover the risks arising from making the investments they promote, the fees they receive for engaging investors, the declaration of their own interests in some of the investments they market, their responsibilities to those who have agreed to become investors, and so on.

One underpinning duty of businesses to shareholders is that of full and accurate disclosure. Others include maintaining and increasing profitability and giving shareholders a reasonable return. These duties may be said to underpin the obligations of shareholders rather than to be on a level with them, because shares are offered to the public on the understanding that the public will be presented with accurate and full information and on the understanding that a dividend will be paid where possible, while members of the public are not understood to commit their goodwill, loyalty or patience in addition to their money simply by their act of buying shares. At most they can be understood to commit their goodwill, loyalty and the rest as long as a firm performs well and keeps them informed.

It is hard to specify the central underpinning duty to achieve and increase profitability, without asking about the relation of this duty to other duties to other stakeholders. This brings us to what was earlier suggested to be the main question raised by shareholders for narrow business ethics: namely, whether achieving profitability for shareholders must be overriding where it conflicts with the interests of others. Another way of broaching the same question is by considering what the content of the duty about profitability is. Is it simply to increase profitability, and/or maintain it at a reasonable level, or is it to achieve *maximum* profitability as quickly as possible? In answering this question about one controversial underpinning duty, it pays to get all the help we can from another and much less controversial underpinning duty, the duty to give shareholders the fullest and most accurate description of the position and prospects of the firm. Discharging this duty, we suggest, affords opportunities for communication that can inform shareholders of the position of the other stakeholders, and that can therefore create greater impartiality about the urgency of enriching shareholders when there are other demands on resources. When the various other demands are known, it may still be urgent to enrich the shareholders – because, for example, they have had to do without dividends for some time, or because the share price has fallen dramatically – but creating a culture in which information about all the stakeholders is considered necessary by shareholders at least encourages objectivity, and it may moderate the pressure from them for ever higher returns.[12]

If there is any plausibility in our suggestion that proper information to shareholders should encourage impartiality abut the weight of various stakeholder demands, and if the encouragement of impartiality means that in some cases a good return for shareholders will seem less urgent than a fair redundancy scheme for employees or a long overdue rise in the salary of the managing director, then, by the same token, it should not be regarded as an underpinning duty to maximize return to shareholders at all costs. The content of an underpinning duty should not prejudice unduly a judgement about the relative strengths of different stakeholders' claims at different times to shares of a firm's resources. This conclusion does not imply that firms can afford to be casual about profitability or about the contentment of shareholders, or to give too much weight to interests that conflict with achieving profitability. This would be self-defeating, since the less profitability is achieved, the fewer resources there will be to make deserving claims upon; the point is only that the claims of shareholders should not be regarded automatically as pre-eminently deserving. Deserving, yes; impossible to refuse, no.

## Management buy-outs

The issues surrounding a business's responsibilities to its shareholders come to a head in the context of management buy-outs (MBOs), in which the existing management of a business seek to purchase it from the shareholders. Management buy-outs can be very profitable – for the managers and the financial advisers who encourage and support them – and this at once makes them suspect to the public. When Allied Steel and Wire, a Welsh steel company, was sold by its owners, GKN and British Steel, to a management-led consortium in October 1987 the management invested just £700,000 (the total package, highly leveraged, was worth about £180 million). In May 1988, when the company was floated on the stock exchange, the management received £4.2 million for its share. In April 1986 Cadbury-Schweppes sold off its non-chocolate food divisions to a management consortium led by Paul Judge, formerly a managing director of one of those divisions and a member of the policy group that had recommended the sell-off. The following year the profits of the divisions, trading as Premier Brands, doubled, and just three years after the buy-out the new company was sold on for £295 million, three times the original purchase price. Paul Judge's personal profit was estimated at over £40 million.

Both these examples raise questions about the motivation of senior management, which seems to have been able to perform dramatically better with the incentive of a major shareholding than without. As management buy-outs became more common in the late 1980s, there was a fear that the managers of companies identified as MBO candidates would be tempted to underperform, to do their jobs badly, in order to hasten the divestment decision and critically lower the price they would have to pay for the buy-out. In the Allied Steel and Wire case there is also the question of how well the parent company directors were doing their job of monitoring the subsidiary. Given the speed of the turn-around, much of the growth potential must already have been implicit in existing performance, though the parent companies were clearly unaware of it. In neither example, however, is there any question of the parent company directors acting immorally or in any fundamental sense irresponsibly. Once the decision had been taken to dispose of the companies concerned, the directors did everything they reasonably could to get the highest prices for them. Thus Cadbury-Schweppes, a company known for its very high ethical standards, openly encouraged bids for the Premier Brands divisions. It was only when these fell short of what the management team thought they were worth that the buy-out option was explored, and thereafter the buy-out team was in open competition with Allied Lyons, the leading external bidder.

Of course, any management buy-out team has an inherent advantage over any external bidder in that it has full access to management accounts and other information while the external bidders, and indeed the shareholders, have to make do with a minimum of information. But in the examples considered so far the presence of a buy-out offer undoubtedly increased the amounts shareholders received for the business divested. The potential for conflict is much greater when it is not a subsidiary or division of a company that is being bought out, but the company itself. An interesting example of this is provided by the largest UK management buy-out to date, that of Magnet, a builders' merchants and DIY company, in 1989.

At the time of the management buy-out Magnet was a quoted public company with a recent history of strong profit growth (from £26 million in 1986 to £73 million in 1989). It had started as a family firm and had been built up by the son of the founder, Tom Duxbury, who was then managing director; but the family shareholding amounted to just 1 per cent, the remaining 99 per cent being in the hands of institutions and individual shareholders. Up to 1989 the focus of the company had been on sales to the building trade, mainly of joinery products, but Duxbury was in the process of refocusing on kitchen and bedroom showrooms with an eye on the DIY market. Despite the recent profit performance, the share price was languishing as the 1980s building boom came to an end and turned into recession, and Duxbury was worried that market short-termism might inhibit his long-term restructuring plans, and that a further fall in the share price might expose the company to an unwanted take-over. With the support of a consortium of banks he and his fellow directors therefore made a bid for the company.

The Magnet bid was worth over £600 million, nearly twice the existing market capitalization of the company. In an attempt to demonstrate some allegiance to shareholders, the buy-out team offered the ordinary share-holders a minority stake in the new company, but the bulk of the bid was in cash. The buy-out team argued that the terms were reasonable, and the non-executive directors agreed, pointing out that the management had no experience of operating under the difficult trading conditions that were to come, and that their previous forecasts had always been optimistic. There were no rival bidders, and there was indeed some sense in the markets that the management was not up to the task of dealing with recession, that the internal controls were poor, and that the offer was actually an over-generous one. (Certainly it turned out that way, as within a few months of the buy-out being completed the company had been forced to refinance, the finance director had been sacked and Duxbury himself had been forced to resign.) But despite all this a group of institutional investors held out for some time against the buy-out bid, concerned not so much by the price they were being offered (though they succeeded in getting that raised) as by the process underlying the buy-out.

In all, four major concerns were raised. The first concerned the infor-mation asymmetry between the buy-out team, on the one hand, and the shareholders, non-executive directors and potential external bidders, on the other hand. The banks taking part in the buy-out were provided with detailed three-year business and management plans, while the management team themselves had complete inside knowledge of the business. Shareholders, on the other hand, were given a bald one-year profit forecast (and in the first instance not even that), together with an outlook statement described by one commentator as having 'a haziness befitting a long-term weather forecast'. Shareholders also had the benefit of advice from the non-executive directors, but they were given no more infor-mation than the shareholders.

A second concern was that the information provided to the shareholders was felt to be quite insufficient to act as a basis for any informed judgement, and was provided in an edited form by a management team that had a clear interest in making the prospects seem unattractive. The third and fourth concerns also related to the conflicting interests of management. It was pointed out that in another sense, too, the management had a whip hand: if their buy-out attempt was rebuffed, what incentive would they have to manage the interests of the shareholders? And it was argued that the time and energy taken up by the management buy-out process, distracting management as it did from the task of running the business, was itself detrimental to the business and its shareholders.

In fact few people doubted the motives of Duxbury and his team, though many questioned the role of his advisers, whose profit would have to be at someone's expense. But the concerns raised go far beyond the Magnet case, to the question of whether a buy-out of this kind is ever morally justifiable. How can a company's directors act at one and the same time in both their own and their shareholders' interests? If they can claim to give better value to shareholders by buying them out than by managing the company for them, then they must, almost by definition, be failing in their duty of management. The discussion has wider implications, too, for it is not only in buy-outs that directors and managers act in their own interests. Take-overs serve to increase directors' salaries (usually measured in terms of company size) and create positions for their protegés. Innovation and change threaten the political *status quo* and are resisted on that account. These and other aspects of corporate life are perfectly understandable, but that does not mean they are morally acceptable in business any more than they would be in any other context of trust or trusteeship.

## Ethical investment

There is more than one way of reaching the conclusion that a shareholder's interest in the best possible return can sometimes be overridden or constrained by other interests. One way is by trying to put oneself in the shoes of the business and seeing all the claims that are made on its proceeds by different stakeholders. From this point of view different interests can take priority at different times. Another way is to look at things from a shareholder's point of view and ask what general ethical responsibilities shareholders might have, quite apart from their specific responsibilities towards the companies in which they invest. One way of doing this is to adopt the standpoint of people who see themselves simultaneously as shareholders and people with strong moral values, people who do not want their shareholding, or any of their other activities for that matter, to be at odds with their morals. Some of these people belong to the ethical investment movement. They were mentioned in passing earlier, in connection with the ethical consumer movement, to which they often also belong. In what follows we shall consider what role individual ethical investors and ethical investment institutions play, can play, or should play, in the financial markets.

Before describing ethical investment in practice, it is worth asking whether the very idea of an ethical investor makes sense. A counterpart of this question arose in the case of ethical consumers. In that connection we considered whether what was morally urgent might be consuming less rather than using one's consumption to make a moral statement to various retailers and manufacturers. In the same way it can be asked whether what is morally urgent might be the redistribution of wealth from the rich to the poor, e.g. through direct donation, rather than making money for oneself through businesses that are relatively respectable morally. This question assumes that ethical investments are always or usually investments in firms with ordinary commercial objectives, though objectives that the firms pursue scrupulously, and for the most part this assumption holds good. But there are perhaps untypical ethical investments which, despite taking the form of shareholdings and despite paying dividends, do not support profit-making ventures.

In the 1980s and early 1990s Traidcraft, a British public limited company controlled by a charitable trust and engaged in the marketing of goods from Third World countries, launched three share issues, two of which were oversubscribed. Shared Interest, an investment society launched to provide funds for anti-poverty, income-generating projects, also raised money through a share issue. Shared Interest guaranteed to repay investments after six months with a return of between 5.10 and 6.75 per cent. Traidcraft has a policy of paying at most 6 per cent gross 'when possible'.[13] Both these share issues channel money in the same direction as some charities, but they may be preferred by people actually working in development projects as a surer and better targeted source of income than funds rerouted to them through charities.

In Continental Europe, 'alternative investments', as the Traidcraft and Shared Interest issues may be called to distinguish them from ethical investments, are well established. There is even an Association of Investors in the Social Economy, to which some of the companies and trusts that make these investments belong. The proceeds of these investments go to co-operatives, such as the co-operatives in Mondragon, Spain, or to small 'green' businesses, or to enterprises dedicated to the principles of Rudolf Steiner. In Britain, Mercury Provident is a Steiner-inspired deposit-taker. Savers hold accounts, rather than shares, and they nominate interest rates within a narrow band. The lower the interest rate nominated, the higher the level of investment in such things as 'green' publishing and bookselling, co-operative light industry, and Rudolf Steiner schools. In 1993 Mercury Provident unveiled plans for specialist investment funds, beginning with a wind energy fund and an organic agricultural fund. Another, this time more mainstream, source of funds for co-operatives is deposits in the so-called ethical savings account offered by the UK Co-operative Bank in association with ICOF (Industrial Common Ownership Finance).

Except for the ethical savings account, none of these seem to be mainstream ethical investments, and mainstream ethical investments may raise questions of their own. Thus, to approach the matter from the angle of the narrow view of shareholder responsibilities outlined by Sternberg, isn't the ethical investor someone who is not, as he should be, really fully committed to the defining purpose of a corporation, namely to increase long-term owner value? And aren't the interests of ethical investors in things other than owner value going to conflict with the interests of those shareholders who *are* concerned with owner value and nothing else? Not necessarily. It is hard to see why an investor cannot be simultaneously interested in increasing long-term owner value *and* concerned with making sure that his money is supporting a firm engaged only in the provision of beneficial goods and services, or, more flexibly, of harmless goods and services. It is hard to see why an investor cannot be interested in increasing long-term owner value *and* in making sure that a firm's other stakeholders benefit from their role in the business. Of course it is possible for some shareholders to show concern for other stakeholders and to show what appears to be relative indifference to increasing owner value. Is it true that in this case people go beyond the legitimate limits of the shareholder role? And when shareholders who are only concerned with increasing owner value complain about fellow shareholders with other concerns, are they right to do so?

These questions have considerable philosophical depth. They raise the issue of how far the obligations that derive from the roles one has, including that of investor, can free one from the obligations that one is under as a human being.[14] There are businesses that do harm – to their employees, to their customers, to the environment – and though investors may not be directly responsible, have they no responsibility at all? When the harm done comes to light, can they blame it all on the directors and continue to hold shares with a clean conscience, knowing the harm does not originate with them? The greater the harm, the less easy it is to shrug off the suspicion that, by investing in the business, one is colluding in the harm and providing resources that make it easier for the business to carry out the activities with the harmful side effects. Of course one can invest and try as a shareholder to get the business to reform, but the activities that justify trying to get the business to reform cannot fail to be reasons (perhaps only weak ones, but reasons all the same) for getting out altogether. In other words, in this sort of case there is no insulating oneself from moral demands by retreating into the role of passive investor.

Matters are more complicated where it is not obvious, or where it is simply not true, that a business in which one has invested harms people. In such a case being an investor is *prima facie* acceptable morally. Of course it is true that even where one has a morally blameless investment in a company, there may be other ways of using the money that would have greater benefits. But except under act-utilitarianism this fact does not make holding the investment morally wrong. In any case the problem of not acting in the way that would be most beneficial is not just a problem for investors of money, but for investors of effort, i.e. for agents in general. For many of the actions we initiate, perhaps most, we could probably substitute others that could have greater benefits, or benefits for more people. That we omit these actions is not always blameworthy even by utilitarian standards, since there may be utility in letting people act for their own benefit or for those close to them at least some of the time. And the same may go for the uses of money we forgo when we make otherwise blameless investments.

The conclusion we appear to be driven to is that there is nothing in the very idea of investment that makes it morally suspect, though there can be cases where to invest in a given business is to collude in or condone harmful activity. Nor is there anything necessarily wrong with expressing one's moral values through investment rather than through donation. The investment may be blameless even if a different use of the money would have been more beneficial.

What about ethical investment in practice? What forms does it usually take and what good does it do? In Europe the main vehicles for ethical investment appear to be unit trusts (mutual funds) and pension funds, most of them based in the UK. There are not many European ethical funds outside the UK, although some UK funds are sold to Continental investors (some regulatory authorities in Continental Europe have, however, objected to the marketing of certain investments as 'ethical', as this appears to denigrate other securities offered to the public). As for the UK itself, 'ethical' funds assume a number of different forms, according to the number and content of their investment criteria. The typical criteria are negative. A potential receiver of ethical investment funds must have no connections with countries ruled by oppressive regimes, or in which basic human rights are disregarded. It must have no connection with armaments, gambling, pornography, tobacco or alcohol, and no history of being a polluter. It must not be a low-wage employer. Some ethical funds are geared to only one or a subset of these criteria such as, until recently, investment in South Africa, or, in the case of some funds directed at doctors, connection with tobacco or tobacco and alcohol. Other ethical funds, a small minority, select companies for the positive worth of their activities, for their provision of pollution control or recycling services, or for their manufacture of health care products. TSB Environmental and Merlin Jupiter are UK funds geared to positive criteria. As the list of criteria indicate, there is not always a firm dividing line between 'ethical' and 'green' investments.

Whether their criteria are positive or negative, ethical funds have, by some measures, access to only a small section of the share market. For one of the most exacting, the Buckmaster Fellowship Fund, administered by Credit Suisse, 82 per cent of the value of the FT Actuaries All-Share Index for the London Stock Exchange is out of bounds. There have been predictable effects on performance. Between 1986 and 1992 the offer price of units rose just over 3 per cent for income units and just over 13 per cent for accumulation units, compared to a rise of over 48 per cent in the FT All-Share Index and 32 per cent in the FT Actuaries World Index. Between August 1991 and February 1992 the offer price dropped over 5 per cent, while the World Index showed a rise of over 8 per cent. In a newsletter distributed by the Fund managers in February 1992 Buckmaster proposed a slight relaxation of most of its criteria for investment so as to improve performance and also take account of political change in South Africa. Companies were ruled out for investment if they employed more than 1 per cent of their workforce in South Africa, if they derived more than 1 per cent of turnover from the production of tobacco or alcohol, or more than 10 per cent of turnover from sales of tobacco or alcohol. In the area of armaments, companies were excluded if they had been engaged in the sale or production of 'strategic' goods or services for military users, or of weapons systems. The one area in which there was no relaxation of criteria was in gambling: Buckmaster refused to have anything to do with firms connected with it. The proposals for change in its investment criteria also included more precise measures of the environmental damage that would make a firm ineligible for investment.

The Buckmaster Fund is relatively small. Its total investment in shares in February 1992 was £4.2 million. On an entirely different scale, The Friends Provident Stewardship Unit Trust had investments of over £109 million in April 1992. This is the largest and oldest of the UK ethical funds, founded in 1984 by the Friends Provident insurance company. Both the insurers and the unit trust are affiliated with the Quakers: the chairman of the finance committee of the Religious Society of Friends sits on the Committee of Reference for the Stewardship Unit Trust, i.e. the committee that advises on the suitability of firms for investment. In addition to the Stewardship Unit Trust, there is a Stewardship Income Trust and Personal Equity Plan, as well as a North American Stewardship Trust, with total investments at the end of 1991 of just over £3 million.

The Stewardship Unit Trust showed modest growth in the period during which the Buckmaster Fellowship suffered a drop in its offer price. From May 1991 to May 1992 its offer price rose nearly 10 per cent. From February 1991 to February 1992 the Stewardship North American Fund showed a gain of over 23 per cent.[15] This was lower than the average gain for US-invested unit trusts, but still an attractive return, and it shows that ethical funds are not only for investors who do not mind losing money. Nor was this relatively good performance the result of relatively lax investment criteria. Friends Provident applies standards comparable in strictness to those of other ethical funds, although it appears to give the Committee of Reference scope to use its judgement.

The N. M. Schroeder Conscience Fund is another strong financial performer among ethical unit trusts, though it is less than a tenth the size of the Friends Provident Stewardship Unit trust. In the six months to 31 May 1992 its price with income reinvested rose over 13 per cent. The fund applies criteria that are somewhat less exacting than Buckmaster. For example, it invests in food retailers that sell tobacco and alcohol. But when its standards are compared to those in force in the whole spectrum of ethical funds, N M Schroeder's seem to be among the stricter being applied. What sets it apart from most other funds is the degree of investor partici-pation encouraged by its managers. Meetings of unit-holders are held every six months, and these are the occasion for debates about the fund's investment criteria, queries about companies in which holdings have been taken, and suggestions about firms in which the fund can invest in the future. Minutes of these unit-holder meetings are published and distributed, and they show a high degree of responsiveness to unit holder questions and concerns. Another distinctive feature of the fund is its practice of donating 10 per cent of the annual management fee to a variety of worthwhile projects. These projects have ranged from disaster relief to assistance for entrepreneurs with environmentally useful business schemes. The fund has a validation panel that advises about the placement of funds in companies, and monitors projects supported by the management fee.

We have been considering some examples of mainstream ethical invest-ments. It is time to get a clearer view on what good they do. It will help to begin with a difference between mainstream ethical investment and ethical consumption. As we saw in Chapter 3, members of the ethical consumer movement sometimes claim that purchases of goods send messages of ethical approval and disapproval to manufacturers and retailers. This claim is doubtful unless manufacturers and retailers have some reason to interpret purchasing behaviour as a channel for ethical opinion. A consumer campaign could endow purchases with this significance perhaps, but purchases would not ordinarily be open to this sort of interpretation. A similar argument could be made here in respect of individuals basing their own shareholdings on ethical criteria. But ethical investment in practice is carried out very largely through the ethical funds, and this places it in a different postion. The ethical funds make clear to the public and to the commercial world what their investment criteria are, and when managers' reports for ethical funds list the firms invested in, those lists *can* be read as giving ethical approval. If ethical funds withdraw investment, or consider investing but decide against, that is at least as much a *prima facie* sign of ethical disapproval as of financial judgement. In short, ethical funds are much more convincingly said to be senders of messages to business than ethical consumers acting outside consumer campaigns. These messages can both raise the ethical standards companies think they need to meet to attract investors, and raise the standards of ordinary investors as well.

A second beneficial effect of the existence of ethical funds is to introduce new types of investor into financial markets: people who might have thought that no good could come of commercial enterprise but have come to have second thoughts. Relatedly, those interested in forming companies that can do good, e.g. by recycling or environmental clean-up, can come to see that there is a source of finance for these activities apart from banks, and can cite investment from ethical funds as evidence of the viability of their enterprises to other providers of credit.

Finally, though this benefit is inspired more by one particular example, the N. M. Shroeder Conscience fund, than by ethical funds in general, ethical funds can provide unusual channels for discussion and influence for ordinary investors, through particularly sensitive relations between unit-holders and fund-managers. This is not the same benefit as the benefit of sending messages to business from investors; it is a benefit in the form of particularly active shareholder participation in investment. Ethical funds may afford a forum for ethically minded unit holders to exercise an influence without necessarily having great financial clout.

## Shareholding as a desirable form of ownership

Is shareholding only morally desirable when it takes the form of ethical investment? Or is even ordinary shareholding a good thing morally? There are those who think that the answer to the latter question is an unequivocal 'Yes', on the ground that ownership is morally a good thing, and that share-holding is a kind of ownership. Margaret Thatcher is one exponent of this view. 'Liberty and property', she once said, 'are intricately bound up in our history; and a country that has no property rights has no human rights... You cannot have freedom without capital and private property in the hands of the people.'[16] In 1986 she looked forward to a time when a whole gener-ation would own their own homes and be able to bequeath them,

> ...so that they topple like a cascade down the line of the family, leaving to others not only their houses but some of their shares, some of their building society investments, some of their National Savings certificates – only on a bigger scale than ever before. The overwhelming majority of people, who could never look forward to that before, will be able to say: 'Look, they have got something to inherit. They have got the basis to start on.' That is tremendous. That is popular capitalism.[17]

Perhaps it was in the same spirit that the privatization of nationalized companies in Britain was sometimes billed as a contribution to a (for Britain) new and desirable form of society, a share-owning democracy.

A belief in the right to the private ownership of property is deeply embedded in Western, and especially in American, culture. But while it seems to be evident that a society that recognizes property rights for all is morally preferable to one in which some people have those rights and others do not, it is not evident that a society that recognizes property rights is necessarily preferable on moral grounds to a society in which no one has such rights. Indeed some people would argue that the existence of private property is one of the most morally harmful features of our society. Moreover, even if we accept that the existence of property rights is morally desirable, it does not follow that being an owner is morally creditable in itself, especially where what one owns is inherited rather than acquired by one's own efforts.

By the same token, share-ownership is not necessarily creditable in itself, even if a society in which one can become a share-owner is morally preferable to one in which no such possibility exists. And if ownership is not necessarily morally creditable, it is not clear why, morally speaking, more ownership should be better than less. Ownership might be morally desirable in its own right, if owning something made one more industrious or responsible, or more virtuous in some other respect. But once again there is no necessary connection. One can be an owner at one remove from what one owns, leaving it to a hired agent to look after or improve one's assets; or one can be an owner and neglect or damage what one owns. Perhaps home-owners look after their homes with more dedication than those who rent them, as the British government used to claim when justifying sales of public housing – or perhaps not. Perhaps those in the private rented market are just as houseproud. Perhaps in countries where much more property is rented and much less owned there is no significantly greater amount of public squalor than in Britain. In any case it would have to be shown that ownership bred special virtues.

If it is not the fact that shares are owned that makes share-ownership a morally good thing, what, if anything, does make it a morally good thing? Our view is that nothing makes shareholding a morally good thing, but that the opportunities for responsibility and active participation in business that shareholding affords, and the fact that it is socially beneficial for there to be private money-raising institutions, indicate that shareholding *can* be a morally good thing, and also that there may be an argument to the effect that it is a morally better form of participation in business than entirely passive and vicarious public ownership through the state.[18]

This position does not imply that privatization of publicly owned businesses is always to be supported, since other things are at stake when these businesses are sold off than turning vicarious and passive ownership into something that is potentially more active and responsible. There is the amount of public investment that has already gone into the business; the need to get a fair price for the business from private investors, not a price that will enable each investor to make a tidy profit; the position of the business in the national economy; the need to retain appropriate levels of public service, irrespective of profit; the question of whether the privatized business will be a monopoly; and many other things. Who owns the shares is not in itself the crucial criterion. These issues will be picked up again in a later chapter, in the context of broad business ethics.

## References

1 See, for example, G. Goyder, *The Just Enterprise* (London: Andre Deutsch, 1987), p.18. One of the clearest statements on ownership comes from Lord Justice Evershed, in Short vs. Treasury Commissioners (1947): 'Shareholders are not in the eye of the law part owners of the undertaking.'

2 'The responsibilities of institutional investors in the UK', *Business Ethics: A European Review*, 1, no.3 (1991), pp. 199ff.

3 *Ibid.*, p.199.

4 *Ibid.*, p.201.

5 *Ibid.*

6 E. Sternberg, 'The Responsible Shareholder', *Business Ethics: A European Review*, 1, no.3 (1991), pp.192-8.

7 *Ibid.*, pp.193–194.

8 *Ibid.*, p.196.

9 *Ibid.*, p.196.

10 *Ibid.*, p.193.

11 N. Cooper *et al.*, (eds), *Takeovers – What Ethical Considerations Should Apply?* (London: Institute of Business Ethics, 1990) p.6.

12 Naturally safeguards are needed to ensure that the information presented can be verified and also challenged in public; but these safeguards are available in principle through mechanisms endorsed by the Institutional Shareholders' Committee, such as the compensation and audit committees of boards of directors, and annual general meetings; perhaps in-house journalism could also be adapted to these purposes.

13 'Autumn attractions', *New Consumer*, Autumn 1990, pp.12–14.

14 Cf. G. A. Cohen, 'Beliefs and Roles', *Proceedings of the Aristotelian Society*, 67, (1966-7); Thomas Nagel, 'Ruthlessness in Public Life', in T. Nagel, *Mortal Questions* (Cambridge: Cambridge University Press, 1979) .

15 Micropal, quoted in 'The Best and Worst of Ethical Funds', *Independent on Sunday*, London, 23 February 1992.

16 M. Daly and A. George (eds), *Margaret Thatcher in Her Own Words* (Harmondsorth: Penguin, 1987).

17 *Ibid.*, p.74.

18 Here, as in other cases, much depends on actual practice in different countries. The influence of a managerial elite in France still vastly exceeds that of shareholders; in the UK, on the other hand, active shareholding is much better established.

# 6 Other businesses

We have so far focused primarily on the relation between businesses and individuals – as customers, employees and shareholders. But what of relations between businesses? Are these the concern of narrow business ethics? Where one business is related to another as a shareholder, the answer is clearly 'Yes', and in the last chapter we looked at the case of one business, an institutional shareholder, investing in another. Another important relation is that between a business and its suppliers, and the responsibilities of a company to its suppliers will be the main focus of this chapter. We shall look in particular at two issues: late payment for goods or services supplied, and non-payment following the liquidation of a company. Finally, we shall look at the ethics of competition between businesses.

## Suppliers as stakeholders

Suppliers are not always included in the list of a firm's stakeholders, but they deserve to be. Any supplier benefits from a firm's custom, but in some cases they depend on it. Consider, for example, the hundreds of clothing manufacturers who supply the UK-based retailer Marks & Spencer or the Italian-based Benetton. They are independent companies but they supply just the one firm. A Benetton supplier is totally dependent upon the orders it receives from Benetton. Similar arrangements operate in the motor car industry and elsewhere; indeed a high proportion of smaller firms rely heavily on one major customer. What responsibilities does the customer business have to its suppliers in such a case?

If the customer has been instrumental in setting up the supplier business, as is often the case with Benetton, or in encouraging it to invest or expand, the responsibilities would appear to be considerable. One of the reasons that Benetton uses sub-contractors rather than manufacturing in-house is that the Italian legislation governing employees is far less strict for firms with under fifteen staff than it is for firms the size of Benetton itself. In an industry in which the manufacturing economies of scale are not great, Benetton effectively uses its suppliers to get employees, but without the legal obligations (in terms of hours and conditions of work, trade union representation etc.) that would be attached to employment as such. In these circumstances there would seem to a *prima facie* argument to the effect that Benetton should, morally speaking, treat its sub-contractors as if they were employees. Indeed, one could argue that the obligation should be greater than to employees, since employees give only of their time while the sub-contractors also invest their savings. Against this it could be argued that the suppliers also benefit from the arrangement, as they have the opportunity to prosper and grow wealthy in a way that they could not as mere employees. The arguments are difficult to weigh, but we would argue that at the very least Benetton and other businesses in a similar position owe their dedicated suppliers a degree of loyalty similar to that which they owe their employees. It would clearly be wrong to take business away from a dedicated supplier without very good reason, ample notice, and in some cases substantial compensation for the investment made.

Even when a supplier is not dedicated to a business's needs, some measure of loyalty may be called for. Suppose that we are in business and one of our supplier companies is going through a difficult time for some reason out of its control (it was perhaps, like thousands of small companies, a victim of the collapse of Bank of Credit and Commerce International), but that it probably has the ability to recover; it has in the past been a good and reliable supplier. Narrow commercial interests might well argue for a switch to an alternative supplier, as this would carry a lower risk. Are there moral grounds for staying with the original supplier, despite the risks introduced by the circumstances? The answer depends not only on our business but on the supplier's other customers as well. If everybody switches, the supplier will go under and its shareholders, employees and creditors will suffer as a result. If everybody remains loyal, it may well recover and all will be well. But if we remain loyal while others switch, the supplier will still go under and we will lose out, in addition. Situations of this kind are difficult but not uncommon, and from a moral perspective it is only act-utilitarians who will need to calculate the probabilities. Ethical egoists will have no hesitation in switching, but from any of the other main moral perspectives it is better to stay loyal to the supplier, providing that the costs or risks to ourselves are not so significant as to severely affect our obligations to our other stakeholders. One would not put one's own business at risk in order to be loyal to a supplier, but one would incur modest extra costs.

## Suppliers as creditors

One circumstance in which suppliers have a very significant stake in a business is when their goods or services have been supplied but they have not yet been paid. Since trade accounts are usually settled in arrears, most suppliers find themselves in this position most of the time, and it gives rise to one of the most commonplace problems of business ethics – that of late payment.

The late payment of creditors is not only commonplace, but in some contexts, and in particular in Europe, it is almost normal. Moreover, it is a problem that disproportionately affects small companies, which are in general those least well placed to cope with it. A quarterly survey of 700 UK firms conducted in August 1992 by Trade Indemnity showed that large firms (turnover over £50m) were paid on average 15 days late, compared with small businesses (turnover under £2.5m), which were paid on average 29 days late. One firm in ten had delays of over 30 days, and the average for all firms was 26 days. The average size of unpaid debt was just over £100,000. In the EC as a whole late payment is also widespread. According to a survey of 5,200 medium-sized and small businesses carried out in May 1993, it took on average 65 days for payment to be made. In Italy the average was 90 days.[1]

Are these delays morally excusable? How quickly should one firm pay its debts to another? The question necessarily has two sides, for there are both a debtor and a creditor to consider. We shall restrict attention to the case where the creditor has already performed by supplying goods or services as demanded by the debtor, and where the debtor intends to pay, but would like for one reason or another to pay at the last possible moment. On these assumptions it seems to us to be very difficult to maintain that delaying payment is all right morally. After all, the creditor has already performed, presumably conferring some benefit on the debtor, and, what is more, he has usually done so on conditions about the timing of the payment known and agreed in advance.

## The principle of paying at the agreed time

One reason for paying at the agreed time or during the agreed period is just that it has been agreed to; for, from the angle of most moral theories, it is wrong to break one's agreements. Different moral theories may give different reasons why it is wrong. Thus utilitarianism would probably focus on the tendency of one broken agreement to foster further broken agreements and weaken trust to the disadvantage of everyone or most people. A latter-day follower of Aristotle might call attention to the defect of character that the breaking of agreements expresses. A Kantian would press the question of whether it can be consistent with the intention of making an agreement that one is willing to break one when it is convenient to do so. But all three theories insist that it is wrong to break agreements. Now in general, if something seems to be the case from many different points of view, that is a reason for thinking it really is the case. The objectivity of a belief is its tendency to be confirmed however one looks at its content. So the fact that from many different points of view it seems right to keep one's agreements is good evidence that one ought to keep one's agreements, including one's agreement to pay debts at a predetermined time.

It is sometimes conceivable, however, that the straightforward principle of paying when one agrees to can be violated excusably. Suppose that, owing to an acquisition or a large short-term call on funds for redundancy payments, a firm finds itself with a problem of liquidity at the time a payment is due; suppose further that the creditor firm, wishing to create goodwill and attract repeat orders, is willing to wait for its money without any penalty to the debtor; suppose, finally, that waiting creates no cash crisis for the creditor firm, and that given the extra time the debtor firm will pay up. In these circumstances, it seems, nothing wrong is done when the payment is made late. What excuses the debtor firm's failure to pay when it says it will? At least three things: (i) the creditor firm is able to withstand the delay, (ii) it is willing to withstand the delay, and (iii) it makes (ii) known to the debtor firm. Let us call a creditor that meets these conditions able and willing. Then to the uncompromising 'pay as agreed' principle we can add an escape clause that allows the payment of debt to be delayed if the creditor is able and willing.

## The able and willing creditor

Though the restricted principle is more permissive than the categorical 'pay as agreed', and though it fits in with the suspicion that the categorical principle can sometimes be broken excusably, the new principle is not *very* permissive. For example, it does not support a firm that considers the cash wealth of a creditor firm to be by itself a sufficient reason for postponing payment: the restricted principle requires that the cash-wealthy firm be *willing* to have the payment postponed. On the other hand, the restricted principle certainly supports the debtor firm in *asking* the creditor firm to wait, given its cash wealth. Again, and more interestingly, the restricted principle does not allow debt payment to be delayed to a creditor firm that is willing to wait but is in fact unable to withstand the wait.

The moral basis for prohibiting the delay in this case is easiest to grasp in the terms provided by utilitarianism, which calculates the harms and benefits that result from different possible courses of action and always makes morally obligatory the action that produces the greatest benefit. What happens from a utilitarian perspective when a firm that is unable to wait expresses its willingness to wait for payment is that the harm that it already suffers by being kept without money is compounded by its doing something that invites bankruptcy. A harm is aggravated. That is why a firm that offers to wait and is unable to should not be made to wait for its payment. Other things, too, are excluded by the principle on current assumptions. The debtor firm is not entitled to delay payment if it merely succeeds in convincing an able and willing creditor that it cannot pay. It must *really* be unable to pay.

There may be reason to restrict further the principle about able and willing creditors. What if the debtor company has an able and willing creditor, and yet finds itself with a liquidity problem because the directors have been paying themselves too much or because managers have committed themselves to a wage increase that the firm cannot afford? Perhaps in the face of these forms of mismanagement there is no justification for even an able and willing creditor to be patient.

In the face of the possibility of making the principle more restrictive someone may object that from a moral point of view it is already restrictive enough, indeed perhaps over-restrictive. In its present form the principle prohibits delayed payments to cash-rich creditors who are unwilling to wait: the ability to wait provides a reason for waiting. In considering this objection we need to distinguish between what is morally right in the sense of being obligatory and what is morally right in the sense of being above and beyond the call of duty. Other things being equal the cash-rich firm does nothing immoral if it decides to be patient and wait. It behaves generously when it is patient. But behaving generously is not something one is obliged to do: on most moral theories to behave generously is to do more than morality requires. So, other things being equal, the cash-rich company that makes the generous gesture is doing something it is not morally obliged to do. In that sense having the ability to wait does not provide a reason, or at least not a strong reason, for waiting. So it may not be morally required of even a cash-rich company that it wait for payment. And of course agreeing to wait for payment may be reckless in view of the character of the debtor firm, or, without being reckless, it may break financial disciplines that shareholders would reasonably want to see upheld.

But if delayed payment is commonplace, even normal, is it not one of the costs that a creditor company, if it is responsible, should make allowance for when it does business with a customer? If so, can a debtor firm not excuse the harm that delayed payment does by describing it as a contingency that the creditor firm should have insulated itself against? The answer seems to us to be 'No', even though it is morally right for one firm to treat another as fully responsible. For one thing, the principle behind the debtor's rationalization cuts both ways: if the creditor should have been prudent enough to make allowance for delayed payment, then by the same token the debtor should have made provision for the payment on time of the debt. Moreover, while the fact that people often act in a certain way may alleviate one's guilt in acting in the same way, it does not in itself excuse the action. Many people fiddle their tax returns, drive under the influence of alcohol, and throw their litter around the countryside. But the fact that these actions are common practice does not justify them.

## Multiple debts, and relative urgency

Though it does not seem to be morally right to withhold payment of a debt to a cash-rich firm that is unwilling to wait, it may nevertheless be morally better to dishonour this debt than to withhold or delay payment to a cash-poor company that is unable to wait. Paying the needier company first does not wipe out the wrong that one does to the rich company, but paying the rich company does compound the wrong of disappointing the poor one; for the unpaid poor company not only has taken from it credit that it cannot afford to extend, but its unpaid debts are much likelier to cause its collapse than the unpaid debts of the rich company.

Since debts are rarely owed one at a time, and since cash shortage often precludes paying all debts at once, firms with more debts than they can pay simultaneously often have to decide which are to get priority. Once things have reached this point, the firm can only avoid doing the morally wrong thing if its richer creditors are able and willing, and if there is enough left over when the debts to these firms are delayed to pay the other creditors. When these conditions are not met, a firm cannot normally avoid doing wrong: the most it can do is cut its losses and avoid doing a greater than necessary wrong, paying off first the firms that cannot survive.

It might be thought that this position is too exacting. What about a firm that cannot afford to pay its debts because it is a disappointed and needy creditor: surely *this* sort of firm cannot be expected always to try to honour its debts to the neediest of its creditors first? Doing that could put it out of business. Surely for the neediest of companies it is too expensive to obey the principle? There is no denying that in order to stay in business a firm must sometimes pay debts first to the least or less needy of its creditors. This fact, however, is perfectly compatible with its being wrong to pay debts first to the least or less needy of its creditors. To see this, compare the case with a case of personal survival. It may be true in a given situation that to save himself from death or ruin a person has to do a particular action which, despite being necessary for his survival, is quite wrong. Consider the case where someone is accused of a murder and where conviction will lead to certain execution. The fact that the accused can avoid execution by incriminating an innocent man does not justify incriminating the innocent man, even if the accused person is also innocent. By parity of reasoning, a firm is not morally justified in causing another firm's bankruptcy to prevent its own. It is not justified in doing this even when it is a needy creditor itself and in danger of bankruptcy. Of course not being justified morally is compatible with being justified in some other way. The point is that when the going gets tough, moral requirements do not lapse.

## Debts and other liabilities

So far, our discussion has restricted creditors to suppliers of goods and services. But what about others to whom payment is owed? In the UK in the 1980s a growing number of firms regarded the Inland Revenue and Department of Health and Social Security (DHSS) as creditors among others, postponing or withholding PAYE and National Insurance Payments deductions in much the same way as payments to creditor firms. In 1987 the fraction of withholding attributable only to companies that went into liquidation amounted to £264 million. The impression that PAYE and National Insurance contributions are the company's until they are paid over is no doubt due to their being held in a company bank account and to their rarely being actively called for by the bodies to whom they have to be transferred. Nevertheless, it is money partly deducted from employees' salaries, and non-payment can disqualify people for unemployment, sickness and maternity pay, as well as state pensions.

Not only is the money withheld not the company's but the Inland Revenue and DHSS are plainly not ordinary creditors. Whereas a supplier's claims on money arise from transactions carried out in the course of business, the claims of the Inland Revenue and the DHSS in some sense come before that, arising from the creation of the conditions necessary to do business at all. Does this mean that if a firm is having difficulties in paying its creditors, the payments to the Inland Revenue and the DHSS should receive priority? On the one hand, the nature of the liability suggests that they should, and this view is supported by the legislation covering company liquidations, in which they have first call on the assets of the company being wound up. On the other hand, they of all creditors are in some sense the most able to wait, or to suffer a loss. It could also be argued, moreover, that since the failure of the company would almost inevitably lead to a loss in tax revenues, as well as to increases in unemployment and social security benefits, government agencies should have particular reasons for being willing to wait for payment, if that will increase the chances of a company's survival.

## 'Phoenixing' and the ethics of limited liability

Mention of the division of assets on liquidation raises a further issue concerning a company's responsibilities to its suppliers. In recent years there has been growing concern over the practice referred to as 'phoenixing', in which a privately held limited company is liquidated and then reformed, carrying out the same business as before but without any obligations to its original, unpaid, trade creditors. This situation typically arises with a company that is heavily dependent on the professional skills of its owners. Some of the most prominent examples have been in the advertising, marketing and design industries. A company gets into trouble, the owners are not prepared to put in any more capital to see it through, so it goes into receivership. The receivers have two tasks: to repay, as far as possible, the creditors; and if possible to keep all or part of the business going. By keeping the business going they hope to save some of the jobs in it and provide a continuing service to customers. They also hope to persuade someone to pay something for the business, the proceeds going towards paying the creditors.

Normally this process introduces no conflicts. Not all the creditors can be paid but there is a legally established pecking order, trade creditors or suppliers coming towards the bottom. In many small firms, however, especially in people-based industries such as those mentioned above, the value of the firm lies principally in the skills of its owners. Customers deal with the firm as a way of dealing with its owners, and the firm is of no value as a going concern to anyone but its owners. Faced with this situation, the receivers appear to have decided in a number of cases that everyone's interests were best served by selling the firm back to its previous owners. Since no one else wanted it, they could pay a relatively small price, and significantly less than they would have had to put in to save it in the first place. They could then regain control of the company, with all its debts either paid off or cancelled, for substantially less than it would have cost them to pay off those debts themselves. The customers were happy, the employees were happy, and the creditors were at least happier than they would have been otherwise, the repurchase of the company having increased the money available for distribution to them. At least *some* of the creditors were happier. For those such as the banks who came high on the pecking list, the arrangement was clearly beneficial. For the trade creditors, on the other hand, it made little or no difference, as they still didn't get paid.

There are cases in which phoenixing is contrived by the receivers and so has a stamp of legitimacy, but the basic practice is much more widespread. Rather than operate on their own account or as a partnership, the owners of a business set it up as a limited liability company. At some stage it gets into serious trouble and goes into liquidation, with suppliers and other creditors remaining unpaid. Shortly afterwards the owners set up another limited liability company in the same line of business, and with the same customers. They proceed as before, but the creditors never get paid. This clearly sounds wrong. But it is a natural if not an inevitable consequence of the existence of limited liability companies and can be and is defended as such. So is it wrong, or is it morally defensible?

To look at the issue more closely, let us consider a case that is not quite phoenixing as we have defined it but raises the same issues, the case of the magazine *Management Week*, which went into liquidation in December 1991.

Six months later a new magazine, *Business Age* was launched, with the same editor, and describing itself as 'incorporating *Management Week*'.

*Management Week* was the brainchild of its editor, Tom Rubython, who saw the need for a different kind of business magazine, focusing on people rather than finance and economics, with a practical 'how to manage' slant, and targeted at middle rather than senior managers – 'a weekly soap opera of business for managers'. Its principal backer in the venture, for which he raised about £2 million, was Paul Judge, the wealthy businessman who had made his fortune from the management buy-out of Premier Brands from Cadbury-Schweppes mentioned in the last chapter. The magazine was brash and aggressive, with a tabloid style. It was also considered by others in the publishing industry to be under-financed, with insufficient investment in promotion costs, and ill-timed, launched as it was in the midst of a deep recession for magazine advertising.

Six months after the magazine was launched, the circulation was reported to be abysmal and the libel actions were mounting up. It seemed as though the magazine could not write about anyone without making it defamatory. Judge, not unreasonably, called for a change of policy, but Rubython would not comply. He tried to sell the title, but no one would buy it. He demanded Rubython's resignation, but could not agree terms for buying out his share of the company. By the time Rubython finally agreed to go, Judge had come to the conclusion that the business had failed, and called in the receivers. The company was wound up, the staff were dismissed, and the suppliers, who were between them owed £0.5 million, went unpaid. Six months later Rubython, with a new set of backers, launched *Business Age*.

In this case Rubython could argue that since the decision to close down *Management Week* was taken against his wishes, and after he had been bought out, he had no obligation to the unpaid creditors. Judge, on the other hand, could argue that he was merely a shareholder in a limited liability company, and that he had no obligations beyond the amount of his investment, which he had of course lost. When limited liability was introduced in the mid-nineteenth century the whole purpose was to encourage businesses to take risks they would not take as unlimited liability partnerships. This enabled businesses to grow and achieve economies and efficiencies of scale, and allowed industry, and so society, to prosper as it could not have done otherwise. The inevitable cost of this is that some businesses will fail and their creditors lose out, but since suppliers always know whether a business has limited liability or not, they can adjust their terms of business accordingly. The suppliers of *Management Week* knew the risks they were taking in dealing with a limited liability company, and could have no cause for complaint if they lost out as a result of the business being wound up.

This argument is a sound one, as far as it goes, but it is not altogether satisfying. Many of the creditors, and many of the public, felt that in the

*Management Week* case Paul Judge should have paid up. True, he had no legal obligation to do so; true, he was only a part-owner of the company (his shareholding amounted to 60 per cent); and true, he had already lost a substantial amount himself. But he was still an extremely rich man, who had had a controlling interest in the company and whose error of judgement in backing Rubython in the first place had brought about its downfall. Of course the suppliers had known that it was a limited liability company but they had also known that it was well backed, by a wealthy, successful and morally responsible businessman. (Indeed Paul Judge had in the past made a point of his moral responsibility. When leading the buy-out of Premier Brands, he had promised the workforce he would launch it on the stock market, and when his fellow directors voted instead for a private sale, he resigned. While they remained tied in to the new parent, he was able to take his profit – estimated at over £40 million.)

The point here is that while the existence of limited liability may be socially beneficial, the way in which it is used may not always be appropriate. The fundamental purpose is to encourage enterprise by protecting the entrepreneur or investor from bankruptcy, not by relieving them of obligations they could well afford. In the case of an ordinary shareholder, who has little influence over the running of a business, it would probably be unreasonable to expect him to pay anything beyond his legally limited liability, however rich he may be. But in the case of an owner or group of owners, whose own actions contribute directly to the downfall of the business, there would seem to be moral grounds for expecting them to pay up, beyond their liabilities, if they could afford to do so.

If, as we are suggesting, someone like Paul Judge does have a moral responsibility to repay his creditors, then the same must certainly be true of those engaged in phoenixing, many of whom seem to systematically abuse the privileged status of limited liability that society affords to a company. Being unable to pay your suppliers and so going into liquidation is one thing, but going into liquidation in order to avoid paying your suppliers is another, and is in our view quite clearly morally wrong. Where does this leave the receiver, with an offer from the former owners to repurchase? As the law stands, he is in a difficult position, but so long as he is allowed to sell to the former owners then, if that is what gets best value for the company, that is what he must do. The moral onus is then on them to make what reparation they can.

## Relations with competitors

We have so far concentrated on the duties of a business to its stakeholders, but in looking at relations between businesses we must consider whether there are obligations to other firms that are *not* stakeholders. If there are such obligations, are they the proper concern of narrow business ethics? We shall take up these questions in relation to firms that are in direct competition with one another. Perhaps there is a difficulty about locating a would-be ethics of competition within *narrow* business ethics, for 'narrowness' was originally defined with respect to stakeholders, and competitors do not seem to qualify. Still, it seems undeniable that some competitive practices are morally questionable, and that some sorts of concern for competitors are morally admirable. It seems undeniable therefore that business ethics has a scope wider than that of the stakeholder relationship. Perhaps competition does not fall entirely within narrow business ethics, but it raises issues closer to those we have already considered than those to do with the environment and developing countries that dominate broad business ethics. After outlining the sorts of issues that might arise within an ethics of competition, we shall consider some examples of responses to such issues by actual businesses.

Morally questionable competitive practices can be divided into two kinds: those that consist of improving market share by immoral means, such as misrepresentation, sabotage, and bribes; and those that consist of employing means that are otherwise permissible commercially, e.g. price-cutting, mergers, and joint sales promotions, for morally questionable competitive ends. In the first sort of case debate centres upon where the boundary lies between means that are morally acceptable and means that are not. In a recent dispute between two airlines, British Airways and Virgin, it emerged that British Airways had been using a computer system to identify customers who were flying with Virgin, and had then approached them directly with inducements to shift to British Airways. Although British Airways is a hard competitor, it is also a very respectable company, and the executives responsible clearly thought that the tactic was morally acceptable. Virgin, not surprisingly, disagreed, and we would argue with good reason. The tactic was a flagrant abuse of confidentiality and of the implicit agreement governing the use of the computer system.

Other disputable cases concern the use of industrial espionage or publicly casting aspersions on the personal lives of a competitor's senior executives. All is fair, it is sometimes said, in love, war or business; but even in war there are accepted ethical standards of behaviour. In business it may sometimes be necessary to go to great lengths to find out about a competitor. The character of a chief executive may have some relevance to a competitive dispute. But if it is not always clear precisely where a line should be drawn, it is at least clear that there is a line, and that some practices are morally reprehensible.

More interesting from an ethical perspective is the second sort of case, where a business uses commercially acceptable means for morally questionable ends. It is not easy, however, to give examples of competitive ends that will be universally agreed to be morally questionable, and where fairly clear cases of such ends *are* proposed, there will usually be rival explanations of why they are immoral.

Legislation is one guide to questionable competitive ends. In the European Community, Articles 85 and 86 of the EEC Treaty and their associated Regulations are the main legal instruments in regard to competition affecting more than one member state, and there is parallel legislation within individual member states. Article 85 is intended to prevent agreements by two or more firms, usually large firms, on price-fixing, market share, and decisions to impose quotas on production. The justification for preventing these practices is not explicitly a moral one – it is that these practices interfere with the desirable effects of competition, such as the efficient use of resources, and commercial innovation. Since efficiency and innovation often contribute to the general welfare, it is plausible to claim that there is an implicit utilitarian justification for the provisions of Article 85, and so an implicit utilitarian explanation of why it is morally wrong for producers to fix prices, settle market share by agreement and limit production.

## The abuse of a dominant position

For a more explicit acknowledgement of the moral dimensions of competition, and of the way that morality requires the regulation of competition, it is necessary to turn to Article 86 of the EEC Treaty, which outlaws the abuse of a dominant market position in the EEC by a particular firm. Dominant position is usually a matter of market share in excess of 40 per cent. A dominant position is abused when a use is made of it that 'causes injury to third parties'. The relevant EEC document[3] gives the following four examples of abusive practices:

- Charging unfair purchase or selling prices. Prices that are unfairly high will be to the detriment of consumers, while those that are unfairly low (below cost) may be aimed at eliminating weaker competitors, i.e. those that do not have the power to match such prices for any length of time.
- Discriminatory pricing, e.g. charging customer A more than customer B for exactly the same transaction, thereby placing customer A at a competitive disadvantage.
- Attempts to hold on to customers, e.g. by granting fidelity rebates.
- Acquisitions of competing undertakings, thereby affecting the competitive structure within the Common Market.

Article 86 has an explicitly moral dimension, because it makes the causing of injury a necessary condition of abuse of dominant position, and because it identifies certain sorts of aims or ends as dubious given the injury they might cause, such as the aim of eliminating weaker competitors.

Let us stick to this example and try to get clearer on what is questionable about the aim of eliminating competitors. What, if anything, makes it wrong? Conventional business wisdom would say 'nothing', provided that the means used are fair: competition is all about seeking to eliminate one's competitors. Most Western governments effectively concur. As regulators, with a regard to the interests of society, they establish limits on competition, e.g. through merger legislation. But they do not argue that a breach of those limits is morally wrong for the company concerned. What they say in effect is that you, the companies, behave as egoists and we, the regulators, will place limits on that where in our judgement it affects the public interest. An analogy might be a boxing match: the referee steps in to protect life where necessary, but there is no requirement for a boxer to limit his blows (providing of course that they are legal blows) and no expectation that he will do so.

Of course a boxer does not set out to kill his opponent, and it is worthy of note that business regulators are more concerned with those situations in which businesses seek directly to eliminate competitors, e.g. through mergers, than with those in which the elimination comes about as a consequence of business success. This suggests that there may be an important difference, from a moral perspective, between aiming directly at the elimination of one's competitors, and aiming at getting the better of one's competitors. When one aims at getting the better of one's competitors, one intends to sell more than one's competitors, perhaps much more. There are various ways of being successful in this aim. One way is to have a greater share of the market than one's competitors at the same time as they each retain a share of the market, perhaps a share that makes each profitable. Another way of being successful is to have a greater share of the market at the expense of the profitability of a minority of one's competitors. These means do not necessarily diminish the well-being of all competitors. The aim of eliminating one's competitors, on the other hand, cannot be successfully pursued except at the cost of the competitors' well-being.

This already suggests that, morally, the policy of getting the better of one's competitors is preferable to the policy of eliminating the competition. The policy of getting the better of one's competitors is not an attack on the competitive process itself, as the policy of eliminating one's competitors is: one can increase market share without necessarily reducing the number of competitors. This itself has moral significance, for reduced competition can be morally undesirable from many points of view. For people in the firms that no longer have a sufficient share of the market, it means unemployment; for people dependent on the spending of the employees, it means further losses, and for consumers, it may mean a rise in prices.

The argument just given is supposed to show that one of two similar policies is morally superior to the other. But it is possible to question the argument; for how can a policy that would be successful if it *resulted* in the elimination of one's competitors be any more valuable morally than a policy *aimed* at the elimination of one's competitors? From an act-utilitarian point of view there may be no real difference: if the results of the two policies are the same, then they are indistinguishable morally. But from the standpoint of certain deontological theories of normative ethics – Christian ethics, for example, or Kantianism – there are certain things one may not aim at, and morality permits them as foreseeable results of what one does only if they are pure side effects. For example, according to certain Catholic teachings, it is morally wrong to aim at taking someone's life; but it is sometimes permissible to do something that will have death as an inevitable but unintended side-effect, as when, in order to spare someone intense pain one administers a dose of a drug that kills the sufferer. The belief that unintended side-effects of intentional actions, even when foreseen, do not affect the moral evaluation of the agent, is sometimes called *the principle of double effect*. In business ethics the principle allows us to distinguish between a policy of outselling one's competitors, whose unintended side-effect is the elimination of a competitor, and the calculated elimination of a competitor. There is, however, no need to stake the moral superiority of the former policy on the principle of double effect. One can say simply that what makes it the morally superior one is its being compatible with the well-being of everyone in the competition.

## Degrees of aggression in competition and the need for restraint

Part of what is wrong with aiming at eliminating competitors is that it is wrong to aim at the ruin, or at a reduction in the fortunes, of others who depend for a living on the competing business. But this, it may be said, is not the whole story. There may, in addition, be harm done to the public; for as a rule, it might be said, the public may benefit from trading conditions in which more rather than fewer enterprises are vying for a share of the market. Because of the consumerist tendency of much public policy and legislation, there is considerable plausibility in the claim that the *main* moral costs of a calculated reduction in competition reside in losses to the public, e.g. losses in the form of increased prices, rather than losses to those directly affected by a firm being driven out of business. But whether the loss to the public really does outweigh the costs to those more directly affected by the business disappearing will depend on a wide variety of factors. For example, the elimination of a single competitor in a market crowded with competitors may make little difference to either consumer prices or the variety of goods and services on offer, while the collapse of a single business may have very serious effects on those who run it or are employed by it and their families, or the local community. Again, the moral seriousness of eliminating a competitor depends on whether the means used are the flatly immoral ones of misrepresentation, sabotage, etc., and also on whether the business bent on eliminating the competitor is much bigger and much better established than the competitor itself. The more immoral the means, and the larger and better established the aggressor by comparison with the targeted competitor, the more likely it is that the wrongness of trying to eliminate the competitor will be weighty quite apart from the effects on price or choice for the public if the aggressor succeeds. Thus, if a large and well established airline starts false rumours about the irresponsibility of the flight crews of one of its smaller competitors, or if its employees accost the competitor's customers at airports and try to persuade them to switch airlines, that is morally wrong even if the accosted customers are made offers of travel terms that they feel are very advantageous. And if the repeated use of these tactics results in the collapse of the targeted airline, that is a big moral wrong – whether or not air travellers have benefited by reduced fares or other inducements.

Not all cases of aggressive competition are easy to adjudicate. To continue with the example under discussion, suppose that the targeted airline had merely had a price-war declared against it, without any hint of misrepresentation in the background or any policy of accosting customers. Then, while the better established airline might still have been accused of abusing its dominant position in the market, the wrongness of the price-war would probably consist in its calculated temporariness, in its leading up to a time when there would be less pressure from competitors to lower prices, and so, to a time of high prices. In other words, the wrongness of the price-war would consist as much in its probable adverse effects on prices in the long run, as in its effects on those working for the competing airline.

As for the ill effects on the airline, it could be objected against what we claimed a moment ago that these are legitimate effects of what is after all competitive rather than co-operative activity. It is true that in price-wars large firms will often lower prices intentionally to such an extent that only they and not their weaker competitors can afford to take the losses; but there are other price cuts that are open to a large-scale firm that do not contribute to a price war and that all participants in the market would agree were legitimate. There are cases, in other words, where advantages of scale that are sometimes ruthlessly exploited against a competitor simply operate to the detriment of competitors – with no aggression or ill-will behind them. These are the cases that are hard to adjudicate: some will think of them as cases of wrongdoing; some will think that they are cases of tough, but permissible, competition. Whichever view is correct, large firms, or firms with large shares of a market, are invariably conscious of their size and the size of their market share, and if they are in a position to discharge a legal obligation not to abuse their dominant market position, as they are under UK and EC legislation, then they are also in a position to exercise restraint in the measures they use to preserve market share. This would seem to be the least that morality demands.

# Altruism and good practice

Restraint does not mean outright altruism, though there do appear to be examples of the altruistic treatment of competitors in the history of British business. In the late 1950s the directors of the glassmakers Pilkington had to decide how to introduce to the world market an extremely advanced manufacturing process. The process – for making plate glass on a float line – had been developed at considerable risk and expense over the preceding ten years. It enabled the firm, if it wished, to cut the costs of manufacturing high quality plate glass to such an extent that an unassailable advantage could be secured over competitors. Pilkington had the choice of keeping the process to itself or making it available under licence to the rest of the glass industry in return for royalty income. It decided in favour of licensing, partly because it seemed morally the better thing to do. Lord Pilkington recalled later that during the deliberations of the Directors' Flat Glass Committee:

> A great deal was said about ethics: that it was not our job deliberately to deny any existing glass competitor the opportunity of living in competition with us. I don't think we were short-sighted or rapacious... There was a great deal of investment worldwide in plate, and people needed to have time to write off this plant, or convert over. The alternative was chaotic disruption of a great industry.[3]

The directors of Pilkington felt a responsibility not to disrupt 'a great industry', and they considered the introduction of their own world-beating process to be disruptive.

More than twenty years after the decision to license was taken, Pilkington was criticised for failing to take full commercial advantage of the float process when it was new. An offer document distributed to Pilkington shareholders to support a BTR take-over attempt in 1986 asked why Pilkington had chosen to license its flat glass technology 'for short-term gain at the cost of long-term ownership and the eventual creation of self-inflicted competition'. Pilkington replied to this question in defence documents, justifying the decision to license the float process on commercial grounds. Earnings from royalties had amounted to £400 million over 20 years, and had helped to finance the expansion of Pilkington's own plants and the acquisition of licensed companies. The ethical dimension of the deliberations about the float process was not revealed, presumably because it would have left the company open to charges of not being sufficiently commercially minded. Whether or not such charges are justified, the Pilkington directors' thoughts for their competitors do seem remarkably generous, and they seem to go beyond what is required for honourable dealings with competitors.

A better model for healthy competitive relations is perhaps that provided by some small businesses in Scotland recently studied by Gavin Reid.[4] The case of small businesses is particularly interesting, because under the EEC *de minimis* rules there is no legal obligation for them to refrain from most of the practices outlawed by Articles 85 and 86: the effect on trading conditions of certain agreements is simply considered too small to require regulation. There are exemptions for small business under the competition legislation of individual EC states as well. For example, in the UK, firms with turnover under £5 million are exempt from the provisions of the Competition Act 1980 unless they have a UK market share of 25 per cent or over. In general, then, compliance with the spirit of competition legislation on the part of small business is, in a clear sense, generous.

To a remarkable extent, however, there does appear to be compliance – at any rate in Scotland. Reid reports that among the small businesses he investigated, established firms were generally reluctant to cut prices in order to discourage market entry by new firms. Collective action by established firms against newcomers was also frowned upon, except in the case where technological innovation by a newcomer might imperil existing businesses. Tactics regarded as fair included aggressive self-advertisement, presenting the appearance of an effective competitor, and matching the guarantees of a rival competitor. The Scottish small businesses seem to give effect to the sort of restraint in their use of market position that sets a good example for businesses large *and* small. Even a mix of competition and fraternity is provided for.

> A concept that was discussed freely under the heading of defensive strategy was that of a 'good' competitor. On the face of it, competitors cannot be good for a given firm because they limit its scope of action. If a firm played a noncooperative game, it would seem that all rivals were 'bad competitors'... however, one finds the owner-manger of a firm which was a specialized knitwear manufacturer saying that one could distinguish 'good' from 'bad' competitors and that the former should be encouraged. A good competitor would, for example, pass on to a rival the surplus of an order over its current capacity that it could not immediately handle. This owner-manager saw his industry as 'a fraternity', even though competition was intense... [He] said he preferred 'to work with my customers rather than against my rivals'. He frowned upon blocking tactics, and thought the best defence was to look invulnerable.[5]

Partly because it does not idealize relations between competitors – the knitwear business owner nowhere suggests a policy of going out of one's way to help one's rivals – this idea of a 'good' competitor appears to have application well beyond the small-business sector in Scotland.

## Competition and co-operation

The last example raises the further, difficult issue of co-operation between competitors. One of the most influential business articles of recent years, published in the *Harvard Business Review*, was entitled 'Collaborate with your competitors – and win',[6] and strategic alliances between competitors are becoming increasingly common, especially in international business. But to what extent do the ethics of competition permit co-operation? If co-operation amounts to a conspiracy of several sellers or producers against a fellow seller or producer, or a cartel that drives up prices for consumers, then it is as morally suspect as conspiracies or agreements to promote narrow self-interest in general. If, on the other hand, co-operation follows the pattern of fraternal gestures between Scottish small businesses, it is probably unobjectionable. In between the clearly permissible and the clearly impermissible practices, however, are many that are hard to evaluate.

Some of these practices, particularly those whose social effects are mixed, and whose value from a utilitarian angle is therefore hard to determine, crop up also as practices that are of borderline legality. For example, the formation of a trade association may be an effective means of bringing a kind of product to consumers' attention, and thereby of increasing sales for individual manufacturers or retailers of the product. These are legitimate ends, legitimately pursued by the formation of a trade association. But the same body that permits these legitimate ends to be pursued may discourage promotional activity on the part of individual producers or sellers, and the collective presence of so many established firms in a market may deter newcomers, so that the unintended effects of forming a trade association start to resemble the intended effects of forming a cartel: higher prices, and less incentive to improve service in order to increase market share. It is for these reasons that the formation of trade associations is explicitly recognized by the EC regulatory authorities as a potential violation of Article 85 of the EEC treaty.

Another example that arises from EEC law is the joint pursuit of research and development programmes by individual companies. This practice is explicitly singled out for exemption from the provisions of Article 85, on the grounds that its anti-competitive or uncompetitive aspects are outweighed by its potential for speeding up innovation and opening new markets for European companies. But the exemption is notable for the weight of restrictions and obligations it carries. For example, if the R & D development programme being pursued by competitors is spectacularly successful, resulting in products that take a market share of over 20 per cent, then the exemption no longer applies. Again, the exemption is supposed to be conditional on there being the possibility of several independent poles of research. The fact that co-operation is allowed only subject to these provisos is not meant to show that EC policy reflects confusion or indecision, but rather that there are many countervailing factors to be taken into account when even limited co-operation between competitors is permitted or encouraged.

On the face of it strategic alliances would seem to be a good thing. Competition between the partners is generally preserved, while a sharing of manufacturing facilities, research and development, or technical expertise leads to an increase in efficiency and productivity. However their effects on other competitors can often be similar to those of a merger, or alternatively of a conspiracy. Especially from a utilitarian perspective, the good of co-operation between businesses can seem doubtful, and this can be so at the same time as the good of co-operation between individuals seems clear.

## References

1 *Independent on Sunday*, London, 4 July 1993.
2 *EEC Competition Policy in the Single Market* (Luxembourg: EEC, 1989), p. 21.
3 Quoted in a case study on Pilkington Bros. PLC in J. B. Quinn, H. Mintzberg and R. M. James, *The Strategy Process* (Englewood Cliffs, NJ: Prentice-Hall, 1988), p.789.
4 Gavin Reid, 'Small Firms and Fair Trade', *Business Ethics: A European Review*, 1, no.2 (1992), pp.117–120.
5 *Ibid.*, p.119.
6 G. Hamel, Y. Doz and C.K. Prahalad, 'Collaborate with your competitors – and win', *Harvard Business Review*, 67 no.1 (January-February 1989), pp.133–9.

# Part Three
# Broad Business Ethics

# 7 Business, state and society

In introducing the distinction between narrow and broad business ethics in Chapter 2 we took up the cases of Grand Metropolitan and Kingfisher, large British firms whose managements believe in corporate social responsibility. The projects funded or directed by these firms are examples of broad business ethics in practice: they directly benefit groups that have no financial connection with Kingfisher or Grand Metropolitan. The question that was pursued earlier about such projects was that of whether they interfered with the commercial objectives of the firms involved. The answer arrived at was 'No' in some cases and 'Not necessarily' in others. The related question that we want to raise now is whether certain ventures in corporate social responsibility saddle business with projects that the state ought to (morally ought to) initiate and maintain.

When business sponsors the arts or donates equipment to schools or hospitals, when business pays for training programmes or subsidizes the construction of a public transport system, isn't business doing what the state ought to do through the proceeds of taxation? And even if the greater business sponsorship is in return for cuts in taxes, isn't the arrangement morally undesirable in certain cases, because it leaves schools and hospitals in hard times having to divert more and more time and resources to chasing scarce private funds and less to doing the vital work of teaching children or treating patients? What is at issue is the morality of dividing up the social responsibilities of state and business in one way rather than another. We shall be concerned primarily with business sponsorship in standard state-provided services, such as education and health, and housing for the homeless. But we shall also consider some of the moral issues surrounding the introduction of commercial practices into the institutions of a welfare state and the privatization of what were once state-run services. Perhaps only the first of these topics – to do with business contributing to public services – is properly classified as 'broad business ethics', but there is a certain naturalness in discussing all of them together.

## Whose responsibility?

Where does the social responsibility of the state end and that of an individual business begin? A case that brings this issue sharply into focus is that of Pilkington PLC after the failed attempt to take it over by BTR in the winter of 1986-7. Before the period of the take-over battle, Pilkington had a formidable reputation as a philanthropic employer in the Merseyside town of St Helens.

Pilkington was a pioneer in the provision of pension funds and hospital services in British industry. Members of the Pilkington family built and endowed theatres and recreation clubs in St Helens. Retired employees received gifts of vegetable seed for their gardens and coal for heating their houses. An elaborate party for employees was mounted each year. By late 1986 specialist services funded by charities or trusts associated with the company included bereavement counselling, a victim-support scheme, a transport service for old people wishing to spend a day out, a gardening and handyman scheme, and a meals on wheels service.

The Community of St Helens Trust is perhaps the most famous of the firm's initiatives. It was formed after Pilkington began a programme of redundancies that reduced its workforce from 15,000 in 1970 to about 8000 in 1986. The purpose of the Trust was to provide finance for small businesses and thereby create jobs to replace those lost in Pilkington's. By 1987 the Trust had helped to launch over 500 small firms and had created over 6000 jobs. It is the prototype of the more than 300  local enterprise agencies that now operate in the UK. A number of the small companies that were formed by the Trust have become Pilkington suppliers or have become profitable by specializing in high value adding processes that would have been unsuitable in scale for Pilkington's own operations.

The firm has also been active in industrial training in the north-west of England, and has directed investment in high technology into the relatively depressed regions of North Wales and Scotland. Pilkington is a founder member of Business in the Community and the Per Cent club. Finally, in at least one Third World country, it has helped to create and fund a community school.

Such was the record of Pilkington up to the end of 1986. After the take-over attempt by BTR, the company began to concern itself more energetically with the bottom line. Since the beginning of 1987 the company has reduced the level of spending on activities associated with its so-called welfare state. Charitable donations, just over 0.4 per cent of profits in 1983, rose slightly in 1986 and then declined sharply after the period of the BTR take-over attempt. In an interview on the BBC current affairs programme *Panorama*, Mary Rimmer, the leader of St Helen's local council, expressed no resentment at the falling-off in Pilkington's giving:

The first time there's a dip in the economy, the private sector will be the first to stop investing in social welfare, and why shouldn't they? It isn't their responsibility – it's the government's responsibility. When that dip comes and when their investment stops in social fabric, then the people will look to the local authority to pick up any shortfall that there may be and we will not have the money to do so.[1]

Gordon Brown, the Labour MP and then Opposition Treasury spokesman, said on the same programme that: 'the first responsibility of business in this country should be to train, to research, to do the work of innovation and to ensure a degree of personal comfort and living standards for the workforces over which they have responsibility'.[2] He went on to deny that business had any role in running the welfare state or in making up for cuts in services offered by the welfare state. Without wishing to be seen to be urging a worse standard of living for workers employed by socially responsible companies, Brown and Rimmer insisted that there are limits to what can reasonably be expected of the private sector. Before 1986 these limits were probably exceeded – exceeded on the side of generosity – by Pilkington.

## The Dragon Award entries for 1992

The view taken by Brown and Rimmer seems a reasonable, even a compelling, one, where what a firm takes responsibility for is the loss or lack of basic necessities that the state has traditionally supplied. The view becomes less reasonable where the firm supplies a service that is less basic and that it is better placed to supply than the state or public sector, as when it makes available business advice or services, or when it donates or discounts goods that it manufactures or retails, or that are connected with what it manufactures or retails. Thus a supermarket chain is an appropriate business to provide recycling collection skips to take the glass and paper packaging its customers buy with their groceries, but not necessarily an appropriate supplier of architectural services to a housing association, even if it has architects on its staff.

Besides making the point that there are limits to what should be expected of a private sector business, Rimmer and Brown also argued, implicitly at least, that for a business to go beyond these limits is morally wrong. By taking on obligations that are properly those of government, it could be argued, businesses discourage government from discharging its obligations itself. If businesses then have to withdraw through financial circumstances, those who might reasonably expect support are deprived of it. Are there cases of businesses offering services or goods that are better provided by the state? The answer seems to be 'Yes', at least to judge by the collection of projects recently submitted for Dragon Awards in the UK. The Dragon

Awards give recognition to London-based firms, usually big businesses, that provide money, expertise, or other facilities to deserving community groups, charities, or schools, sometimes in British inner cities outside London. It is a joint venture between Business in the Community and the Corporation of the City of London. In 1992 there were seventy entries for the awards, and the descriptions of the entries are a good guide to the range of initiatives thought suitable for the expression of corporate social responsibility.

There was a striking variety of projects: help of various kinds to the ill, handicapped and elderly; sponsorship for community arts programmes; youth training schemes; land reclamation and building restoration; aid to women in business; the provision of funding and expertise for local enterprise; community publishing and radio and television projects; and the provision of free office space and meeting rooms for charities and community groups. Many of these schemes, especially those concerned with providing business services, facilities and expertise, neither duplicated state provision nor provided things that the state could just as easily or appropriately have provided itself. For one thing, not many of the things provided were basic goods and services. Again, many schemes complemented state schemes without taking their place. Others, however, are harder to assess.

Several Dragon Award entries consisted of business sponsorship of city technology colleges. The Mercers' Company, along with the construction group Tarmac, sponsored a school in Telford, Shropshire, and put four of its members on the governing body. BAT Industries is the major sponsor of Teesside City Technology College in Middlesbrough. It has an employee seconded to the school and provides two of the school's governors. Both schools emphasize technology training, and pupils from the school are likely to provide a skilled workforce for local employers.

In the UK the very idea of having city technology colleges has attracted criticism on the ground that it diverts resources and the best pupils to a few showcase schools, leaving other schools to make do with inadequate buildings and equipment, and with pupils who are less talented or have less support at home, and so who need more help. Even if these criticisms are set aside, however, and it is assumed that it is desirable to have city technology colleges, it is not obvious why they should not be funded entirely by the state, since it is plausible to say that it is the responsibility of the state to provide, through its education system, a technologically trained workforce. A further issue is whether it is desirable to have members of sponsoring firms in positions of great influence in school governing bodies: perhaps the attitudes and political leanings of big business will produce hostility towards, or incomprehension of, the demands and interests of the inner city communities that in theory are meant to benefit by the presence of the schools.

Finally, it is unclear whether a school might not be affected by the changing financial fortunes or ownership of a sponsoring firm. Whether or not with quite these reservations in mind, the Director of the UK Confederation of British Industry, in a speech in September 1992, said that 'the CBI wants the long-term funding of *all* schools to be on a secure and adequate basis', and rejected the idea that the right relation between business and education was one of sponsorship. The Director also confessed to having doubts about the concept of a sponsor-governor.

A second area in which it may be asked whether the commercial firm is the proper supplier of a welfare service is in the area of homelessness. The ten-year corporate review of Business in the Community, published in 1992, says that 'companies such as British Rail, Kingfisher and Grand Metropolitan are tackling the homelessness problem by offering accommodation linked to training schemes'.[3] Granted that it is beneficial to the homeless to be given accommodation at the same time as they are trained, and generous of the firms to offer it, can it really be their *responsibility* to do so? Surely they could not be criticized if they did not provide it? And cannot the government be criticized for failing to provide the accommodation even when Grand Met and Kingfisher make it available? A reasonable answer would surely be 'Yes'.

This does not mean that absolutely every business that tries to help the homeless is operating beyond its proper sphere. Much depends on the firm and the nature of the initiative. John Laing is a construction firm, and its Dragon Award entry describes very concrete help to the homeless through the supply of building materials and labour as well as money. In a clear sense this particular business has skills that are highly relevant to homelessness, and so in that sense its initiative is appropriate, but the question of whether it is not really the government's responsibility to *buy* those skills is perfectly legitimate. Far less easy to evaluate is a Body Shop initiative in relation to homelessness. The Body Shop contributed funds and office space for the launch of a newspaper, *The Big Issue*, sold on the street by homeless people. The proceeds of sales support the homeless and allow them to avoid begging. This seems to be a case not of the Body Shop taking over the responsibilities of a housing ministry or a social services department, but of supporting what is turning out to be a paying enterprise that alleviates some of the conditions that homeless people face – apart from the lack of a place to live. We cannot see a good objection to it.

## The ethics of privatization I: for-profit public services

We have been considering initiatives by UK business in areas traditionally occupied by the welfare state, initiatives intended not to replace the institutions of the welfare state but to assist those institutions or to assist people insufficiently helped by the welfare state. We have considered reasons for thinking that business behaves generously but beyond its proper sphere when it takes over the funding of schools, or when it houses the homeless. We now turn to the question of whether it is right for the institutions of the welfare state not only to be assisted by business, but to be put on a business footing themselves.

What is in question are activities that have not previously been conducted on a commercial basis, or that have not recently, or that have not generally, been run on a commercial basis, and which certain people want to turn *into* commercial activities. In Britain these activities range from the provision of medical services to street cleaning and rubbish collection to the management of public housing. Some further and rather different cases that might be mentioned are sport and the running of cultural institutions, such as art galleries and museums. In these areas profit is often thought to pollute.

Before considering the reasons that might lie behind the thought that profit pollutes, it is important to give due weight to the context in which the thought arises. By context we mean at least time and place; for of course it's not believed everywhere, even if it is widely believed in Britain, that profit pollutes the activities just mentioned. Some of the activities that have not recently been conducted on a commercial basis in Britain, and that it would be controversial to privatize, have always been in the private sector in some other countries, such as the USA. And even if one sticks to Britain, it may not *always* have been widely believed that profit pollutes. The experiences of other countries now and experiences in Britain in the past are relevant to saying whether privatization is a practical possibility at all, and relevant also to claims about the consequences of putting previously non-profit-making activities on a commercial footing. But the experience of other countries or of Britain in the past may not be decisive, because cultural differences may underlie the acceptability of, say, a national health service in one place or at one time and its unpopularity in another place and another time; and it may be that, quite apart from the rights and wrongs of profit, we want to preserve these cultural differences.

It is at the very least arguable that facts about culture have a great deal to do with the attraction in Britain of the thought that profit pollutes in the public services. This does not invalidate the thought. Indeed the considerable value that British people in large numbers manifestly place on their culture – a welfare-state culture if you like – is a very good reason for not disrupting it. But there can be disputes about whether the welfare state culture is authentic, and about whether its value is purely contrived. Some people who believe in privatization think that the effect of following their policies would be to restore free-market values to a dominance in British life that they have lost during a supposedly temporary flirtation with socialism. The same people ascribe to the merely temporary appeal of socialism the appeal of the thought that profit pollutes. Whether these people are right or whether their opponents are, the question of which ways of providing medicine are true to values held by Britons has considerable relevance if culture or tradition does. We shall have more to say later about these kinds of issues.

In the meantime let us try to make explicit the logic of the dispute between those who think that profit pollutes and those who think it doesn't. By the logic of the dispute, we mean the pattern of reasons given for conclusions on both sides. We also mean the issue between the two sides. When people complain that profit pollutes a given activity, e.g. hospital services, they are not drawing a distinction between loss-making private hospitals on the one hand and private hospitals whose revenues exceed costs on the other, and saying that the loss-makers are morally superior to the profit-makers. They are saying that it is wrong to run hospitals with the *aim* of making a profit, and wrong also to run other enterprises – art galleries, say, or museums or schools – with the aim of making profits.

### Why should profit pollute?

Let us stick to the case of hospitals and ask what is wrong with aiming to make a profit by running them or what is wrong with running them on a basis other than that on which they are run by, say, the UK National Health Service at the moment. One answer might be that people who need hospital care are suffering with certain disorders, or perhaps have been struck down in accidents and are in acute pain, and that it is wrong to try to make money out of their misery, or even charge them when the service has to be used and they are at a low ebb. Instead, one should aim at most at covering costs, and the service should be free at the point of delivery. A problem with this answer, however, is that it seems to tell against the provision for profit of other activities that have almost always been conducted privately, and that few people feel strongly should be on a not-for-profit basis. Surely 24-hour plumbers, automobile breakdown services, roofers, and glaziers make money out of people's misery in some sense; yet that fact does not seem to make it tempting to have a state-run plumbing service or a tax-funded national roofing service, free at the point of use, or an automobile breakdown service on a not-for-profit basis. A borderline case in this area may be funeral services: state funding for burials for the indigent exists in Britain and other countries, and its rationale may not be completely unrelated to a rationale for a state-funded hospital service. But whatever that rationale is, it is not that misery should never be an occasion for someone else to make money; otherwise we should run into the incongruity of a national roofing service.

It might be thought that what makes a national health service necessary, or a public hospital system necessary, but not a national roofing service, is that lives can depend on having hospitals, and it is morally wrong that people should die for lack of money to pay for medical treatment. This rationale is relevant, however, only to that fraction of hospital treatment that might make the difference between life and death. It does not by itself justify the provision of hospital services for non-life threatening but unpleasant conditions, such as some orthopaedic complaints or even some treatment dispensed by casualty wards. Enlarging the scope of the principle that we are appealing to, so that it covers different kinds of pain and discomfort, would help to give us a rationale wide enough to justify a public health service with the range of treatments that the NHS offers. But once again it might be asked whether other activities that help to prevent pain and discomfort and death have to be on a not-for-profit basis or brought into the public sector if the rationale of preventing death and pain is a sufficient justification for having most *hospitals* run on a not-for-profit basis and for having them in the public sector.

To appreciate the difficulties, we do not have to return to the glaziers and roofers, though their case is relevant. Think instead of the pharmaceuticals and the food production and distribution industries, to speak of a huge swathe of commerce all at once. Surely these are essential to the prevention of pain, and the prevention of death by starvation. Surely our lives and the quality of our lives depend on them. Indeed, in the case of the pharmaceutical industry, our lives depend on it if they depend on the health service, for the health service depends on the pharmaceutical industry. But must it, for that reason, be taken into public ownership? Must it, for that reason, be run on a not-for-profit basis? The argument is scarcely compelling.

We are still without a principle that justifies a non-profit hospital system or health service and perhaps the difficulty of finding such a principle is that a principle by itself will not provide the justification we are looking for. Perhaps the case for the National Health Service depends on the moral importance of its life-saving, life-prolonging and pain-preventing powers, only in *combination* with the fact that some life-prolonging, life-saving and pain-preventing treatments, while morally necessary, are simply never going to be profitable to offer. Or perhaps there are some treatments that could be sold for a profit in some parts of the country and not in others, so that under a profit-making system it would happen that there were parts of the country that hospital services simply would not reach. Then the moral arguments for treating the expensive conditions, even at a loss, and for servicing the commercially unattractive parts of the country, even at a loss, would be arguments for keeping the National Health Service in its present, non-profit form.

Notice, however, what these arguments do not show. They do not show that a for-profit alternative to the National Health Service would *necessarily* be polluted. All that is in question is those parts of for-profit medicine that, because they might run at a loss, might be dropped despite their moral necessity. We do not have a reason to think that just any essential treatment might be dropped on a profit-making scheme; we only have assumptions that make it plausible that *loss-making* essential treatments might be dropped. And even these reasons do not definitely rule out a morally acceptable for-profit service, since loss-making essential treatments might still be offered in a service that made profits.

Is there no tension at all, then, between the profit-making aims of a commercial health service, and the pain-preventing and life-saving aims of such a service? Is there no sense in which profit pollutes? We would have a reason for supposing that profit polluted if in a commercial hospital service the prospect of a loss or of merely breaking even were always a decisive reason for dropping a treatment. But the most that seems to be plausible in this area is that the prospect of no profit or of a loss is *a* reason for dropping the treatment, not that it is a decisive reason. It is true that in the thinking behind the National Health Service as it now is in the UK, the prospect of break-even or loss might be no reason for dropping a treatment. To that extent there is a difference between the for-profit and not-for-profit conceptions of treatment. But the tension is not severe. That is, the thinking that we are attributing to the National Health Service, while it is admittedly morally purer than the thinking in the commercial health service, is in the same moral universe as the commercial thinking, since both sorts of thinking can attach great value to the saving of life or the prevention of pain, and even more value to this than the making of profit. The difference comes in the values they attach to other things.

Now it might be objected that while the commercial health service can attach great importance to pain prevention and the enhancement and prolonging of life, it cannot attach much value to these things in comparison to the value of making of profit, since, being a commercial entity, its *raison d'etre* is to maximize its profits. However, this line of thought seems to confuse two different things, only one of which is essential to the conduct of a commercial enterprise. The two things are (1) running a health service on condition that one makes a profit, and (2) running a health service only for the sake of profit. Running a health service on condition that one makes a profit is compatible with putting a high value on whatever goods are promoted by the existence of health services: goods such as longer lives and decreased pain. But running a health service only for profit makes the value of these goods irrelevant to running the service, and perhaps even denies their value. However, a commercial entity does not have to conduct its activities for the sake of profit alone.

Suppose that it is granted that there is nothing in the very idea of a commercially run health service that must make it subordinate everything else to profit. Still, might it not be true, e.g. for institutional reasons, that a commercially run health service is always in *danger* of letting the pursuit of profit be a decisive reason for having or dropping a treatment, or even for remaining in business or going out of business? Suppose that our hypothetical commercial health service has a management with its heart in the right place but that its shareholders are dissatisfied with the level of profit. Or suppose that it has taken loans out with a bank, and that the bank's credit managers believe that profit-making counts for too little with the management, so that the bank is unwilling to extend further credit until a higher level of profitability is aimed at. These suppositions are not at all far-fetched. Even if a company is in the unusual position of having a management, shareholders *and* banks all with their hearts in the right place at the same time, they may not always be in this position. For these reasons we must admit that even a morally conscientious business is likely at some point to be at the mercy of stakeholders for whom profitability is decisive or overriding. And so we concede that there is always a risk of profit polluting. But this seems to be a much weaker and in some respects more contingent basis for thinking that profit pollutes than any opponents of privatization would usually appeal to.

### Profit does not purify

If the message of the preceding discussion had to be summarized briefly, it might be put by saying that profit does not necessarily pollute, but that it at worst carries a risk of polluting. This is a weaker conclusion than anti-privatizers are likely to welcome, but it also falls short of what pro-privatizers are likely to welcome. And there is worse to come for the pro-privatizers – for at the same time as it is true that profit doesn't necessarily pollute, it is also true that profit doesn't necessarily purify. For some elements of the privatization lobby, on the other hand, there is not only supposed to be a gain in efficiency as a result of privatization, or as a result of the introduction of market forces; but there is also supposed to be a morally improving enlargement of choice for consumers, a morally improving dedication to service on the part of sellers of goods,[4] a morally improving willingness to take responsibility and a morally improving increase of concern with value for money.

The reason these things are supposed to be morally improving, we take it, is that it is morally good for people to make choices, exercise responsibility, and not waste money, and that in a situation in which market forces prevail and profit is pursued, there is more scope for these things than in a situation in which they are absent. This has a plausible sound to it, but where it is correct, it does not contradict anything an anti-privatizer would have to assert, and where it does contradict the anti-privatizer, it depends on kinds of choice and responsibility that do not have any particular moral significance.

Where the line of thought just outlined is correct and uncontroversial is in its implication that it is wrong to waste money. One does not have to believe in profit to believe that money is sometimes squandered in the public sector, and that it is wrong for money to be squandered. However, it is not necessary for people who are only out to cover their costs to have a less exacting conception of waste than people who are out to make money. The wrongness of waste can, it seems to us, be common ground. Perhaps as a matter of fact people in the public services are less preoccupied with preventing waste than those in the private sector – we do not know. Perhaps there is a range of cases in which what is regarded as prudent expenditure in the public sector might be seen as wasteful in the private sector. Suppose these things are true: it still isn't clear why it must be so. The reply that in the public sector workers and managers are spending other people's money, and are for that reason likely to be profligate, while in the private sector they do not and so are less likely to be profligate, seems hugely disputable if one is looking at big business, or, for different reasons, at some sections of the financial services industry or even solicitors' practices: here the spending of other people's money is commonplace and profligacy not unknown. The reply that in the public sector no one feels enough of a stake in the organization to take a keen interest in cost-cutting might also be met with the reply that in a sufficiently huge and impersonal and seemingly endlessly solvent private company – a Shell or a Unilever or a Philips – one could find the same thing.

The war on waste, we are suggesting, should not in principle come any more naturally to big business than to big public services, and even if measures are more readily taken against it in the private sector, there is no reason why the fact that waste is wrong should be more readily acknowledged in the private than in the public sector. So any claim that it takes the market or the profit-motive to recognize or to combat waste seems unconvincing.

What now of the idea that the market-oriented, profit-motivated approach is morally improving because of its tendency to promote choice and responsibility? This idea is very familiar from the rhetoric of the political right in the UK in the 1980s, and repetition may have given it an air of self-evidence. To question the rhetoric, we need to distinguish between the extension of consumer choice, which has no particular moral significance, though it may be desirable, and the extension of autonomy, which does have moral significance. When privatization is said to extend choice, what is meant is an enlargement of the range of things to choose from. Under the new health service reforms, doctors are supposed to be given a wider range of treatments, hospitals and so on to choose between for their patients. Is this a morally better situation than the one it replaces?

Consider the case in which a small corner shop is demolished and what takes its place is a large supermarket. The supermarket offers more things to choose from than the corner shop, perhaps the things one can choose from are also cheaper, perhaps the turnover is higher and the produce is on the shelf for less time. One can see that the supermarket might be preferable to the corner shop – but on *moral* grounds? Has the supermarket more of a stake in our well-being than the corner shop? Are we necessarily treated with more respect? Is the larger store fairer or more scrupulous in its dealings with its customers? Maybe, maybe not: the larger choice of goods by itself does not settle the matter. By the same token, the extension of choice in the health service is not necessarily a moral improvement either. The rhetoric makes it sound like a moral improvement because of an equivocation on 'choice' – that is because it makes use of more than one sense of the word 'choice'.

A different sort of choice from consumer choice does have moral significance, and the extension of this choice can accordingly constitute a moral improvement. Choice in this sense is extended if people's actions and omissions are less and less determined by things outside their control and more and more determined by things under their control, i.e. their choices. Things outside one's control include coercion by other people, compulsions and addictions, unwanted habits, illnesses, physical handicaps and so on. Against this background, we may say that building a ramp in a building that previously had only stairs and was inaccessible to wheelchair users extends choice. Once the ramp is built, wheelchair users are on a par with able-bodied users of the building – free to use it or not as they choose. Even if no one in a wheelchair does use the building, that is from choice rather than due to circumstances outside their control. Or to take another sort of case entirely, it is morally better if a marriage that two people would have been forced into anyway takes place without the pressure ever having to be applied – because the two people choose to do it. And it is morally better still if the two people choose to get married and there is no compulsion in the background at all. Now it is quite unclear that privatization, or the rolling back of the state, or the profit motive promotes the extension of this kind of choice. On the contrary, there is quite a good *prima facie* case for thinking that the unrolled-back state has more of a record of extending wheelchair users' choices than the minimal state.

What goes for the privatizers' use of the concept of choice goes also for the privatizers' use of the concept of responsibility. It, too, may lack the moral significance it appears to have. It may be true that when a public service is put on a more commercial footing, whether in the run-up to privatization or afterwards, lines of managerial responsibility become clearer. That is, it may be true that people inside the organization have a clearer idea of who is in charge of what and who is answerable to whom. Perhaps, though this is more controversial, it even becomes clearer to consumers who precisely the people in charge *are*. Thus, in the Network Southeast sector of British Rail, platform advertisements carry photographs of local managers and even station personnel, as well as the man in charge of Network Southeast himself. This practice is commonplace in the private sector: the Nationwide Anglia Building Society does something similar in relation to its branch staff. The rationale for this publicity probably includes the consideration that putting a face and a name to a management position personalizes, and so makes more friendly the service being offered; it probably also includes the consideration that by being able to identify who is in charge, consumers know who to blame or admire for the way the system runs. They know who to hold responsible. The managers in turn are supposed to expect that they will be held responsible and are supposed to act in that knowledge. It is in this sense that privatization or the preliminaries to it might increase people's willingness to take responsibility. Is this a morally improving spin-off of privatization?

Once again, we must not let ourselves be captivated by the use of words with ostensibly moral senses. In particular we must not be transfixed by the word 'responsible'. There is a big difference between having responsibility for a thing, in the sense that a certain task is part of one's job description and is known to be part of one's job description, and, on the other hand, actively taking charge and dedicating oneself to the task. There is a difference, in other words, between being charged with a responsibility and being conscientious. There is even  a difference between conscientiousness and being willing to take the blame in public. One can be masterful at taking the blame in public just because, through lack of conscientiousness, one has taken the blame again and again. An increase in conscientiousness, other things being equal, is a definite moral improvement. But the change that accompanies or precedes privatization, and that consists of a simple clarification of job descriptions, an openness about job descriptions, and an openness about job-holders, and about who is to take the blame – let's call it 'clarifying lines of responsibility' for short – is less obviously a moral improvement, and is compatible with no change in conscientiousness.

Not only may clarifying lines of responsibility not be a moral improvement; it may also have aspects that are morally questionable. For example, one by-product of saying that a particular individual is responsible for Network Southeast is that he may be perfectly conscientious and competent and yet be let down by someone else who is not.  In these circumstances it is not clear that the manager ought to be blamed, even if he is, as we say, the responsible person, the person in charge. The same of course applies when things go well, and the person in charge is singled out for praise that, properly speaking, belongs to many other people, and often to the other people exclusively. In other words, there is a kind of illusion, and a high risk of unfairness, in holding people individually responsible for the success and failure of complex activities that are well outside one person's control.

Another questionable aspect of the thinking about responsibility that we are considering is its lack of impartiality in the essentially consumerist framework that the pro-privatizers and many of the rest of us in daily life take for granted. Within a consumerist framework managers are supposed to take the blame when things go wrong but they are not held to be good judges of when things go wrong. Instead the consumer is supposed to be authoritative, sometimes incorrigible, about when things go wrong. This is the line of thought according to which the consumer is king, or the customer is always right, a line of thought well represented in the rhetoric of the privatizers. The trouble with this line of thought, as we saw in Chapter 3, is that while it's very convenient for us as consumers, it's undoubtedly false. The customer is not always right.

### The costs of undoing successful social engineering

Here, as elsewhere, there are limits to what philosophy can do in exposing what underlies a particular controversy or even in making clear the relative strengths of the two sides. There are the reasons on both sides, but there is also the broader culture or climate in which the controversy is located. This can matter in a large number of ways. It can matter, for example, in assigning the burden of proof. Thus, there is a welfare state in the UK and considerable support for the welfare state. Similarly for other countries in Western Europe. This is the position that debate in the UK and Western Europe has to start from, and so the burden of proof, as usual, falls upon those who want something different. It is for the privatizers to show why there should be less of the welfare state, and more of something else. It is for the privatizers to show this even if it's hard to come up with convincing arguments for the *status quo,* and even if it is easy to come up with facts and arguments to show that the *status quo* is not ideal.

Now facts about the *status quo* and the burden of proof are important to many arguments, but they are important in a special way to the new-right thinking that supports privatization. This is because it is part of the new-right case for privatization that the welfare state is a product of something bad, namely social engineering, or a process of remoulding society in the image a government has. Social engineering is supposed to differ from a policy of letting people order their own activities according to their own images, and not an image imposed from on high. Since the new-right in Britain often presents its policies as a means of undoing the social engineering of postwar governments, its proponents are able to present the policies not only on their own merits, as better ways of providing housing, health care and the rest, but as a way of restoring a freedom from state interference. What they overlook is that when a piece of social engineering has really succeeded, as it has in the creation of the postwar welfare state, it is social engineering to undo the social engineering. The attraction of a certain image of a new sort of British society, new in the sense of being different from the welfare state, but old in the sense of returning people to their supposedly vigorous Victorian roots, is taken to override the attraction that the present – admittedly socially engineered – state actually has for the British people or many of them.

In philosophy this disregard of what people actually want or prefer is an occupational hazard, because one gets into the frame of mind in which one is interested only in what it is rational to prefer or want. In morals and politics and real life, on the other hand, it makes a great difference what people actually think and want, whether for good or bad reasons; and the greater a departure from the actual that one is recommending, the more the importance to people of the actual must be taken into account. So the privatizers must prove their case. So far, in our judgement, they have not succeeded in doing so. But this is not because there is always something wrong with profit, but because there may be something wrong with trying to pursue it everywhere.

## The ethics of privatization II: sales of state-owned business

How strong is the case for privatization where what is in question is not an activity or institution associated with the welfare state but a state-owned industrial enterprise?  In such an instance the enterprise may already operate on a for-profit basis, though its organization and management may not conform to an orthodox commercial pattern. Its principal sphere of operation may be markets in which the other enterprises represented are all or mostly privately owned. Isn't the state-owned enterprise in this case properly turned over to the commercial sector?

The matter is in fact more complicated than it looks. The economic case for privatization can differ from firm to firm and market to market. There are well-known economic objections to privatizing firms, such as the typical public sector telephone or gas company, which would have a monopoly position in the private sector. There are fewer economic objections to returning to the competitive part of the private sector companies that started out there and were taken into public ownership only to save them from outright failure. On the other hand, some firms whose privatization makes sense on public sector economic grounds – to privatize them would be to reduce the public expenditure, and sometimes the public borrowing, needed to finance them – could only survive commercially at huge costs in unemployment, and so significant losses in well-being to individuals and communities, amounting to something of a utilitarian moral case *against* privatization. Sometimes the transfer of a publicly owned firm to the private sector can be for the best on balance, and yet the actual sell-off be influenced by considerations of political advantage or the partiality of financial advisers, so that the net financial returns to the state are lower than they might or should have been. Here, too, there are utilitarian considerations against privatization, as well as arguments from justice.

Whether there can be good general arguments for or against the privatization of just *any* state-owned industrial enterprise in just *any* circumstances seems to us to be doubtful. Yet very general arguments for and against privatization *are* mounted. In the UK, privatization has been attacked on the ground that the sell-off of state-owned enterprises is always a case of asset stripping. This argument is less than compelling across the board, since some companies in public ownership are hugely expensive to maintain, and are probably better regarded as liabilities than assets. On the other side, privatization has been defended in the UK on the ground that any rolling back of the frontiers of the state is desirable. It has also been defended on the ground that the widening of share-ownership in particular, and of ownership in general, is a good thing. At the end of Chapter 5 some reasons were given why neither share owning nor ownership in general is necessarily morally desirable. Earlier sections of the present chapter contain reasons why rolling back the frontiers of the state is not necessarily a good thing either: if the state is the vehicle for certain welfare institutions – a health service, a social security system, a social work service, a network of recreation facilities and adult education services – and these command wide public loyalty, as they do in the UK, then rolling back the state to the extent that these institutions are transferred to the private sector has much to be said against it. Unless any state – even a popular welfare state – has latent in it the makings of the fully homogenized, fully centralized, highly authoritarian states that once existed in Eastern Europe, a suggestion sometimes made by those in favour of rolling back the state, then the claim that the less extensive a state is, the better it is, is not easy to defend in full generality.

More convincing than a fully general argument is detailed testimony, even anecdotal testimony, that calls attention to the weaknesses of particular intrusions of particular state institutions, leaving it open whether all state institutions are intrusive or whether all states have frontiers in need of rolling back. Testimony of this kind exists, testimony with a bearing on some controversial UK privatizations. Sir Ian MacGregor, who ran some large nationalized companies, has given some examples:

All of [the] dangers [of state ownership] stem from the fact that once a property passes into state ownership, it becomes the victim of different influences. There is the immediate management who would normally try to avoid constant battling, and one cannot fault them for this. Most people like to live a reasonably peaceful life. If enough pressure is applied, one will try to compromise. Many of the past relationships in both the steel and the coal industries where compromises were achieved involved two groups putting enormous pressure on each other. This made for dramatic inefficiencies... The civil service also creates problems. When private enterprises passed into state ownership, the civil servants became the *de facto* managers. Many of them were, if you will, frustrated managers. These civil servants had not entered the managerial ranks through the orthodox way of joining a company and working their way up. They were vicarious managers; they loved to practise managing; and they had one great advantage: they could make decisions about what to do. But somehow or other, when it came to responsibilities, these civil servants were totally anonymous. The person who was responsible could never be identified and, therefore, there was no accountability. A committee decided things, and the committee was a long list of names... Then there is the public.

...There are large areas of England where buildings on the surface are slowly sinking and how much they sink depends on how much coal has been removed from below. In some buildings, cracks appear in the ceiling. In others, the windows do not move up and down as they once did. Traditionally, the British Coal people compensated the owners of these properties for such damage. Then, there came political lobbyists... These lobbyists, who depicted the coal industry as totally vulnerable, would take claims for compensation and win large settlements... The managers could only take the line of least resistance; they did not want to get into the subsidence debate... Consequently the coal industry was prepared to pay. In some cases, for every ton of coal extracted £10 was paid for fixing living rooms...[5]

The instances MacGregor gives have considerable force, but they do not seem unique to state-run business. Plainly companies in the private sector can be targeted by lobbyists, and there is no firm dividing line between some sorts of lobbyists who have no direct claim to determine the direction of a business, and some stakeholders, who do. Besides, MacGregor's testimony about the influence of outsiders is not always hostile. Though the civil servants appear to have been a nuisance, the politicians are sometimes described as allies:

Thanks to a very enlightened Minister of Energy, Mr Nigel Lawson, management was able to offer to the workforce a transition structure which presented a person who had been in the industry for 30 years an opportunity to retire early with £1,000 for every year of service.[6]

Evidently the actions of the civil servants were interference, while the action of a sympathetic politician was assistance.

Not only do MacGregor's views about state intervention differ, depending on which representative of the state is under discussion; it is clear from his account that his difficulties as a manager in charge of a nationalized industry were as much to do with unions as with the state.[7] It is true that in the 1970s the British government encouraged a pattern of industrial relations that kept unions in touch with top management even in minor disputes, apparently at great cost to managerial efficiency. But a strong active union might have been an obstacle to the efficient running of the Coal Board or British Steel, whether nationalized or not.

MacGregor's view is that of someone who knows from the inside the limitations of some nationalized companies, and who is in favour of their privatization partly on the ground that the resulting efficiencies are in the public interest. Alongside his examples, however, must be set cases of firms that have been subject to little state regulation once they passed out of the public sector, arguably at some cost to the public interest. A detailed study of the privatization of British Airways shows that enthusiasm for reducing state ownership of business can sometimes produce blindness to the actual effects of privatization on competition.[8] Although the transfer of businesses to the private sector is supposed to increase competition, there is evidence to show that, in the case of British Airways, privatization ushered in predatory behaviour that reduced competition among UK airline operators on international routes. What is more, some of the adverse effects on competition were predicted by the regulatory agency in charge of the pre-privatized British Airways, and these predictions were apparently ignored by the government when the agency recommended that privatization be accompanied by appropriate regulatory safeguards on competition. The difficulty of introducing competitive pressures into the post-privatized electricity-supply and gas industries in the UK was also foreseen, but it did not obstruct the relevant sell-offs either.

The conclusion of a recent survey of privatization schemes throughout the world suggests a variety of conditions for the success of privatizations, many of which fail to be met by the schemes it investigates.[9] In Western Europe in general and the UK in particular the problems of achieving the right level of competition and regulation are claimed to cancel out some of the supposed cost-efficiencies.[10] Revenues to privatizing governments are often swallowed up by the costs of meeting international environmental standards, and privatization can take place without the creation of a culture among stakeholders that makes them receptive to it. Popular resistance in Portugal to sales abroad of shares in nationalized companies is a case in point, as is popular resistance in Sweden to a tax reform that would allow for private sector participation in what is reportedly a widely disliked public health care system.

# References

1  Quoted in Tom Sorell, 'Strategy and ethics: Pilkington Plc', in D. Asch and C. Bowman, *Readings in Strategic Management* (London: Macmillan, 1989), p.289.
2  *Ibid.*
3  CBI, *Ten Year Corporate Review* (London: CBI, 1992).
4  D. Green, *The New Right* (Brighton: Wheatsheaf, 1987).
5  Quoted in P. MacAvoy et al., *Privatization and State-owned Enterprise: Lessons for the United States, Great Britain and Canada* (Boston: Kluwer, 1989), pp.270–1.
6  *Ibid.*, pp.260–70.
7  *Ibid.*, pp.267–8.
8  Robert Baldwin in J. Richardson, (ed.), *Privatization and Deregulation in Canada and Britain* (Aldershot: Dartmouth Publishing, 1990), pp. 96–111.
9  D. Gayle and J. Goodrich, *Privatization and Deregulation in Global Perspective* (London: Pinter, 1990), pp.435–6.
10 *Ibid.*, p.437.

# 8  Green business

A central issue in broad business ethics is that of a business's responsibility
to the society in which it operates, and also to the physical environment on
which that society depends. In Europe ecological issues have been brought
to bear on business by 'green' political parties, by pressure groups, and,
partly independently of these, by the laws of various Western European
governments. Measurements of environmental damage traceable to
business activity have been made routinely since the 1970s, and targets for
reductions in damage, or for the reversal of damage, have been set by
governments, industries and individual companies. Not all these developments, however, belong to broad business ethics in the sense previously
defined. A business that sets itself a target for the reduction of emissions or
that cleans up some of its own pollution is not necessarily motivated by the
interests of people other than its own stakeholders. It is not necessarily
acting for the sake of society or in the interest of the environment. It may be
acting simply in order to avoid damaging legal action, punitive fines, or
publicity that would have adverse effects on shareholder returns. Even
when the wider world does weigh with a company, when its environmentally related activities do reflect a commitment to broad business ethics,
that commitment may still fall short of what environmental groups would
consider ethically appropriate.

In this chapter we shall begin by reviewing some of the environmental
issues faced by Western European countries and some of the legal
responses to these issues. We shall then survey a range of environmental
initiatives in business, and shall consider some of the ethical issues raised.
We shall ask to what extent the initiatives described have moral value; to
what extent the contributions of a business to society or its responsibilities
to its stakeholders may reasonably override its responsibilities to the
environment and to what extent the determination of what is morally
acceptable in this respect should be the responsibility of businesses, and to
what extent of governments. Finally, we shall look at the relation between
business ethics and environmental ethics and at what light this sheds on
the social tensions between business and environmentalism.

## Environmental issues in Western Europe

Western European countries have long faced a variety of environmental problems, some of them recognized centuries before there was a green movement. In The Netherlands, for example, 48 per cent of the land area lies below sea-level. Civil engineering works to defend this land against flooding and salination have for a long time consumed large quantities of sand, the removal and spreading of which harms the few wooded areas in the country.[1] The Netherlands also suffers from industrial pollution of the rivers Rhine and Maas. In Spain environmental problems are also formidable and of long standing. Although environmental legislation and an interministerial commission for co-ordinating it have been in place since the early 1970s, an EC directive in 1988 required the country to spend no less than 300,000 million pesetas in industry and technology to improve the environment.[2] From emissions of pollutants into the air to forest fires and soil erosion, the threats to Spain's environment continue to be numerous.

More prosperous European countries than Spain have not been spared either. A quantified 'ecological balance sheet' was drawn up in 1986 for what was then West Germany. It estimated the total cost per year of all environmental damage, from atmospheric and water pollution to soil damage and noise, at DM 103,500 million.[3] A similar balance sheet, drawn up for a unified Germany, would of course show a much higher total.

In the UK the pollution of air, water and soil is also significant. Water pollution incidents – more than 22,000 occurred in 1991 – are recorded, analysed and investigated by the National Rivers Authority. The NRA recognizes three degrees of severity of pollution incidents, and classifies them by source: farm, industrial, oil, sewage, and water industry. Figures given in the 1992 NRA report show that the water industry was responsible for the largest proportion of incidents (23 per cent), followed by oil pollution (20 per cent), with farms and industry accounting for about 11 per cent of incidents each. The most consistent industrial polluter was the minerals industry, followed by the chemicals industry.[4] When pollution incidents are classified by severity, the NRA found that in 1991 industry accounted for about 21 per cent of serious pollution incidents.[5] Given the artificiality of the NRA distinction between 'industrial' and 'oil'-related pollution, the true figure (combining oil and industry) may be closer to 40 per cent.

The NRA deals with pollution by court action  often leading to fines and the award of legal costs against offenders, and by the issue of formal cautions. By March 1992, 356 prosecutions for pollution incidents occurring in 1991 had been undertaken, almost all of them leading to convictions. The level of fines for offenders cannot be considered high. The largest fine imposed on a company for an incident occurring in 1991 was £200,000, for oil pollution in the Welsh region, and that fine was exceptionally high. In no other UK region was the maximum fine imposed in that year over £15,000. Not all pollution incidents led to prosecutions. Water companies sometimes used a defence of third-party release of sewage, or exercised prerogatives to protract the time necessary to improve levels of water purity. Again, some pollution incidents did not come to the attention of the NRA. A legal initiative taken in 1993 by Greenpeace UK will test the viability of private prosecutions under UK legislation that empowers the NRA to take action against a polluter.[6] Greenpeace issued a summons against the UK chemicals multinational, ICI, alleging discharge of unlicensed chemicals into the Wyre Estuary and the Irish Sea, and, at another ICI plant, into the Tees Estuary and the North Sea. According to the newsletter *Greenpeace Business*, Greenpeace had analysed the ICI discharges, and had discovered forbidden chemicals in the discharges of around twenty other companies operating in the UK.[7]

Are prosecutions of companies in the UK likely to increase? Greenpeace has claimed that the transfer of discharge monitoring from the relatively active NRA to an inspectorate that relies much more than the NRA on self-regulation (Her Majesty's Inspectorate of Pollution) will set back the cause of effective pollution-regulation in the UK. What about legislation in the rest of Europe? EC legislation geared to protecting the environment consisted by 1990 of more than 120 different Acts, based on a three-pronged policy of (1) promoting the prevention rather than the clean-up of pollution, (2) 'subsidiarity', or the tailoring of legislation to the requirements of EC member states, and (3) making the polluter pay, a policy realized in part in fines, and in part in eco-taxes.[8]

Governments have not been the only institutions with green agendas. Businesses, too, have had their ecological initiatives. Unsurprisingly, many have been in response to, or in anticipation of, legal regulation. These include the mainstream activities of emission control, such as the installation of desulphurization plant in West German power stations in the 1980s, and a host of energy saving measures. Less conventional initiatives should also be mentioned. They range from the exploitation of under-used sources of energy to environmental campaigning. After describing some examples of these initiatives – both conventional and unconventional – we shall consider the sort of criticisms that they might attract from conventional moral philosophy and from the green movement. We shall ask to what extent business objectives and green objectives must be deeply at odds, and we shall argue that the greens have better reason to want a world in which business operates defensively than a world in which business disappears.

## Conventional green initiatives in business

The German programme of desulphurizing power-station processes in the 1980s has already been mentioned. At about the same time, UK business involvement in the development of methods for controlling emissions was also significant. In the late 1980s the UK Central Electricity Generating Board (CEGB) was interested in processes for treating nitrogen emissions at all its coal-fired power stations, and sulphur emissions at three 2000 megawatt power stations. Three sulphur-removing processes were developed by competition among eleven consortia of engineering companies from Europe and the USA: a limestone gypsum process, using limestone to absorb the sulphur from stack emissions and produce gypsum, a material suitable for plasterboard construction; a spray-dry system, which removes sulphur and produces a non-usable waste product; and a regenerative method, which extracts sulphur for re-use in the manufacture of sulphur-based chemical products.[9] Here beneficial technology was developed for the UK, sometimes with associated success in export markets. Another, much more recent case of beneficial reduction of emissions concerns ozone-destroying CFC and HFC gases in refrigerators. German domestic refrigerator manufacturers introduced new CFC-free technology at the Domotechnica trade fair in Cologne in February 1993.

The control of emissions is one well-established 'green' initiative. There are others. Waste management is probably more widely implemented, especially in the form of recycling schemes, and it appears to be the most commonly studied and discussed throughout UK industry. But it is also, as we shall see in a moment, a subject that tends to be considered from a narrowly economic and corporatist perspective with which the green movement is out of sympathy. An indication of this approach is given in a recent Working Party Report on Waste Management in the UK, published in June 1992 by Business in the Environment, a subgroup of Business in the Community specializing in environmental subjects. The Working Party Report took the UK government's aim of recycling half of all recyclable household waste – 25 per cent of all waste in Britain – by the year 2000, and suggested three methods of achieving this target. Foremost among the measures was that of drastically increasing the price of landfill in the UK, estimated to be about a sixth of the cost per ton of landfill on the Continent in 1992. Although increasing the price of landfill was not the only means of encouraging the rate of recycling, it was regarded as the most fundamental one:

> The importance of landfill economics cannot be overstressed, for while landfill remains the last resort in a hierarchy of waste disposal options, it arguably sets the framework against which other options, e.g. minimisation, re-use, recycling and energy recover, are judged.[10]

The Working Party also urged the introduction of financial incentives, mostly in the form of tax credits, for the manufacture of recyclable products.

Apart from price and fiscal mechanisms, the Working Party recommended national and local government guidance on recycling tailored to different regions, purchasing policies that would favour the use of recycled material in products and services bought by the public sector, and the adoption nationwide of the best practices being piloted throughout the country at the local level. Action that could be taken in the private sector was also sketched: companies could themselves encourage recycling by showing a preference for suppliers of products using recycled material; companies with developed waste-management policies could publicize them within their sectors of business, and business associations could play a role in encouraging consciousness of the need for recycling among small and medium-sized firms. Finally, industries most closely concerned with markets for recycled materials were urged to set targets for collecting and re-using these materials.

Measures for controlling emissions and managing waste are two of the most characteristic types of mainstream or conventional 'green' initiative in British businesses. Then there is energy-saving. Recent illustrations of good practice in energy-saving in the UK are given in a publication produced by Business in the Environment and KPMG Peat Marwick, *A Measure of Commitment: guidelines for measuring environmental performance.*[11] This report gives the case of Hydro Aluminium Metals Ltd, a firm involved in reprocessing used aluminium into primary product form. In conjunction with the Polytechnic of Wales, the company was able to arrive for the first time at measures of gas and electricity consumption per tonne of aluminium processed; it was also able to identify possible savings in energy use through the recapture of waste heat in stack emissions. A reduction in gas consumption of at least 10 per cent was forecast as a result of its monitoring activities. *A Measure of Commitment* also mentions two companies, Bluecrest Convenience Foods and Scott, the paper maker, that reduced effluents in manufacturing processes.

Do these initiatives really amount to a show of commitment to ecological protection over and above what is required by an obligation not to pollute? As in the case of the Dragon Awards, *A Measure of Commitment* provides a mixed bag of cases. There are initiatives, particularly in the formulation of performance measures, that go beyond what a company should be doing anyway to protect the environment, and that may help other companies to further a creditable 'green agenda'. But there are also cases of initiatives that, apart from being worth imitating, are only what companies that pollute owe to those who are suffering or would suffer the pollution.

# Less conventional green initiatives

Less conventional 'green' business initiatives range from environmentally friendly technological innovation, 'green' investment services, 'green' trading and 'green' tourism, to 'green' community initiatives, environmental counselling and environmental campaigning. Among the technological innovations, some, like Johnson Matthey control systems and catalytic converters, respond to conventional demands for reductions in emissions. Other measures, such as processes for recycling toner cartridges in laser printers, respond to conventional demands for waste-saving. Still, certain innovations stand apart. Boots Microcheck is responsible for the development of environmentally acceptable anti-fouling chemicals used to keep oil wells and cooling systems clean.[12] Novo Industri, a Danish pharmaceuticals firm, is developing safer, species-specific pesticides,[13] and the Belgian-based Plant Genetic Systems is working to produce an insect-repellent lettuce variety.[14] Ecoschemes, a UK design group, has developed turf as an ecologically sensitive and effective domestic roofing material, and Architype Design Co-operative and Pinke, Leaman and Browning of Winchester, in the south of England, are two architectural firms that have succeeded in the UK Green Building of the Year Award. Architype is responsible for an energy-efficient self-build scheme.

Environmentally acceptable technological innovations are sometimes supported by investment from the 'green' or ethical funds discussed in Chapter 5. TSB Environmental and Merlin Ecology are specialists in such investment, and, as we saw, management fees from the N. M. Schroeder Conscience Fund are sometimes donated, at the request of investors, to non-commercial green initiatives, such as the Centre for Alternative Technology in Wales. Certain deposit-takers, such as the UK Co-operative Bank and Mercury Provident, also channel money into 'green' enterprises. The Ecology Building Society, only 14 years old in 1994, and the second smallest provider of mortgages in the UK, lends on 'environmentally sound' property in a variety of locations. Its loans are relatively modest and are repaid at interest rates slightly higher than market rates.

A large number of retailing firms have tried to establish 'green' credentials by introducing environmentally friendly versions of familiar household products, by 'green' purchasing policies, or by 'green' labelling. In the UK most of the major supermarket multiples have introduced 'green' schemes of this sort. Some are also active in recycling packaging and product containers. Again, a number of European DIY retailers, such as those belonging to the UK Kingfisher group, have policies requiring the sources of their timber to be environmentally friendly. Other companies are going further. A leader in environmentally acceptable timber importing in the UK is the Newcastle-based Ecological Trading Company (ETC). Its aim is to import timber from sustainable logging operations in the developing world that are run for the benefit of local people. In East New Britain, a large Pacific island off the northeast coast of Papua New Guinea, the Bainings tribe owns a forest in which it runs carefully controlled logging operations. ETC imports timber from this tribe and has identified other suppliers from among community-based forestry projects in the Solomon Islands, Brazil, Mexico and Honduras. It acts as importer for Milland Fine Timbers, which also pursues policies in line with 'green' development principles. ETC is acknowledged as a pioneer by the Worldwide Fund for Nature, which is lobbying the timber industry to use only well-managed forest sources by the end of 1995.

Green tourism or 'eco-tourism' is another manifestation of 'green' business. It takes a number of different forms in the UK and Continental Europe.[15] Some firms offer conventional holidays and tours and make a donation for each such booking to a 'green' organization or charity; some companies (such as EcoTrails in London) combine conventional tours in the developing world with visits to charity projects and some organize voluntary help for scientific projects around the world concerned with the study and protection of wildlife. Weekends and longer periods away are also marketed to those who wish to work directly at repairing degraded landscapes in Europe or cleaning up litter in more exotic locations. World Challenge Expeditions and the Survival Club book expeditions for those wishing to clean up the Base Camp on Mount Everest. Finally, in the UK, there are opportunities for people to help at weekends on organic farms.

Initiatives that find a market among the ecologically minded for beneficial ways of spending leisure time are to be distinguished from initiatives that moderate the effects of ordinary 'penetrative' tourism on sites of great natural beauty or on local communities in the developed and developing worlds.[16] These do not assume or necessarily encourage green values on the part of tourists, but they are attempts to foster 'responsible tourism' among travel companies. Although these initiatives can have benefits, they sometimes introduce a pattern of tourist growth out of keeping with what is supported locally, and are not always easy to distinguish from a marketing ploy.[17]

Green community service projects are another example of what is being done in the private sector to demonstrate concern for the environment. The News International Greenforce project, one of the entries for the 1992 Dragon Awards, called for significant investment in landscape improvements in and around Knowsley, the location of its Merseyside printing plant. The Royal Bank of Scotland has contributed money and staff volunteers to a campaign organized by an environmental organization, the Groundwork Trust, to improve and rehabilitate various countryside sites. Finally, there is the RTZ Corporation's Community Forest Initiative, another joint venture with environmental charities. This entailed the development of a woodland site and the secondment of staff for the benefit of a local community in East London.

We come finally to environmental counselling. This was pioneered on the Continent by the leading 'green' business in Germany, the diamond tool manufacturer Winter and Sohn.[18] The company had one policy for its employees at work, and another for them in their homes. At work employees were given talks on environmental issues, the company newspaper published many articles on 'green' topics, and competitions were introduced to encourage ecologically sensitive innovations in working practices. There was even a scheme for selling organically grown produce at the factory gate. Winter and Sohn also hired five environmental counsellors who advised on how employees could save energy at home and change their buying pattern so as to benefit the environment.

Only a few companies make it their business to promote 'green' thinking or policy in the community as a whole. Winter and Sohn is an example. Its activities led to the formation of the first 'green' business grouping in Germany – BAUM – and it has sponsored environmental initiatives outside business as well. Perhaps better known as a green campaigning company in Europe and elsewhere is Bodyshop International. In conjunction with highly visible environmental pressure groups such as Greenpeace and Friends of the Earth, Bodyshop has campaigned through publicity at its shops for measures to combat acid rain and to promote recycling.

## The moral value of 'green' business

In assessing the moral value of the various initiatives just described, we have to put the apparatus of business ethics alongside the apparatus of environmental ethics. Environmental ethics is the attempt to apply moral theory to the human treatment of natural objects. Theories in environmental ethics come in different shades of green, according to the kind of value they ascribe to different natural objects. So-called light green theories assign value to things like mountains, rivers and deserts to the extent that those things promote the welfare of human beings and other creatures with conscious states and purposes. Deep green theories, on the other hand, say that mountains, rivers and deserts are intrinsically valuable, quite apart from the human and animal welfare to which they contribute. These theories imply that certain kinds of treatment of the environment are morally wrong, though the things wronged are capable of neither pain nor reason. Their light green counterparts imply that mountains and rivers can be mistreated because creatures that depend on them suffer as a result. The light green theories are generally extensions of standard moral theories developed to cater for the treatment of humans; the deep green theories depend on a theory of moral value that breaks from what is standard or traditional, and that even denies that it is always unfortunate for human life to be lost or for human life to be taken.

When theories from business ethics are set alongside those of environmental ethics, the first thing that emerges is that both light and deep green theories identify obligations that would not be recognized within narrow business ethics. These include obligations to refrain from polluting rivers, lakes and seas; to preserve the rain forests; to keep the ozone layer from depleting; and to consume natural resources only in a sustainable fashion. According to light green theories, these obligations arise from the harm that would otherwise be done to human beings the world over, both in our own and in future generations, through the impact on food stocks, energy and other resources, and through the climatic effects of greenhouse gases in the atmosphere. According to deep green theories, the obligations arise from the intrinsic value of the environments concerned and, though controversially, of the biological diversity they support. These obligations would confront individuals as a reason why they should not, for example, add to the demand for timber from rain forests, or perhaps as a reason why they should boycott goods from countries whose governments encourage the cutting down of the rain forests.

To what extent are the obligations on individuals identified by environmental ethics also obligations on businesses? Like individuals, businesses are required to refrain from harming people, and if cutting down the rain forests harms people, businesses have a reason not to cut down rain forests, and not to add to the demand for timber from them. Businesses are also in a position to make *greater* demands on the rain forests than individuals, if they make any demands at all; and so they might be thought to be under an even greater obligation not to exploit the rain forests than individuals. The same goes for the pollution of seas or the depletion of resources.

From the perspective of environmental ethics, then, the initiatives discussed earlier might have some value, in that it is morally better to do them than not to do them, but still fall short of what is morally required. For example, it is certainly better for the CEGB to treat power-station emissions than not to treat them, but, even with the treatment, they are still polluting the atmosphere and depleting non-renewable energy resources in a way that is unacceptable, whether from a light green or from a deep green perspective. The same goes for many other conventional initiatives in the field of pollution control, waste management and energy-saving. On the other hand, some of the less conventional initiatives would seem to be much more in tune with the demands of environmental ethics. Schemes to repair past environmental damage or to manage forests and other resources on a fully sustainable basis would appear to fall into this category.

This is the conclusion we reach, at any rate, when assessing 'green' initiatives from the viewpoint of environmental ethics, which assigns the same sort of obligations to businesses and individuals. From the perspective of business ethics, on the other hand, businesses are, in important respects, in a very different position from individuals. They may make greater demands on the environment, but in doing so they also make greater contributions to the welfare and prosperity of society. If a manufacturing company produces goods for which there is a demand in society, then the environmental costs of production have to be set against the social benefits of meeting that demand. Businesses also have obligations to their stakeholders, and it is possible that any harm done through damage to the environment may be outweighed by the harm done to these stakeholders by refraining from the productive and presumably profitable activities concerned. Both these arguments could be used by the CEGB or others engaged in pollution control, waste management or energy-saving initiatives to claim moral value for what they are doing.

## The weighting of environmental factors in business

Business ethics identifies sources of obligation and constraint, then, that can compete with and override those exposed by environmental ethics. But how are these competing constraints to be weighed against one another? As we have already seen in our consideration of narrow business ethics, the problem of weighing up obligations to different stakeholders or communities is one that is endemic to business ethics, but in this situation it raises particular difficulties. From a deep green perspective, indeed, it would appear to be insuperable. The value of biodiversity is still so controversial that it is difficult to give it any objective weighting, and how is one to compare the intrinsic value of a river, say, with the happiness or well-being of a group of humans? If we adopt a light green perspective, we can at least consider the arguments within conventional moral theories, but the task is still formidable. For how can a business possibly weigh its impact on the happiness and well-being of those now living against its unknown share of the as yet unknown impact of environmental damage on unknown numbers of people, in an unknown number of future generations?

Perhaps it is not reasonable to expect businesses to make such calculations. Perhaps it is, rather, for governments to decide what degree of impact on the environment is acceptable to society, and to legislate and regulate the activities of businesses accordingly. Since governments are appointed to represent the interests of society, and since it is only through governments that a global consensus can be reached on these issues, which are very largely of global concern, this argument has considerable force. It has its limitations, however. First, governments are not in a position to weigh up the factors affecting each and every business. They can only prescribe minimum levels of environmental obligations that every business can reasonably be expected to accept, regardless of the strength of any counter-obligations to its stakeholders. A business that met its regulatory obligations would not necessarily thereby meet its moral obligations. Indeed a reasonable case could be made out that for most businesses something more would be required; the responsibility on businesses to weigh up the conflicting obligations for themselves would remain.

Secondly, governments are no more immune than businesses from the pressures to meet short-term needs at the expense of long-term ones. There is always a likelihood that the interests of future generations, who cannot after all speak for themselves, will be underestimated as against the interests of the day, and if this is reflected in regulation, it will encourage businesses to make the same error.

Thirdly, the effects of environmental damage tend to fall disproportionately on the poorer and less powerful nations of the world, while the economic benefits accrue to the rich and powerful. This again leads to an under-representation of environmental factors both at the national level, within the developed countries, and at the international level. Finally, within the developing countries, poverty and economic deprivation are frequently such that environmental considerations receive little weight there either, a situation that is often compounded by ignorance and naivety as to what the environmental effects of a business activity might be.

If environmental considerations are to be given appropriate weight in business, it would appear that both businesses and governments must take responsibility for this. Governments certainly have a responsibility for those whose interests they are there to represent and protect, but businesses may also have to take explicit account of obligations beyond those to their immediate stakeholders. In some cases, e.g. when a sophisticated multinational is operating in a small developing country, the business might be much better placed than the host country government to recognize and analyse the effects of environmentally damaging activities. To argue in such a case that an environmental obligation was satisfied merely by adherence to local regulations would not be an ethically acceptable response.

## Business ethics and environmental ethics

The tension between environmental ethics, in which any damage to the environment is morally questionable, and business ethics, in which environmental responsibilities have to be weighed against responsibilities to stakeholders and the social benefits of business, is particularly apparent when we compare popular conceptions of business and popular environmentalism. In Chapter 2 we concluded that ethical egoism did not provide a satisfactory basis for business ethics, but that it did cohere with the popular rhetoric of business and with how businesses often behave in practice. Ethical egoism, or the theory that one should act only in one's own interest, is, however, completely at odds with both light green and deep-green environmental ethics. Under this theory no harm to others, whether they be humans, animals or plants, living now or as yet unborn, is morally signif- icant unless it rebounds on oneself. Environmental ethics, on the other hand, of whatever shade of green, is based upon a respect for others and a prohibition on harming them.  One consequence of this conflict is that many 'greens' are opposed not only to specific business activities, but to business *per se*, while many business people are opposed not only to specific environmental constraints, but to the green movement as a whole.

So long as self-interest is held to be a legitimately strong value in business, this conflict would seem to be inevitable and adherence to green values precarious. It is not that the green agenda and the business agenda can never coincide. Rather we would argue that when the agendas do coincide, it is an accident, and that for as long as the agendas agree, the agreement is superficial. Some evidence for this exists in our survey of 'green' business initiatives, especially at the conventional end of the spectrum. Thus, the Business in the Environment approach to waste management, with its emphasis on pricing and on fiscal incentives to recycling, appears to assume that the areas of human psychology most important to motivating people to recycle are their desire to make money and their aversion to paying more and more for current methods of waste disposal. The idea of organizing the general public at grass roots level to demand recycling and to practice rubbish separation themselves, and the idea of making people think twice about the amounts that they consume, seem entirely foreign to the BIE approach, but entirely at home in the policies of green campaigning groups. At the level of popular thinking, both in business and in the green movement, the tension between green approaches and business approaches to the environment seems to be even more acute than at the level of the corresponding branches of moral philosophy.

It is perhaps ironic, then, that it is from the angle of the popular green movement that the real common ground between the business community and the green movement is most readily seen. The popular green movement obliges itself to answer the question of how society is to get from its present, barely ecologically conscious state, to a state which more nearly embodies green ideals. Can the passage from here to there dispense with all the institutions of society as we have it in the West?  Can it, in particular, dispense with trade and a money economy, with industrialization and technology?  If the answer is 'Yes' and the transformation that society must undergo is so radical, how, voluntarily, can people bring about that transformation in time to avoid the ecological catastrophes that the greens predict? How can they be expected to do this willingly, given the drastic changes in their way of life they would have to put up with?

For certain *red* revolutionary groups these questions would not be particularly troublesome; since they would subscribe to the idea of a party in the vanguard of a struggle that aims at transformation by force, if necessary. Force and violence are among the phenomena that the greens tend to repudiate at the same time as they repudiate the strongly materialistic character of society in the West. What is there for them to resort to instead? Persuasion is one thing, leading by example is another: thus the successful experiments in green living that are available for public scrutiny in places like the Centre for Alternative Technology. Mainstream political action, through the formation of 'green' parties, is another means of bringing green values to bear on society as a whole. Being less than revolutionary in the traditional sense, however, all these measures run the risk of being or becoming too mainstream; representatives of the green movement engaged in mainstream politics run the risk of being seduced by it. Indeed, disillusioned supporters of and activists in the German Green Party have said that elected officials from their party *have* been seduced.[6] What is more, they run the risk of being seduced to no purpose, idealistically underestimating the strength of opposition among powerful groups to the measures, especially tax measures, that they propose, and not seeing clearly what economic programme could sustain their plans in a world anxious to attract business and people away from any country that came under green government.

To sum up, the very forces that keep greens apart from reds propel them either in the direction of piecemeal and local green advance, usually in the form of a back-to-the-land separatism, or tamed reformist lobbying in and around legislatures. Not that there are no militant greens prepared to pursue their aims violently, but their claims to reflect authentic green values are in a sense just as shaky as those of the Business in the Environment Working Party on Waste Management.

It is not clear whether there is a satisfactory 'green' way out of the impasse, but it does seem that when the question of how to get from an unsatisfactory present to a green future is raised, it pays to take account of how one has got *this* far. In particular, it pays to take account of how there have come to be the variety of 'green' initiatives in business that there now are. Without committing oneself to the view that any initiative calling itself green is therefore valuable, or that all the initiatives surveyed above are equally valuable, it is fair to say that green thought and practice from a range of sources – from militant to the reformist – has gradually become more influential, both among the general public and in the business community, through the ordinary processes of writing, broadcasting, public campaigning, and political lobbying, and, occasionally, the use of shock tactics.

The result of this pressure has been the gradual enlargement of the potential sources of green influence, sources extending to 'green' business initiatives. It should not of course be thought that these new or potential sources of pressure will ever be firmly controlled by green values; as we have seen, the values that are dominant in business are unlikely to be green or even consistent with green values, and even some 'green' initiatives are decidedly pallid. Nevertheless, the pressures of the greens can make business defensive enough to play down or conceal its un-green business values, those attached to efficiency, growth and profit. What of a more militant alternative, aimed at eliminating business? Not only is this unlikely to be very effective on its own, but its success would be wasteful. It would be wasteful of the great reserves of intelligence and effort at the moment willingly dedicated to business that would be unwillingly dedicated to other things in the short term, and that, from both a moral and a green point of view, are better rechannelled than undercut, i.e. rechannelled though the multiplication of 'green' business initiatives. This unashamedly reformist and gradualist programme for green change will not reduce damage to the environment at the rate at which it is required, but at least it does not scrap all the institutions of the known world for the sake of a supposedly preferable but completely uncharted green one.

## References

1   C. Randlesome, W. Brierley, K. Bruton, C. Gordon and P. King, *Business Cultures in Europe* (London: Butterworth-Heinemann, 1990), p.304.
2   *Ibid.*, p.263.
3   G. Winter, *Business and the Environment* (Hamburg: McGraw-Hill, 1988), p.18.
4   National Rivers Authority, *Annual Report* (1992), p.20.
5   *Ibid.*, p.13.
6   The Water Resources Act 1991.
7   *Greenpeace Business*, vol.13 (July 1993), p.2.
8   John Donaldson, *Business Ethics: A European Case Book* (London: Academic, 1992), p.157.
9   J. Elkington, T. Burke and J. Hailes, *The Green Pages: The Business of Saving the World* (London: Routledge, 1988), p.113.
10  *Working Party Report on Waste Management in the UK* (London: Business in the Environment, 1992), p.10.
11  *A Measure of Commitment* (London: Business in the Environment, 1992).
12  Elkington, Burke and Hailes, *op. cit.*
13  *Ibid.*, p.93.
14  *Ibid.*

15  See Katie Wood, *The Good Tourist* (London: Mandarin Books, 1991).
16  See Robert Proser, 'The ethics of tourism', in David Cooper and Joy Palmer, (eds), *The Environment in Question* (London: Routledge, 1992), pp. 37–50.
17  Marion Wheeler, 'Applying ethics to the tourism industry', *Business Ethics: A European Review*, 1, no.4 (1991), pp.227–34.
18  See Winter, *op. cit.*

# 9  Development and the ethics of capitalism

Just as the concerns of business ethics and environmental ethics overlap when what is in question is the goal of reducing or repairing industrial damage to the environment, so the concerns of business ethics overlap with those of development ethics in regard to reducing the disparities of wealth between the West and North, on the one hand, and the East and South, on the other. As in the case of solutions to ecological problems, solutions to development problems have in the past been widely thought to depend on the repudiation of capitalism. No longer. The collapse of the Soviet bloc is taken by some people to leave capitalism as an economic system with no rivals, and capitalist development as the only sort of development open to poor countries. Indeed the newest of the international development banks, the European Bank for Reconstruction and Development, is legally bound to fund initiatives that will hasten the transition in central and eastern Europe from a command to a market economy.[1] Lending to the industrial remnants of the old communist regime is, if not outlawed, less of a priority for the bank than starting new entrepreneurial ventures from scratch. The USA insisted that 60 per cent of EBRD lending be directed at the private sector in Eastern Europe, yet very little of a private sector exists to receive this money. The policy is understandable in an atmosphere in which strategies for development that bypass the market are widely argued to be out of tune with reality. In this chapter we want to encourage second thoughts about rhetorical appeals to 'realism' in development ethics.

## The argument from realism

The collapse of the Soviet Union has been taken to show that the command economy of socialism does not work, and that the only successful marriage of economics and politics is democratic capitalism. This is the form of society that the former communist countries of Eastern Europe are widely expected to adopt, at times with the enthusiastic support of local converts to the free market in such places as Poland and Hungary. Democratic capitalism is also the form of society being urged on the *older* developing world. It is being urged not for the reasons that used to be given, reasons that reflected uncertainty about the outcome of the competition between socialism and capitalism, but for the new reason that capitalism has won that competition, and is now the only game in town. Combine this with the claim that democracy is the natural political counterpart of free-market economics, and that free-market economics is realistic about human nature while socialism, in its economic and political forms is utopian, and you have the argument from realism for the desirability of progress toward democratic capitalism. This turns into a moral argument when democratic capitalism is held to be the most effective means of eradicating poverty – in the East as well as in the South.

Clearly many different versions of this argument could be constructed. We are going to consider a formulation due to Sir William Ryrie, who is Executive Vice President of the International Finance Corporation.[2] IFC is a Washington-based affiliate of the World Bank, which was established in 1956 to promote increases in the standard of living of its developing member countries. These now total around 110 of over 140 IFC member countries in all. IFC provides funds for investments in public/private sector partnerships in the developing countries of Africa, Asia, Latin America and, more recently, Eastern Europe. In the early 1990s it has been active in implementing privatization in the former Soviet Union as well as in its more traditional Third World sphere of operations. It is heavily involved in projects, often to do with mining and oil development, that produce net in-flows of hard currency to developing countries. It is also active in creating financial services markets where they do not exist, and in tapping the re-sources of the established financial markets for investment in the developing world.

This, then, is the organization that Ryrie operates in. We choose his version of the argument from realism, not only because it comes from someone who is a forthright and confident exponent of the benefits of capitalism in development, but also because, as Ryrie presents it, the argu-ment has at least the appearance of evenhandedness. It concedes that capitalism is not perfectly suited to eradicating poverty, and that the poorest in a free-market system, especially a pre-industrial one, need protection and help that are not provided by market forces on their own. These concessions are meant to signal Ryrie's openness to a critique of capitalism, so long as the critique is anchored in the economics and politics of the real world.

## Capitalism, warts and all?

The paper in which Ryrie presents his views falls into two parts. The first part begins with the claim that the contest between capitalism and socialism has now been settled, settled not by argument, but 'by a kind of trial by ordeal in which one system has proved itself to be superior to the other in practice'. This trial by ordeal has reached a conclusion only recently in the former Communist countries of Europe, Ryrie says, but the trend of capitalism proving itself superior to socialism was well established in the Third World for most of the 1980s. His review of the economic performance of Third World market economies compared to that of state-run economies occupies him for much of the first part of his paper. Not everything he says here is indisputable. A recent OECD report emphasizes the importance of government intervention in some of the economies (South Korea, Taiwan, Singapore and Brazil) that are routinely cited as free-market successes.[3] Ryrie does not, however, confine himself to the economic record alone. He takes up the question of how capitalism, which is so effective in generating economic growth and thereby acting against poverty, can be cured of some of its major ills. Ryrie considers four of these: the tendency of capitalism to create monopolies; its tolerance of inequality; its treatment of the unemployed and of the weak and vulnerable generally; and its occasional glorification of the profit motive.

We are going to concentrate on Ryrie's discussion of the ills of capitalism rather than his survey of economic growth. The main theme of this discussion is that capitalism at the best of times has its shortcomings, and that these, like its benefits, are likely to be felt more intensely in the developing countries than in the developed ones. In enlarging on these shortcomings, in elaborating his moral and social critique of capitalism, Ryrie returns again and again to the point that such a critique had better be, and that his is, realistic, i.e. in harmony with hard facts about human economic and political behaviour and in tune also with the realities of the developing world.

Now the question of what comprises a realistic critique of capitalism is far from straightforward. Being realistic means seeing things as they are; but criticism depends on seeing beyond how things are and insisting on a certain conception of how things should be. This tension between the realistic and the critical attitude can be acute in the case of moral criticism; for some conceptions of how things morally ought to be are utopian and some conceptions of the sort of moral improvement that people are capable of may idealize human beings. Thus a moral critique of capitalism risks being, on the one hand, over-critical or over-moralistic, and, on the other hand, under-critical and complacent. The danger of being under-critical and complacent is particularly pressing in a climate in which capitalism is taken to have won a trial by ordeal, and in which criticisms of capitalism tend to be dismissed as attempts to revive the losing side in the contest between capitalism and socialism. Ryrie, in his realism, does not consider every aspect of capitalism to be morally tolerable, given how human beings and economies are, but he does accept many, perhaps too many, aspects of capitalism as they are, and so he sets the threshold for moral criticism higher than it need be set.

Consider Ryrie's view of the first of the four ills of capitalism, its monopolistic tendency. In considering this shortcoming, Ryrie quotes Adam Smith:

> There is a passage from the *Wealth of Nations*… which I like to quote: 'People of the same trade seldom meet together… even for merriment and diversion, but the conversation ends in a conspiracy against the public or in some contrivance to raise prices.' But you really cannot fault businessmen for that: making sure there is fair competition is not the responsibility of business people, but of the government and the law. No one can be player and umpire at the same time.[4]

Ryrie's point is that one has to face up to the behaviour of traders and not be disappointed or censorious when, in the absence of a law to ensure fair trade, they act in their own interests by forming cartels. They cannot be blamed for not policing their own activities. They cannot be, as he puts it, players and umpires at the same time.

This sounds like the height of realism. But what Ryrie says is false, and false in a way that may encourage moral complacency. Far from its being true that no one can be player and umpire at the same time, it is utterly routine for these roles to be adopted simultaneously. In observing the most commonplace precepts of morality – not to lie, not to steal, not to break promises – we are constantly our own enforcers of the moral rules, and we are in a clear sense responsible for observing these precepts even if no one is around to catch us, expose us or punish us if we don't, and even if there is no law to prohibit these things. Of course we often lie, steal and break promises anyhow; in a way it is only human. But the relevant sense in which it's only human and only to be expected – the very same sense in which it is only to be expected that people in the same trade will gang up on the public and fix prices – doesn't excuse the lying, stealing or breaking promises, and it doesn't excuse the traders' conspiracy either. It is all wrongdoing, whether or not the rules broken are backed up by an external enforcement mechanism. So, contrary to Ryrie, the rule-breakers can be faulted, even if it is no surprise when they lie, steal, break promises or fix prices.

In pressing this obvious line of thought against Ryrie we don't believe that we are pouncing on a mere slip. We believe that the sort of realism expressed by Ryrie's comment on Adam Smith, the sort that licenses the inference from 'People can be expected to do such-and-such' to 'People can't be blamed when they do such-and-such unless there is a law against it' – the sort of realism that underlies the point about players and umpires – is very widespread, and that it is morally over-permissive. It makes it into a fact about human beings that we have to accept and not moralize about their going to great lengths to pursue their self-interest. Whereas it seems to us perfectly intelligible to accept that people go in for a lot of self-interested activity, *and* to criticize them for doing so.

Ryrie's questionable realism surfaces again when he considers the reliance of capitalism on the profit motive. Here his point is that, whatever elevated incentive, such as the desire for freedom, may actuate capitalism, the desire to make money, a somewhat less noble motive, is necessary for capitalism to succeed. Capitalism is based on a kind of realism:

> I am not going to speak of original sin but it surely behoves Christians to be realistic about human nature. The market philosophy not only recognizes some less admirable aspects of human nature, but seeks to use them for the common good. This realism contrasts directly with the illusions on which communism was based, illusions about the ability or willingness of human beings to act unselfishly. The exposure of the hypocrisy, misuse of power and sheer corruption of the communist systems in Eastern Europe demonstrated how unrealistic that view really was.[5]

A good question to ask is what capitalist realism consists of. Does it consist of recognizing that human beings have some less than admirable motives, such as greed? If so, then neither Christianity, which has a very vivid sense of base human impulses, nor Communism, which was constantly and openly proclaiming the need to protect the revolution from reactionary, bourgeois or capitalist-road tendencies, can be accused of being unrealistic about greed.

The realism that Ryrie has in mind consists not only of acknowledging the existence of less than noble motives, but of not condemning them, given the good effects they can bring about. But this realism really does go quite far in the direction of outlawing the moral criticism of greed. After all, it is quite commonplace for bad motives and bad institutions to have good effects, but these good effects do not cancel out the badness of what produces them. To take what we hope will be an uncontroversial case, slavery in ancient Greece helped to support a society with great cultural achievements, yet condemnations of slavery do not have to deny the greatness of the achievements. Similarly, moral criticism of the profit motive does not have to deny the benefits of the profit motive. One can be realistic in the sense of acknowledging the benefits without holding back all criticism. Ryrie tends to suppose that, when properly understood, the benefits of the profit motive will silence criticism of all but its most extreme manifestations: only the money-mad will come in for criticism, not the common or garden greedy. And this is another case, we think, of redrawing the limits of fair criticism of capitalism more narrowly than they have to be drawn. For consider what Ryrie says:

> People who are not involved in business should be very careful about taking up an attitude of moral superiority about the profit motive. For the market system to work efficiently, we *need* the profit motive. It is a powerful engine which can bring great benefits for society. Of course, we are right to condemn

it when it takes extreme forms, when businessmen or stockmarket operators appear to be consumed by greed. Obviously it can and does corrupt some people.[6]

The clear implication is that we are not right to criticize greed when it falls between the extremes; that a kind of unreality takes hold of us when we do. This, we are suggesting, is the kind of realism that assists moral complacency.

Now Ryrie's sort of realism, the sort that issues in very lenient criticism of the free-market system, has considerable force in the present moral and political climate in the West, for in the mainstream opinion of the West the following four claims are widely accepted: first, that the only alternative to the free-market system is some state-run economy; so that, second, criticisms of the free-market system are indirect arguments for state-run economies; third, that a state-run economy demonstrably fails as a system for producing and distributing and enabling people to afford goods that they actually want to buy; and fourth, that the political system of the state-run economy – socialism – is demonstrably inferior to democratic capitalism as a political-cum-economic system, since people who know socialism at first hand prefer capitalism.

How does Ryrie, who purports to give a critique of capitalism, avoid appearing to support the rival system? He does so not only by praising capitalism as an instrument of economic growth, but by criticizing those who adopt a morally superior attitude toward it. On the other hand, he does not forfeit all claim to be critical of capitalism, for he is dismissive of those who idealize the profit motive and who think that there are market solutions to virtually every economic and social problem. More, he claims that non-idealized versions of capitalism need to be civilized. What he thinks this civilization consists of, however, is market forces plus anti-monopolies legislation, and a tax system that finances education and a modest welfare state on the proceeds of economic growth. By a modest welfare state is meant a health service for the poor and vulnerable and measures to alleviate the effects of unemployment. For this to be possible in the Third World what needs to be achieved is 'the kind of virtuous circle of growth which will ensure that, as jobs are lost, new jobs are created in new enterprises or growing ones and that the country gradually produces enough to enable the government, by a balanced prudent use of taxation, to put the necessary safety nets in place.'[7]

This conception of civilized capitalism puts Ryrie slightly to the left of the most fervent of the free-marketeers – but not very far to the left. And it is notable that when he urges provisions for safety nets, he makes it clear that his point is not exclusively a moral one: 'Safety nets are not only a matter of social justice; a good employment safety net makes the labour market more flexible and the economy more efficient.'[8]

Once again it is realism as much as morality that calls for the civilization of capitalism. In fact Ryrie's treatment of capitalism and the Third World is from start to finish an essay in realism: first, there are the facts attesting to the superiority of capitalism rather than socialism as an engine of growth; then there is, as Ryrie thinks, a frank acknowledgement of the excesses of the free market and the identification of tried and tested mechanisms – regulatory legislation and a tax system – for dealing with these excesses.

Capitalism comes in for more discussion in Ryrie's paper than democracy or democratic capitalism, and Ryrie concedes that there is no necessary connection between democracy and the free market. Capitalism can flourish in an undemocratic Korea or Chile, and a state-run economy can co-exist with democracy, as in India:

> But whatever the historical record, we can surely say that there is an affinity between democracy and the market economy. They are both systems of choice and realism. By his choices as a consumer the citizen determines what will be produced in the economy, and through his choice at the ballot box what sort of government he will have. Well-regulated capitalism and political democracy are both based on realism about power, which is diffused at the same time as it is constrained.[9]

Ryrie does not dwell on the failure of some democracies to reflect the political preferences of significant proportions of people who are narrowly outvoted by majorities; and he does not say in what way a democracy is more realistic about power than one that is very repressive: that, regime too, can acknowledge that power is diffused as well as constrained. In the end it is not as a defence of democratic capitalism but as a defence of capitalism that Ryrie's views need to be confronted.

## Scepticism about realism

A rebuttal of Ryrie would naturally focus on his faith in growth as an answer to poverty, for this is what makes the growth rates of capitalist developing countries seem so telling to him, and also why capitalism seems to him the right form for a developing economy to take. A rebuttal would also naturally aim at showing that Ryrie's criticism of capitalism is anaemic, even for someone who has no sympathy for socialism. Now we have already suggested that by a questionable use of arguments from realism Ryrie persuades himself that *no more* than an anaemic criticism of capitalism is in order. Ryrie persuades himself, and he may well persuade others if they adopt the perspective of a triumphalist West surveying the world, and especially the former Communist world, in the wake of the Cold War. Fortunately, this is not the only perspective in town. There is another perspective, available to those who have lived unhappily under a succession of elected right-wing governments in the West in the 1980s, and this makes room for facts that Ryrie does not mention, facts that call into question not only the wonders of capitalism but also the value of growth.

Many such facts were mentioned in the course of election campaigns in the West in 1992. In Britain these include, for example, the adverse effects of tax cuts in the form of a decline in the public provision of health, transport, and education, and a disproportionate increase in the wealth of the richest at the expense of those with middle and low incomes. In the United States the adverse effects of deregulation could be mentioned as well. Thus the deregulation of the savings and loans industry led to fraud and losses on a colossal scale in the 1980s. No two policies could be more characteristic of recent free-market governments than tax cuts and deregulation, and yet neither can claim to be a conspicuous success.

The questioning of market economics and new right politics after Reagan and Thatcher has been accompanied by increasing criticism of business practices, especially in the financial markets in the West in the 1980s. This criticism is heard not only from the moralizing individuals that Ryrie criticizes for taking a dim view of the profit motive from a sheltered position outside the market place. It is heard increasingly from many members of the business community who do not want to be tarred with the same brush as a Robert Maxwell, an Ivan Boesky or the many and varied villains in the scandals involving Guinness and the Bank of Credit and Commerce International. Newspapers in the developed countries are only one source of evidence for a growing acknowledgement of a need to demonstrate what is called social responsibility in addition to profitability. This book has provided much more evidence.

We call attention to ways in which criticism of business is both growing and being responded to in the developed countries for several reasons: first, because some of this criticism is developing quite independently of the ending of the Cold War, and quite independently of the obstacles that post-Cold War rhetoric puts in the way of criticizing capitalism or business; second, because some of the criticism directed against multinational business has generated ideas about sustainable development and development through trade that are much more critical of growth than Ryrie is; and third, because trying to accommodate these ideas is much higher on the agendas of some First World businesses than trying to fend them off with tributes to the free-market system. Indeed it is because the realities of the Boeskys and the Maxwells are taken to make general defences of the system seem unduly abstract or, if one may borrow the term, unrealistic, that businesses are putting new concerns on their agendas.

In a climate in which business is turning toward social responsibility in self-defence, there is a natural alliance between some increasingly influential critics of business in the developed world and the countries of the developing world. The critics we have in mind are not usually political parties, but pressure groups or campaigning groups, such as, in Britain, the World Development Movement, which are able to bring public pressure to bear on governments and which have joined forces with some of the new consumer groups – notably New Consumer in Britain – to encourage businesses to assist sustainable development through, for example, their import policies. Unlike the pro-growthers that Ryrie represents and the no-growthers in some of the European green parties, the World Development Movement advocates development (contrary to the pro-growthers) and trade with the North (contrary to some no-growthers).[10] The idea is that Third World countries should first develop agricultural production for a home market, together with some rural-based, low-technology processing of agricultural produce, such as sugar, for home, regional and international markets. Cottage industry – the successful Botswanan home-brewing of sorghum beer is an example – can be encouraged simultaneously, and both agriculture and light industry can be developed not on national but on regional lines, on the model of the Southern African Development Co-ordination Conference.

In the case of Third World industries that are already able to produce for markets in the rich countries, such as the textile industry in Bangladesh, the World Development Movement suggests consumer and campaigning group pressure for the lowering of trade barriers put up by the rich countries. It also urges the extension of schemes in the European Community for compensating Third World losses in export earnings arising from falls in commodity prices.

## Development ethics and businesses

The measures proposed by the WDM make an important contribution to applied development ethics, but they are ideas primarily for governments and individuals, not firms. Where does business ethics come in? With the involvement of the banking sector in Third World debt, to begin with, and also with multinational manufacturers and firms operating in the commodities markets on which so many Third World economies depend.

In the UK the four large clearing banks – Barclays, Lloyds, the Midland and National Westminster, all have outstanding loans in the Third World. According to a discussion paper published by the United Nations Conference on Trade and Development, these generated net payments to the banks of £8.5 billion between 1982 and 1987.[11] Lloyds is the most heavily committed of the four. Provisions in the balance sheets of the major banks for defaults on these and other loans took a heavy toll on their profits at the end of the 1980s. In the case of Lloyds, provisions against default in the Third World accounted for much of a huge loss of over £700 million in 1989.

By 1991, 75 per cent of Third World debt was covered by provisions in the Lloyds accounts. According to a survey of the UK financial sector up to the end of 1991 carried out by New Consumer, Lloyds has forgiven portions of its debt to several countries, including Mexico and Costa Rica.[12] But it has ruled out forgiveness of the rest of the debt, on the ground that it would weaken incentives for future commercial lending and postpone financial reform in some debtor nations. Lloyds has not resold much of its debt on secondary markets, as some of its UK counterparts have, and it has made only limited use of the opportunity to trade debt for equity in the Third World.

The Midland Bank has been more innovative than other UK banks in regard to debt, which is to say innovative relative to extremely conservative practice. It has sold debt on secondary markets, it has accepted in-kind rather than cash payments for debt service from Peru, and it has been involved in debt-for-equity swaps. These measures have reduced the level of outstanding loans on its books, but have apparently not significantly affected the level of indebtedness of its client governments in Latin America. On the other hand, in 1990 it effected a highly unusual though extremely small-scale 'debt-for-development' swap, by which it donated to UNICEF the £800,000 owed to it by Sudan. The donation paid for a water and reafforestation scheme there.

Debt-for-development swaps belong to a range of measures introduced by banks early in the 1980s and then given an official seal of approval in 1989 in the form of the Brady Plan (named after the then US Treasury Secretary) for debt reduction in the Third World. The Brady Plan provides for 'market' inspired means for reducing debt, and consists of:

● Selling debt at a percentage of face value to (i) new buyers, who are still entitled to collect the full face value, or sometimes (ii) the debtor nations themselves.
● Exchanging debt for shares in a company within the debtor nation, shares denominated in the local currency.
● Exchanging doubtful debt at a discount for debt more certain of repayment in the form of 'bonds'.
● 'Debt-for-nature' or 'debt-for-development' swaps, whereby non-governmental organizations, usually charities or campaigning groups in the developed world, take on a portion of Third World Debt and cancel it by funding a 'green' or development project in the debtor nation.

The Midland is not the only UK bank to avail itself of Brady Plan measures; Barclays and the National Westminster have done so as well, the latter on rather generous terms in some cases. For instance, it resold its Bolivian debt to Bolivia for 11 per cent of face value, and co-operated in the partial forgiveness/debt-for-bond swap strategy pursued by other banks with loans outstanding to Mexico.

The WDM and other Third World campaigning groups have urged outright forgiveness of loans and, short of that, the repayment of tax relief that the major UK banks have received on their provisions against default on Third World loans. There are strong moral arguments for these courses of action, and for partial but significant forgiveness on the model of the National Westminster treatment of the Bolivian debt.

To begin with, there is the consequentialist or utilitarian argument. Easing or wiping out the debt burden would create the possibility of increased investment in essential medical services and education in the developing world, would make available foreign currency earnings for necessary imports, would ease the pressure for short term environmental degradation for the sake of cash crops, and would help to end the cycle of repeated devaluations in local currencies. All these things would increase welfare on a large scale.

There is also an argument from justice. It is just for banks to take losses on loans that were irresponsibly and at times cynically extended to poor countries, often after the banks carried out research to establish which countries were able to withstand a higher burden of debt; and there is also the matter of treating people in the markets in which banks operate with equal respect. It cannot be morally acceptable for banks in the developed world to win over caring customers in the developed world by programmes of social responsibility, and yet for them to be casual about benefiting communities in the developing world, where needs are more urgent and social responsibility correspondingly more obligatory as well.

The banks are in a position to affect the welfare of the Third World much more dramatically than other businesses. But it still matters what other businesses do. Companies engaged in the growing, export and retailing of cash crops, such as coffee, sugar, and bananas, from Third World countries, often command resources that enable them to win highly favourable terms of trade for themselves, at considerable cost to the economies of countries in the developing world. These companies are also able to carry out research that enables them to introduce effective policies of import substitution. Thus the development of artificial sweeteners by the UK sugar refiner Tate and Lyle, in co-operation with Unilever, has reduced demand for sugar crops from the Third World; so have techniques for extracting a sweet syrup from corn: the syrup is now used extensively by the big US soft drink manufacturers in preference to sugar formerly exported by the Philippines.

The power of multinational corporations extends to the manufacturing sectors of the developing countries. A computer assembly plant established to take advantage of cheap labour in Southeast Asia, for example, can be put out of business by a transfer of the assembly operation to a highly automated and, in the long run, cheaper production site in the developed world. This is what happened when Apple started assembling its Macintosh computers in California after having previously run an assembly operation in Malaysia.

In the short term the only effective weapon within the framework of business ethics – as opposed to the ethics of international relations – for changing these trends may be the use of campaigning pressure on multinational corporations in forums (such as shareholders' meetings and the press in the developed world) where the case for better trade terms and compensation for lost markets can be put effectively, and where companies may be embarrassed into changing their ways. Then, relatedly, there is scope for the establishment of more ethical business. We have already seen that it is possible to go into business as a timber importer and be able to give weight to sustainable development. The Ecological Trading Company is doing that in the UK on a modest scale. Oxfam has successfully marketed a premium coffee, Café Direct, that pays South American growers a much higher proportion of the sale price than they have traditionally received. Traidcraft has introduced a 'Fairtrade mark' for products that give good returns to Third World producers. Other models of organizations promoting defensible, and sometimes very unusual, strategies for development come from the Third World itself.[13]

Apart from action to put trading relations between the developing and developed world on a better footing, there is scope for much more complicated action to reduce environmental damage in countries in which companies have located partly to evade the expense of complying with environmental legislation in the developed world. A number of European companies have acted to raise the emission standards of some of their Third World plants to the levels achieved in countries with exacting regulations. In the chemical industry the British-based ICI claims to have designed for the virtual elimination of waste at its terephthalic acid plant in Taiwan, while Ciba-Geigy, a Swiss multinational with operations in more than eighty developing countries, has successfully reduced the emission of polluted wastewater at the Chandra River dyestuffs plant in Jakarta, Indonesia.[14]

## The ethics of development in Eastern Europe

We said earlier that there is a natural partnership between groups such as the World Development Movement and New Consumer in Britain and enterprises in the developing countries, but perhaps what we should have said is that there is a natural partnership between these groups and enterprises in the *older* developing countries. The newer developing world of Eastern Europe seems to be far more in tune with the Ryries and the International Finance Corporations, with the World Banks and IMFs, than the countries of Africa and Latin America. Not only the governments of such countries as Hungary, Poland and Czechoslovakia, but also their general populations, seem committed to a transition to a full market economy. According to opinion polls taken in Poland in September 1991, 74.1 per cent of those who responded believed that privatization of the economy was necessary.[15] In Hungary, where the encouragement of small firms was government policy long before state privatization schemes were adopted, public support has been shown by actual entrepreneurship. Matters are less clear elsewhere, but in Russia the first experiments in the sale of state assets to individuals have proved popular. The *IFC Review* for March 1993 reports the sell-off of the regional trucking monopoly by auction in Nizhny Novgorod at the end of October 1992: 'Large crowds attended the auction, held in the historic trade hall... All the trucks on offer were sold in hectic bidding'.[16] It seems that ordinary citizens as well as governments regard privatization as a symbol of their emergence from Communism and of membership in the wider civilized world.

Nevertheless, the difficulties of creating an environment for privatization do not end with enlisting public support. On the contrary, the problems of selling off state-owned enterprises in countries with a non-existent private sector and a backward state of industrial development, countries such as those of the former Communist block in Eastern Europe, are formidable. Jacques Attali, the first head of the EBRD, has warned of the dangers of a mafia economy, in which protection rackets and cartels dominate economic activity.[17] The authors of a recent study of the most advanced privatization programmes in the newly democratized Eastern European countries note that, in a sense, privatization works best in economies that are already significantly privatized:

> The lack of a market environment, which is a strong argument for privatisation, also appears at the same time as an obstacle to it. The virtual absence of well-established and functioning financial markets, and the lack of an established and well understood legal and regulatory framework require great care to be taken in the sequence of new policies. Security of private property, with its associated legal rights, responsibilities and liabilities, is an essential first step. In addition it is important to establish the key financial markets, at least at a rudimentary level. Finally, anti-monopoly policy (which may entail breaking up larger firms into smaller units), domestic price liberalisation, and reforms of the tax system can all be expected to influence enterprise behaviour.[18]

Without the legal, fiscal and competition policies that usually provide the background to the existence of a private sector in the West, without a pre-existent private sector in the form of a financial services market, the sell-off of shares in state-owned enterprises cannot be expected to operate smoothly. Or, in other words, privatization of the Western European kind may be an effective means of enlarging a private sector, but not of creating one from scratch.

Privatization of the West European kind – usually the selling off of large-scale public utilities, nationalized extraction or manufacturing businesses, or government-provided services – is to be distinguished from legal measures that make possible the ownership of small businesses, especially in the service sector. In Poland powers to sell and rent premises suitable for shops and restaurants were introduced in 1990, and left to local government to administer. Many new businesses have started as a result. Local consumers have not always benefitted from these changes, however: the provision of unprofitable basic goods and services has often given way to the sale of luxury items that are widely unaffordable.[19] Prices of even basic goods and services at first rose to levels beyond most people's means. In response to these difficulties *ad hoc* restrictions on the use of rented and sold premises had to be introduced by local government, indicating the need for state regulation to accompany privatization even in the small business sector.

The irony that privatization can require action by the state if the economy is to grow (at least temporarily) is particularly evident at the level of large state-owned enterprises. In Eastern Europe these are popularly perceived as national assets regardless of their true commercial worth; as a result governments are under pressure to sell them only after careful valuations, which no domestic Eastern European institutions are usually able to carry out. Valuations apart, financial institutions are required for the privatization themselves, some of them needing to enlist combinations of skills that are unheard of, even in the West. The privatization funds called for by Polish plans for a three-year transfer of a large part of the state industrial sector to the public illustrate the problem, as Grosfeld and Hare explain:

> Privatization funds, the key element in the [privatization] programme, do not yet exist in Poland (and even in Western countries, such an intermediary institution combining the skills of a merchant bank, an investment bank, a venture capital manager, and an auditing and consulting company, is hard to find). The Ministry of Ownership Transformation intends to invite foreign financial intermediaries, possibly in cooperation with Polish counterparts, to establish such funds in Poland. The 'constitution' of the intermediaries should be carefully designed to assure, on the one hand, that they have sufficiently strong incentives to come in and, on the other, that their strategy is compatible with the interests of the Polish economy.[20]

Grosfeld and Hare describe the creation of institutions such as the privatization funds as 'institutional engineering', and contrast such engineering with the organic growth of these institutions outside the sphere of the state.

The contrast identifies important questions about the process of privatizing from scratch, as in Eastern Europe. How authentic a private sector is going to be created by the process of privatization if the instruments of the process are government-created or government-inspired, and if it is left to governments to decide which businesses are transferred to private ownership? On the other hand, how authentic a local culture of investment and ownership is going to be created if market mechanisms, which are all concentrated abroad, are left to set the agenda for privatization? Finally, how stable can the result of the privatization process be if concessions are not made to the legacy of the past, which in the case of Eastern Europe means a long history of official corruption, and of cushioning the population against the normal capitalistic phenomena of price rises, bankruptcies and, especially, unemployment?[21] In other words, how stable can the process of privatization be if it does not continue to interfere with the operation of these market forces by a self-denying discipline of 'social protection'?

Grosfeld and Hare note that the success of Hungary's privatization scheme will be threatened so long as there is institutional interference with the market forces that drive firms with unsaleable products out of business. Yet the Hungarian government fears that the cost of letting these forces operate will be unmanageably high levels of unemployment, a fear shared by other privatizing, former Soviet bloc governments. The case of the former East Germany suggests that this fear is only too well-founded. There an unparalleled deindustrialization led in 1992 alone to a 40 per cent drop in GDP. From the time of unification in 1990 to mid-1993 the number of those employed in industry dropped from 3.3 million to 750,000. To reduce the speed of the decline, the German government has begun to slow down the programme of privatizing large-scale industries from the former East Germany and of winding up unsaleable companies. The newer policy of 'preserving industrial cores' calls for Treuhand, the state privatizing agency, to form firms from outmoded industries into holding companies under western managers, with Treuhand acting as major shareholder and guarantor of losses in the forms. One ill effect of these arrangements is that firms in the shielded holding companies are able to underbid unsupported companies for business, threatening to drive into bankruptcy precisely the independent firms on which the new German economy depends. It is easy to describe the policy of preserving industrial cores as perverse, but it is also easy to see why the German government thinks it is out of the question to do nothing in the face of a massive decline in jobs in the East.

Questions about the reasonable limits of privatization are not just questions about which measures will actually be effective in establishing some kind of market economy. They are also questions about what is morally tolerable. The hardship of people who have to live on reduced incomes when they are unemployed in the West is bad enough; but it must be worse in countries such as those in Eastern Europe, where unemployment has been unknown, where prices have risen so as to make even basic goods expensive, and where the quality of ancillary services for those who are unemployed and ill or unemployed and badly housed are very poor at the best of times. From the point of view of effectiveness *as well as* from the point of view of morality, the process of privatization in the newly emerging countries of Eastern Europe has probably got to proceed as if in the context of an extensive welfare state. And, as in some parts of Western Europe, it must be a question whether the ultimate objective, given local history and local expectations, can be the minimal state or the maximally rolled back state that the advocates of privatization sometimes claim is their ideal. It may be that the mixed economies and welfare states of Western Europe – the social economies of Western Europe, for short – are preferable, both because they are in principle receptive to the criticism of the free marketeers and open to further privatization without massive 'institutional engineering', and also because they are in principle obstructive of the most radical measures suggested by free market criticism.

# References

1   See I. Shihata, *The European Bank for Reconstruction and Development: a comparative analysis of the constituent agreement* (London: Graham & Trotman, 1990), p. 43.

2   Sir William Ryrie, 'Capitalism and the Third World', in R. Roberts (ed.) *Capitalism and the Resurgence of Capitalism,* forthcoming.

3   *The Newly Industrialized Countries: Challenge and Opportunity for OECD Countries* (Paris: OECD, 1988), p.80.

4   Ryrie, *op. cit.,* p.9.

5   *Ibid.,* p.18.

6   *Ibid.,* p.20.

7   *Ibid.,* p.16.

8   *Ibid.*

9   *Ibid.,* p.20.

10  See Ben Jackson, *Poverty and the Planet* (Harmondsworth: Penguin, 1990), Ch.4.

11  Juan A. Castro, 'Protectionist pressures in the 1990s and the coherence of North–South trade policies', United Nations Conference on Trade and Development, Discussion paper 27 (Geneva, 1989), p.22.

12  Sean Hamil, *Britain's Best Employers* (London: Kogan Page, 1993), pp. 65–104.

13  See P. Ekins, *A New World Order* (London: Routledge, 1992), Chs 5 and 6.

14  S. Schmidheiny et al., *Changing Course: A Global Business Perspective on Business and the Environment* (Cambridge, Mass: MIT Press, 1992), pp. 287 ff.

15  I. Grosfeld and P. Hare, *Privatisation in Hungary, Poland and Czechoslovakia* (Edinburgh; Centre for Economic Performance, 1991), p. 30.
16  *IFC Review,* March 1993, p.2.
17  *Business Ethics: A European Review,* 2, (1993), p.114.
18  Grosfeld and Hare, *op. cit.,* p.3.
19  *Ibid.,* pp.34ff.
20  *Ibid.,* p.43.
21  *Ibid.,* p.62.

# 10 International business ethics

So far in this book we have treated business ethics from the point of view of a single culture. Although we have not been slow to criticize some of the practices and attitudes we see around us, the arguments we have used and the values we have adopted are essentially consistent with the assumptions, beliefs and social context of a late twentieth-century democracy, and in particular of the UK and Northwestern Europe. Many international businesses, however, find themselves operating in a range of cultural environments, some of which are very different from our own. Sometimes it is just the circumstances that are different, leading to different trade-offs between stakeholders or between morally desirable objectives. Sometimes the very beliefs and assumptions upon which society is built are different, leading to different values and different conceptions of what constitutes an appropriate moral argument. In these circumstances the directors and managers of a business often have to decide how far to conform to the standards of the culture in which they are operating, the standards let us say of the host country, and how far to insist upon the standards of their own culture, the standards of the home country.

This situation frequently arises in the context of employment practices. The normal and socially acceptable conditions of employment in a developing country may be far worse than would be considered morally defensible at home. The wages might be well below what we would consider subsistence level, even after allowing for differing costs of living. The hours might be long, grievance procedures non-existent, and holidays unheard of. Child labour might be normal. Health and safety precautions, if they exist at all, might be minimal. How should a European-based multinational respond to circumstances such as these? Should it simply adopt the standards of the host country? Should it stick rigorously to its own, home country, standards? Or should it adopt some middle path? If the last of these options is appropriate, how should it go about deciding what standards to adopt, and how far should considerations of profitability enter into these decisions?

A different type of question arises in respect of equal opportunities and the non-discriminatory treatment of employees. We argued in Chapter 4 that where there are no differences between people relevant to the treatment they receive, they should receive the same treatment. But what is considered relevant varies considerably from society to society. In some societies the difference between men and women is considered so fundamental that sexual equality in employment is unthinkable. In some cultures the caste or tribe to which people belong determines the type or level of job they can do, even though it has no effect upon their working skills. In many societies status and seniority are considered more relevant to promotion than expertise and ability. Moreover, for societies in which the criteria of maleness, caste, seniority or status are considered important, our employment practices are every bit as unacceptable as theirs are for us. Once again, the multinational company has to make a decision whether to stick by its own standards, adopt those of the host country, or find some middle way. The only thing of which it can be sure is that someone will be upset whatever it does.

Another area in which cultural differences lead to difficult ethical decisions is that of bribery. From our Northwest European perspective, bribery is morally unacceptable, but in other societies it appears to be a necessary part of doing business. In the Middle East or South America personal payments to petty officials, such as customs officers or policemen, are normal and accepted practice. In many cases the rates appear to be standardized, and the monies received treated as part of the standard remuneration or rewards of the job, a sort of compulsory tipping. In many countries much larger bribes or kickbacks, to politicians, government officials, agents or managers in customer organizations, may be necessary if contracts are to be secured. Sometimes, though accepted practice, these are illegal and frowned upon by the community at large. The well-publicized kickbacks to politicians in Italy and Japan fall within this category, as do the backhanders to managers that are common in a number of southern and eastern European countries. Sometimes, however, they are completely open and apparently legitimated by the state. In all these cases businesses may have to compromise their own moral standards and those of their home country societies if they are to do business in the country concerned. They have to decide whether the benefits to their shareholders and other stakeholders are sufficient to justify the compromise or not.

Issues of environmental ethics, discussed in Chapter 8, also have a particular relevance to international business. As is the case with conditions of employment, the environmental control and pollution standards prevailing in developing countries are often far looser than we would consider acceptable. Once again, the international firm has to make a choice between home and host country standards, or find a way of settling on some middle path.

212 BROAD BUSINESS ETHICS

## Moral absolutes, ethnocentricity and cultural relativism

Responses to these issues have varied considerably. They have varied in particular between those engaged in multinational enterprise, who have traditionally argued for the adoption of host country norms, and those not so engaged – indeed those usually not engaged in business at all – who have taken what they have seen as the moral high ground and have argued for the maintenance of home country standards. Neither of these positions appears to be tenable, however.

At first sight, the maintenance of home country standards, given that these are generally higher, in our terms at least, than host country standards, appears morally attractive. And if it were possible to equate home country standards with some absolute standards of morality, this would indeed be an appropriate starting point. It would *only* be a starting point, as varying circumstances would still call for varying solutions. For example, the desperate need for income and employment in a very poor society might justify lower safety levels than were felt appropriate – and could be afforded – in a much richer society. But we could account for such variations by asking what we would consider morally acceptable were we to be faced ourselves with the circumstances of the host country. However, the assumption that our moral standards – the standards of north-western Europe or North America – are in some sense absolute, or even just exemplary, is rather difficult to defend. Many writers on business ethics, most of whom adopt a North American perspective, take the assumption for granted, and write as if their own values were absolute, but the result is an ethnocentric morality rather than a universal one.

To see this it is useful to look both at the value systems of other cultures, and at the historical development of our own culture. The idea of moral absolutism has always been attractive, if only because, as we shall see below, the opposite idea of moral relativism is so unattractive and socially dangerous. Most moral theories assume some absolute basis for morality, and most moral philosophers have accordingly written as if the values prevailing within their societies, or within some subgroups of their societies, were in some sense absolute. From a historical perspective, however, it is easy to see the extent to which those values were conditioned by the social context of the period.[1]

For Aristotle, for example, slavery was morally acceptable, and to release someone from slavery was, in general, morally wrong. Aristotle's choice of virtues (courage, temperance, liberality, magnificence, greatness of soul, gentleness, being agreeable in company, wittiness) was also a reflection of his society, as was the very idea of a morality founded upon virtues. The Christian ethics of Jesus and St Paul, with their heavy emphasis on equality and self-sacrifice, may be seen as a product of early Christian society and a religious expectation of an imminent day of judgement. Kant and the

Utilitarian philosophers represent responses to the intellectual challenge of Enlightenment rationalism as much as to their social contexts, but Kant's moral strictness also seems to owe much to his pietist Lutheran background, while the Utilitarians' concern with the greatest good for the greatest number can scarcely be divorced from the political turmoil of late eighteenth-century Europe.

It is very difficult of course to see our own society in historical perspective, but we can compare it with other contemporary societies. We have already mentioned that the equal treatment of men and women, which features so strongly on our own moral agendas, would be considered positively immoral within an Islamic society. Christian and Islamic societies also have very different approaches to moneylending. Looking across the world and moving outside business we can also see a range of attitudes to issues of monogamy, sexual relations, birth control and the consumption of alcohol and other drugs; to the treatment of elders or those of social standing; to the merits of private ownership of property as against the sharing of property within a community or society; and, more generally, to the relative importance of the individual and the community.

The existence of different sets of values does not in itself imply that each set is equally good. We noted above that the circumstances of an economically undeveloped society might lead to a balance of judgement that would be morally unacceptable in our own wealthy society but morally defensible in the host country, and this argument can be turned the other way around. It can be argued, in other words, that the morals of other societies are a reflection of their relative lack of development, and that even if our own values are not absolute, they are at least exemplary, in the sense of being the best so far developed. This is, however, a dangerous line of argument, for who is to say which of the world's cultures is the 'most' developed? Only in economic terms can any kind of objective answer be given, and it is far from obvious why economic development should provide a touchstone for morality: 'rich' is not necessarily 'right'. Moreover, even among the economically most advanced nations, such as Japan, the USA, Germany and Sweden, there are strong cultural differences, and we have only to look at some of the issues touched on in Chapter 4, such as equal opportunities or employee participation, to see how these can be reflected in different approaches to business ethics. Many of the most striking moral differences between cultures are related to different religious beliefs, and here again it is difficult to prove that one system is better than another. Even though the society in which we live in north-western Europe is now largely secular, the values characteristic of that society are essentially Christian (and, indeed, Protestant), and they differ in many respects from the values of an Islamic, Buddhist or Hindu society.

Does it follow, as cultural relativism maintains, that all cultures are equally good, morally speaking? As the above argument indicates, there appears to be an extent to which ethics are culturally relative, and it is tempting to go further and say that they are entirely so. It is particularly tempting for the pragmatic businessman or woman, under pressure to perform on the bottom line, simply to adopt host-country standards even when these fall significantly short of what would be required in the home country. The old adage 'When in Rome, do as the Romans do' has often been seen not only as a licence to adopt host country standards but also as a positive reason for doing so, out of respect to one's hosts. It is also tempting for the ethical theorist to argue that any moral system is simply a product of its society or culture, with no import or significance beyond that society or culture.

Logically this argument is difficult to refute. In trying to refute it, philosophers opposed to cultural relativism will sometimes argue that by pursuing it to its extremes its weakness becomes obvious. Thus, if we were to believe in ethical relativism we would have to accept as valid the ethics of any society imaginable, however abhorrent these may be, e.g. a society in which murder and torture for pleasure were deemed morally good. But the fact that such practices are abhorrent relative to our own values does not necessarily imply that our values are anything other than socially derived. It may indicate the strength and passion with which they are held, but it says nothing about their origin. Another argument sometimes made is that the degree of moral common ground between cultures, and the recourse to moral language in international dispute and debate, indicate some common transcendental values. Despite their visible differences, the cultures concerned also have a lot in common. They are the products of very similar social and biological processes, and it would be very surprising if these did not lead to similar moral systems and to enough of a common moral vocabulary to make moral debate between societies meaningful. Once again, the objection misses the point.[2]

The real problem with cultural relativism lies not in any logical inconsistency but in its opposition to the very fundamental and almost universally shared belief in the moral nature of human existence, for to accept the relativist position is in some sense to deny any objective grounds for morality at all, and so to reject the very concept of morality as commonly understood. If moral values were merely the products of a society's behaviour, if they were no more than codifications of accepted customs and practices, they would lose completely their imperative force. If ethics were culturally relative, then there *could* in principle be a culture in which torture and murder for pleasure were good, and we would have no grounds for objecting to it at all. Moreover, once we allow ethics to vary between societies, it is difficult to argue convincingly against variations between subcultures within a society: if a group of people in Cornwall or Tuscany were to develop their own set of values different from those in the rest of Europe, they could argue quite reasonably that these values were as valid as anybody else's. A further concern relates to the importance of religion, for dispensing with morality as we know it would lead us also into dispensing with religion as a foundation for morality, other than in a purely sociological sense, and this is something that most religious believers find unacceptable.

There may be such a thing as an absolute standard of morality, there may not. In writing this book we have assumed that there is, and from this perspective we would argue that it is morally irresponsible for businesses to act on the basis of 'anything goes'. We would also argue, however, that in many areas of business practice there is an element of cultural relativism, and that for a business to assume that its own values are necessarily the only or best ones is also irresponsible. By avoiding the two extremes of cultural relativism on one hand and ethnocentric arrogance on the other, we can open the way for a reasonable approach to the problems of cross-cultural business ethics.

## Characteristic types of ethical dilemma

Given that we cannot rely unquestioningly either on our own home-country values or on those of the host country, how are we to decide what is an appropriate compromise in any given situation? To answer this, we shall begin by characterizing a number of different types of situation that commonly arise in international business. We shall then consider a variety of responses to such situations in the form of criteria or procedures for judgement.

A first type of situation is where there are cultural differences with ethical content, but where each culture would consider its own standards not only acceptable but morally better than those of the other. This might arise, for example, in the case of employment and promotion practices, which in one culture might be based solely on technical ability, in another on seniority, and in another on gender, caste or social status.

A second type of situation arises where practices unacceptable in the home country are acceptable in the host country, but where these practices have no moral connotations for the host society. This might be the case with personal payments to government officials or other individuals, or with some aspects of employment practices. It might also arise in connection with more general social attitudes, such as those to do with alcohol or other drugs, with sexual morality, or with decency in dress, in so far as these impinge upon the workplace. Even within Europe there can be significant differences in this respect. In the traditionally Protestant countries of Northern Europe, for example, the underdeclaration of income to the taxation authorities, though widely practised, is generally thought to be morally wrong. In the traditionally Catholic countries of the South, however, it is largely a matter of social custom, with little or no *moral* significance; in these cultures moral weight is attached only to more important matters.

A third, and very common, type of situation arises where there is no fundamental moral conflict between the two societies, but where differing circumstances or cultural nuances lead to dramatic differences in the societies' interpretations of what is or is not ethically acceptable practice. Examples here would include the differences between the developed and developing worlds in terms of acceptable safety standards in mining, chemical plants or construction projects, acceptable terms and conditions of employment, or acceptable levels of pollution and environmental damage. These differences might result from a variety of factors. Most obviously, the costs and benefits of imposing high standards of safety or pollution control look very different to people who are poor and hungry, and who may die anyway if there is no employment to sustain them, than they do to people living in a wealthy society with the buffer of a highly developed welfare state.

Some of the basic industries on which developing countries most depend are also some of the most polluting, and the costs of controlling this pollution can actually be higher than in developed countries. Cement, for example, is a basic need in developing countries, but without expensive pollution-control equipment cement factories will pollute heavily whenever there is a break in the electricity supply – something to which most developing countries are prone. The cost of the necessary equipment, however, would put the product out of reach of the local economy. In some cases there may be considerable ignorance in a developing country as to the real risks entailed in process, especially where the consequences are not immediately visible. There may also be cultural or religious differences, which lead to a different weighting of present as against future interests, of wealth as against health, or of individual lives as against communal welfare. In all these cases the home-country standards might appear very desirable were they to be accompanied by home-country circumstances, but not in the circumstances actually existing.

In describing these three types of situation we have assumed that the values characteristic of a society are freely held throughout that society. When this is not the case of course, the situations can appear very different. If differences in employment practices are upheld by a forcibly imposed system of apartheid, as for many years in South Africa, or by the forcible suppression of religious or ethnic groups, such as that of the Jews in the former Soviet Union, then this has to be taken account of in reaching a judgement as to what type of business activity or behaviour is ethically acceptable. The same also applies when, as in many developing countries, the benefits of multinational operations are captured by ruling elites, often leaving the majority of the population worse rather than better off.[3]

# Criteria for judgement

None of the situations we have described are morally straightforward, and it is not surprising that most multinationals approach them with a degree of pragmatism. What typically happens is that local managers in the host countries are left to make judgements that they think are appropriate to the circumstances, within the constraints imposed by an international code of corporate ethics. In many cases, as we saw when we looked at codes in general, in Chapter 1, these codes are not ethically very constraining. They generally require that the company abides by the laws of the countries in which it operates, and by internationally accepted standards of human rights. They may require that some account be taken of the well-being of employees and the welfare of communities, but without being specific as to how this should be measured. Sometimes there is a requirement that the standards imposed should not only be acceptable within the host country society but should conform to the best practices obtaining there.

All this is very well as a minimum requirement, but it does not go much beyond what would be called for by the adoption of ethical relativism. And when companies do go further, and impose absolute standards or prohibit or require specific practices, it is usually with an eye to their public image rather than as a result of ethical considerations as such. The calculation, in other words, is an economic one. Where the adoption of host country standards is likely to cost more, as a result of the tarnishing of the company's image at home, than the gain that would result from cheaper operating costs or the development of business that would not otherwise be possible, the company takes a supposedly moral stance and insists on the standards that its public would expect.

It is easy to criticize this approach as cynical, but much harder to come up with a satisfactory alternative. For those situations in which there is no essential moral conflict but only a difference of circumstances, moral judgement has to be left to those with the best knowledge and understanding of these circumstances. For those situations in which there is an essential moral conflict, or in which the practices concerned have moral import only for the home country culture, a more comprehensive and ethically based code would risk being inappropriately ethnocentric. The use of public opinion as a determinant of what departures from home-country values are acceptable does at least provide one way of 'drawing a line', of deciding which of one's own values are important enough to insist upon, and which can be more readily sacrificed. But public opinion is not always a good guide as to ethical priorities. It follows fashions, and is open to manipulation by pressure groups. More seriously, it is limited by what is and is not disclosed by companies. A company may prohibit some activities which are in the public eye, or the consequences of which are publicly visible, while continuing to pursue ethically far worse ones which are not.

A company may also conceal from the public information about an unethical activity, rather than abandon that activity.

One way round this difficulty might be to adopt an ethical criterion suggested by Sir Adrian Cadbury, chairman of the UK-based multinational Cadbury-Schweppes.[4] Addressing the issue of bribery and corruption, and of how far a company can go morally in obtaining business in societies in which private payments to individuals are accepted practice, Cadbury argues for 'two rules of thumb to test whether a payment is acceptable from the company's point of view: Is the payment on the face of the invoice? Would it embarrass the recipient to have the gift mentioned in the company newspaper?' Underlying these rules of thumb is Cadbury's belief in the value of openness as a criterion for ethical judgement, a belief that 'openness and ethics go together and that actions are unethical if they will not stand scrutiny'.

Not all societies place a high moral value on openness, but few would argue that it is ethically undesirable. By using it as a criterion for determining what is acceptable in cross-cultural business, we can remove at least one of the drawbacks of the pragmatic economic approach described above. Instead of relying on the actual state of public opinion as a guideline for what it morally important, we can think in terms of what public opinion would be, given the appropriate information. If an activity can be pursued only by keeping it secret, there must be at least a suspicion that it is ethically undesirable. If it can be pursued openly and above board, then, even if it entails a departure from home-country standards, there is a presumption that it is at least defensible. We would still have to work out the pros and cons in each case, and weigh up the benefits and costs to different stakeholders and communities before deciding whether something was morally acceptable or not. But a criterion of openness does at least encourage us to make such a calculation, which we might not otherwise do.

Another approach to this problem has been proposed by the philosopher Tom Donaldson, in his book on *The Ethics of International Business*.[5] Donaldson proposes an algorithm in two stages. The first stage is to assign a situation to one of two categories, depending on whether or not the cultural differences are dependent on the stage of economic development:

[In type 1 conflicts] the moral reasons underlying the host country's view that the practice is permissible refer to the host country's relative level of economic development.

[In type 2 conflicts] the moral reasons underlying the host country's view that the practice is permissible are independent of the host country's relative level of economic development.[6]

Donaldson's type 1 conflicts correspond roughly to the type of situation we have identified in which there is no essential moral conflict, only a difference of circumstances. Economic development is not the only source of such differences, and the weight a society puts on economic as opposed to other benefits is not purely a function of its economic development, but the definition is easily generalized to take account of this. In the case of such conflicts, Donaldson argues, 'The practice is permissible if and only if the members of the home country would, under conditions of economic development [we would say, more generally, in economic and social circumstances] relevantly similar to those of the host country, regard the practice as permissible.'[7]

This criterion seems very reasonable, in that it makes due allowance for local conditions while still being ethically demanding. It is ethically demanding because we are not simply asked to put ourselves in the position of the host country society, but to apply to that position our own knowledge and experience. A multinational company operating in a developing country is often in the position of having access to far better information than the host country authorities about the health and safety or environmental risks associated with certain practices or processes. It may also be in a position to form a clearer judgement as to the social and economic implications of setting up or carrying out a business in a certain way, and may even be able to weigh up the resultant costs and benefits more objectively than can the ruling elite of the host country's government. In Donaldson's criterion it is the members of the home country society who have to make the ethical judgement, and to do so they have to take all these considerations into account. Passive acceptance of the standards adopted by the host country is not a sufficient response.

To illustrate this, let us consider just some of the factors that might have to be taken into account by a multinational business operating in an economically deprived developing country in dealing with issues such as pay rates, health and safety standards and pollution levels. The business will have to ask to what extent the interests of its local employees and the communities in which it operates will be better served by the provision of a number of jobs at local pay rates, and with locally acceptable safety and environmental standards; or by the provision of fewer jobs, or of no jobs at all, but with the maintenance of higher standards. It will have to balance those local interests against those of its shareholders, customers and other stakeholders. In making its judgements it will have to take account of the influence of the business on the host-country society: to what extent do its position and power carry a responsibility for leadership in the setting of standards; and to what extent will its decisions affect, either directly or indirectly, the decisions of other companies, both local and multinational? If the business is inclined to operate at or close to the locally accepted standards, it will have to satisfy itself that these do not amount to the exploitation of the workforce or community, and that their acceptability is not influenced by ignorance as to the possible consequences, e.g. in the case of environmental pollution, or the exposure of the workforce to chemical or other hazards. If ignorance is a factor, the business will need to consider whether it has a moral responsibility not only to make a more informed judgement in its own case but also to educate others and to apply pressure for the general raising of standards. If the business is inclined, on the other hand, to pay its workers significantly more than the local going rate, or even to insist on significantly higher safety or environmental standards, it will need to consider the potentially disruptive effects of this on what might be a very fragile economic and social base of the host country community.

Donaldson's type 2 conflict embraces the situations we have described in which there are essential moral differences between societies, either because morals conflict or because practices have moral content in one society and not the other. The criterion he proposes in such cases is that the practice concerned is permissible *only* if it is impossible to conduct business success-fully in the host country without undertaking the practice and if the practice is not a direct violation of any fundamental international right.[8] To qualify as a fundamental international right, a prospective right must protect something of great importance that is subject to substantial and recurrent threats. It must also meet a 'fairness-affordability' condition, which in essence requires that the right must be strictly speaking affordable by the moral agents concerned – i.e. affordable absolutely, not merely affordable having taken account of other economically desirable ends – and that there must be some fair arrangement for sharing the cost of honouring the right between the moral agents concerned.[9]

As a minimal list of such rights, Donaldson proposes the following:[10]

1  The right to freedom of physical movement.
2  The right to ownership of property.
3  The right to freedom from torture.
4  The right to a fair trial.
5  The right to non-discriminatory treatment (freedom from discrimination on the basis of such characteristics as race or sex).
6  The right to physical security.
7  The right to freedom of speech and association.
8  The right to minimal education.
9  The right to political participation.
10 The right to subsistence.

Many people, he suggests, might want to add to such rights, including such things as the right to employment or to a certain standard of living, but few would want to subtract from them.

Donaldson's recourse to the language of rights derives from an attempt to identify moral standards that can be applied across different cultures, and that can be subscribed to by nation states, individuals and corporations alike. To the extent that it succeeds in doing this, however, it inevitably sets the standards required rather low: whether within or across cultures, actions can be unethical without necessarily breaching basic human rights. As Donaldson's list of rights indicates, moreover, the identification of international rights comes up against the very problems it is intended to solve. Either the rights reflect the values of his own, North American culture, in which case they are in danger of being too restrictive, or they allow for distinctly different interpretations within different cultures, in which case they are in danger of being too permissive. Donaldson's first criterion, that to be permissible a practice must be necessary if a business is to be conducted successfully in a country, is also subject to different interpretations of the word 'successfully'. It would be remarkable if a business did not claim to be adhering to the highest moral standards consistent with operating successfully, but who is to define 'success' in this context?

To illustrate these points, let us look at a couple of the examples we noted above. Let us suppose, first, that to do business at all in a country (so that a definition of 'successfully' is not an issue), large cash payments must be made to a senior government official. This is unlikely to entail a breach of international rights, directly at least, and so, being necessary for successful business, it would seem to be allowable on Donaldson's criteria. But is it possible to make such payments without corrupting the recipients, and so maintaining a corrupt government? Perhaps, but Donaldson's criteria do not appear to give weight to corruption. As a second example, let us suppose that to do business in another country it is necessary to appoint and promote people on the grounds of their gender, caste or social status. From a North American point of view this would seem to fall foul of the fundamental international right to non-discriminatory behaviour. But from a host company perspective, what is called for may not be considered discriminatory at all. Again the criteria fail to resolve the issue.

What this discussion tells us is that there are unlikely to be any simple rules or algorithms that can determine what is ethically acceptable practice across cultures and what is not. As Sir Adrian Cadbury says, managers must make their own rules in the light of the prevailing circumstances. What we can do is to use different criteria or thought processes to guide that rule-making process. Cadbury's criterion of openness is a useful counter to the dangers of relativism. So too is Donaldson's criterion for his type 1 conflicts, which requires that we put ourselves in the position of the host country.

Another useful guide, which can help to protect us from the opposite danger of ethnocentrism, is to transpose the situation from one in which ours is the home-country culture to one in which ours becomes the host-country culture. From a UK perspective, for example, we could ask how we might respond to an Islamic multinational operating in the UK and criticizing our immoral lending practices, our practice of depriving men of jobs by employing women, or the social pressures to consume alcohol. If in such a case we were to argue that the Islamic multinational should accept UK norms when operating in the UK, then this might suggest that on issues of this kind we should accept Islamic norms when operating in an Islamic state. When looking at cases in which there is no essential moral conflict but a difference in economic and social circumstances, it might be useful to remember that the UK is not among the world's economically most advanced nations; nor, as we saw in the discussion of the Social Chapter in Chapter 4, can it claim particularly high standards in respect of the treatment of its employees. For a Swedish multinational, say, operating in the UK, there may well be an issue as to whether to adopt home country standards on salary levels, the minimum wage or worker participation, or whether to accept the lower standards of the host country.

## Political considerations

So far in this chapter we have assumed that there are no apparent moral objections to operating in a country as such, only to the adoption of certain practices when doing so. But in many cases businesses do also have to ask whether it is morally acceptable to operate in a country at all. As the debate that raged over whether companies should operate in South Africa in the 1980s indicates, this can be a very contentious subject. If a country is ruled by an oppressive regime whose policies are ethically unacceptable not only by home-country standards but by the standards of many of its own inhabitants, it can be argued that any involvement in that country by a multinational business constitutes an endorsement of the regime and is thus unacceptable. On the other hand, for a business already established in such a country to pull out carries costs not only for its shareholders but also for the local communities who depend upon it, and who are the very people its withdrawal would be intended to help.

As with other issues of cross-cultural ethics, many businesses are guided in practice by the strength of public opinion and the potential impact of this on the bottom line rather than by ethical considerations. When public opinion equated doing business in South Africa with endorsement of apartheid, many companies, who shared the public abhorrence of apartheid but who believed that they could do more to change the system from within than from without, had little option but to withdraw – while in many cases retaining a presence in other countries subject to equally objectional regimes but not to the same public scrutiny.

Of course the impact of public opinion in this case may well have been beneficial. For businesses whose South African operations were very profitable, the argument that more could be achieved from inside than from outside the system must have had considerable appeal and may well have been given more weight than it could carry objectively. But the argument is not one that can be dismissed out of hand. In such cases a policy of simple acquiescence to the standards of the regime is unlikely to be ethically acceptable. Where government policy is immoral, the multinational business must have a duty to speak out against that immorality and to use its influence to correct it, and to protect those who are disadvantaged by it. But whether that influence is better exerted through participation or withdrawal depends on the particular circumstances of the case and on a careful analysis of the impact of alternative decisions on all the stakeholders concerned. In these circumstances as in many others, businesses find themselves in a position of social power such as few individuals can achieve. It is incumbent upon them to exercise that power with responsibility.

## References

1   See Alasdair MacIntyre, *A Short History of Ethics* (London: Routledge and Kegan Paul, 1967).
2   Both these arguments are expounded in Tom Donaldson, *The Ethics of International Business* (Oxford: Oxford University Press, 1989), but without any recognition of their basic flaws.
3   See Louis Turner, 'There's no love lost between multinational companies and the Third World', *Business and Society Review* (Autumn 1974), reprinted in W. M. Hoffman and J. M. Moore, *Business Ethics*, 2nd edition (New York: McGraw-Hill, 1984), pp.531-6.
4   Sir Adrian Cadbury, 'Ethical managers make their own rules', *Harvard Business Review* (September-October 1987), pp.69-73.
5   Donaldson, *op. cit.*
6   *Ibid.*, p.102.
7   *Ibid.*, p.103.
8   *Ibid.*, p.10
9   *Ibid.*, p.81.
10  *Ibid.*

# Index

Absolutes, moral, 212–15
Accountability:
  of shareholders, 120
  see also Responsibilities
Acquisitions, see Takeovers and mergers
Act utilitarianism, 41–2, 81, 131–2
Active honesty, 89
Acts of Parliament, see Regulations, laws etc.
Advertising tobacco, 60
Affordability of rights, 220
Age of consumers, 82–3
Aggressive competition, 151–2
Agreements, 140–1, see also Contracts
Agriculture, developing countries, 201
Agriculture, Ministry of, 65
Airlines:
  competition, 176
  overbooking, 63–4
Alcohol, 60, 61
  and ethical investment, 132, 133, 134
Alliances, strategic, 155–6
Alternative investments, see Ethical investments
Altruism, 47, 153
Aluminium production, 182
Analysis, philosophical, 19
Animal Health Act, 74, 75
Annual percentage rate (APR), 70
Apartheid, see South Africa
APR (annual percentage rate), 70
Argument, philosophical, 19
Aristocracy, moral, 44
Aristotle/Aristotelianism, 24, 42–4, 45–6, 140, 212
Armaments manufacture, 60, 61
  and ethical investment, 132, 133
Arrears in repayment of debt, 66, 67–72, 201–3
Asset stripping, and privatization, 174
Association of British Travel Agents (ABTA), 11, 15
Attali, Jacques, 205
Autonomy:
  and morality, 37
  and privatization, 169

Baby milk, Third World, 61
Banal codes of ethics, 14–15
Bankers' Association, 66

Banks and banking:
  and developing countries, 201–3
  loans, 67
  scandals, 3, 4–5
BAUM, 185
Beauchamp, T., 42
Benedetti, C., 3
Beneficence, 75
Bentham, Jeremy, 23
Betting, see Gambling
The Big Issue, 163
Biodiversity, 187
Blame, 171
Boesky, Ivan, 200
Bolivia, debt, 202–3
Borrie, Gordon, 68, 75–6, 77
Borrowing, see Debt
Bowie, N., 42
Boycotts:
  and ethical consumption, 81
  Nestlé, 61
Boys' Clubs, National Association of, 30
Brady Plan, 202
Breadth, see Broad
Breast feeding, 61
Bribery:
  cultural differences, 211, 218, 221
  Italy, 5–6, 211
British Sports Association for Disabled, 30
Broad ethics, 28, 29–31, 39, 50, 51–2, 158–223
Brown, Gordon, 161
Buddhist ethics, 213
Building societies, 69
Business associations, codes of ethics, 11–13
Business codes, see Codes
Business in the Community, 30, 160, 162, 163
Business in the Environment, 181, 182, 189, 190

Cadbury, Adrian, 218, 221
Cagliari, G., 5–6
Calvi, R., 3
Capitalism:
  critique of, 195–201
  democratic, 193–4, 199
  and developing countries, 198, 199, 200–1
  ethics of, 8–9, 135–7, 193–209
  popular, 135
  and socialism, 194–5, 198
  see also Market

Cartels, 73, 155, 196
Caste discrimination, international differences, 211
Categorical imperatives, 35, 50
Catholic ethics, 215–16
*Caveat emptor*, 77
Central Europe, *see* Europe
Centre for Alternative Technology, 183, 190
CFCs, 32
Chandler, H., 29–30, 38, 47
Character, virtuous, 23, 45–6
Charitable giving, 29–30, 32, 33, 40, 46–7, 48, 49, 107, 160
 and ethical consumers, 78
Charters, *see* Codes
Chickens, salmonella, 64–5
Choice, 168–70
Christian ethics, 75, 81, 197, 212, 213, 215–16
Churchill, C., 7
Cinema, moralizing, 7
Citizens, and consumers, 57
Citizen's Advice Bureaux, 75
 National Association of, 66
Citizenship, corporate, 13–14, 21
City technology colleges, 162
Civic Trust, 30
Civil Service, 174–5
Client confidentiality, 12, 15
Closed shops, 111
Clowes, P., 4
Co-determination, employers and workers, 91–2
Coal industry, 175
Codes, 217
 consumer protection, 74–5
 investor relations, 12
 moral, 11–16
 of practice, 11–16
 voluntary, 13
Collusive pricing, 73
Commission for Racial Equality (CRE), 106
Commodity prices, 201, 203
Common practices, 142
Communism, 197
Communist countries, former, *see* Europe, Central and Eastern
Community:
 companies' relations with, 13, 19–22
 companies' responsibility to, 25, 28
 green projects, 184–5
 *see also* Society
Companies, codes of ethics, 13–15
Competition, 147–56
 aggressive, 151–2
 airlines, 176
 and consumer protection, 72–3
 and cooperation, 155–6
 good practice, 153–4
 and pluralism, 33
 and prices, 73, 149, 152, 154
 and privatization, 176

regulation of, 72–3, 149–50, 151
 restraint, 152, 153, 154
Competition Act, 72, 154
Competitors:
 disparagement of, 14, 148
 elimination of, 149–52
 relations with, 147–56
Complaints by consumers, 77, 78
Confederation of British Industry, 29, 96, 163
Confidentiality, 12, 15, 148
Conflict:
 environmental and business ethics, 188–91
 of interests, 15, 28
 of responsibility, 28, 52
 of self-interest and morality, 51
 of values, 19–22, 215–22
Conscientiousness, 171
Constraint, 23, 24, 187
Consultation with employees, 94–9
 good practice, 109–10
Consumer Credit Act, 73, 74, 75
Consumer Protection Act, 74, 75
Consumer watchdogs, 74
Consumerism, 65, 151, 171–2
Consumers, 57–84
 choice, and privatization, 168–70
 complaints, 77, 78
 and corporate social responsibility, 30–1, 38
 credit and debt, 65–72, 76–7
 demands, moral costs of, 59–63
 education of, 71
 ethical, 78–82, 129, 130, 134
 exploitation by, 62–3, 77
 as kings, 57–8, 172
 protection, 58
  commercial costs of, 63–5
  and competition, 72–3
  and credit, 71, 73–4
  and trading standards, 73–8
 responsibilities of, 78
 unfairness of, 62–3, 77
 as victims, 57–8
Consumers' Association, 78–9
Consumption, reduction of, 80–2
Contractors, minority-run, 104, 105
Contracts:
 of employment, 85–7
 fairness of, 77–8
 *see also* Agreements
Control of firms, 122
Control of Pollution Act, 74
Cooperation between competitors, 155–6
Corporate citizenship, 13–14, 21
Corporate interest:
 and corporate social responsibility, 31–4, 49–50
 *see also* Self-interest
Corporate social responsibility, 159–63
 and consumers, 30–1, 38
 and corporate interest, 31–4, 49–50
 environment, 50, 178–92
Costa Rica, debt, 202

Costs:
  of consumer protection, 63–5
  of employee participation, 96–8
  of !ate payment, 142
  of Maastricht social chapter, 93–4
Courage, 45
Credit, consumers, 65–72, 76–7
Credit cards, 68, 71
Credit insurance, 71–2
Credit reference agencies, 68–9, 71
Credit unions, 71
Creditors, 139–44
  interests of, and employees' interests, 86
  and phoenixing, 144–7
Critique of capitalism, 195–201
Cultural differences, 212–15
  and economic development, 218–19
  and ethical dilemmas, 215–22
  Europe, 102–3
  and multinationals, 211
Cultural relativism, 212–15
Culture, and public services, 164
Cultures, respect for, 39
Customers, 57
Czechoslovakia:
  privatization, 205
  see also Europe, Central and Eastern

Debt:
  consumers, 65–72
  debt–for–development/equity swaps, 202–3
  developing countries, 201–3
  see also Creditors
Debt-for-development/equity swaps, 202–3
Decency, 44, 45
Deep green/light green, 185–6, 187, 189
Defective products, regulations, 74
Deindustrialization, Germany, 207
Democracy, 44, 199
  share-owning, 135
Democratic capitalism, 193–4, 199
Deregulation, 200
Developing countries:
  baby milk, 61
  and banks, 201–3
  and capitalism, 198, 199, 200–1
  and corporate responsibility, 49–50, 160
  and environment, 188, 211, 216, 219
  ethical investments, 130
  growth, 198, 199, 200–1
  moral standards, 213, 216
  trade, 200–1, 203–4
  wages, 219, 220
Development:
  and ethics of capitalism, 193–209
  sustainable, 183–4, 200–1, 204
Development ethics, 201–8
Dialogue with employees, 94–9
Dilemmas, ethical, 215–16
Directors, 121, 127, 129
Disabled people:
  as consumers, 83
  employment, 104

Discrimination, 89–90, 101–2
  gender, see Gender
  indirect, 101–2
  international differences, 211, 221
  positive, 104–7
  racial, 61–2, 91, 99, 102–3, 216
  religious, 104, 216
Discriminatory pricing, 149
Dividends, 115, see also Return on investment
Dominant market share, 149–51
Donaldson, Tom, 218–19
Double effect, principle of, 151
Dragon Awards, 161–3
Duty, 37, 39
Duxbury, Tom, 127–8

Eastern Europe, see Europe
Economic costs:
  of employee participation, 96–7
  of Maastricht social chapter, 93–4
Education:
  of consumers, 71
  role of state, 162–3
  see also Training
Efficiency, and competition, 149
Eggs, salmonella in, 64–5
Egoism, 98
  ethical, 47–9, 51, 54, 188–9
Elderly consumers, 82–3
Elimination of competitors, 149–52
Emergencies, and corporate responsibility, 49–50
Emission control, 180, 181, 186, 204
Employees, 85–112
  Avon Products Inc., 107
  consultation and participation, 94–9, 109–10
  discrimination between, see Discrimination
  equal treatment, 98–108
  John Lewis Partnership, 19–22, 109–10
  Littlewoods Organization, 107–8
  loyalty of, 87–8
  Marks & Spencer, 108
  morale, 18
  part-time, 111
  personal needs, 87
  redundancy, 86, 111
  responsibilities of, 87–9
  safety, regulations, 74
  Scott Bader, 110
  in social chapter, Maastricht, 90–102
  of suppliers, 139
  training and education, 86, 111
  welfare:
    and company codes, 13
    and ethical consumers, 78
  see also Discrimination; Equal opportunities
Employment Appeals Tribunals, 100
Employment contracts, 85–7
Employment practices, international differences, 210, 219

Energy saving, 180, 182
Enlightened self-interest, 31, 39, 54, 78
Entry to market, 72, 154
Environment:
  corporate responsibility, 50, 178–92
  and developing countries, 188, 211, 216, 219
  and ethical consumers, 78–82
  and ethical investment, 132, 133
  effects of tourism, 15, 184
  see also Green
Environmental counselling, 185
Environmental ethics, 185–6, 189, 211
Equal opportunities, 99
  good practice, 103–4, 107–8
  international differences, 211, 213
Equal pay, 91, 92, 100, 101
Equal treatment of employees, 98–108, see
    also Discrimination
Erskine, Keith, 17–19
Escape clauses, 77
Essentialist approaches to ethics, 8–10
Ethical Consumer (journal), 79–82
Ethical Consumer Research Association, 79
Ethical consumers, 78–82, 129, 130, 134
Ethical dilemmas, 215–16
Ethical egoism, 47–9, 51, 54, 188–9
Ethical investment, 53, 129–35
Ethical savings, 130
Ethics, 10
Ethnocentricity, and cultural relativism,
    212–15, 221
Europe:
  alternative investments, 130, 132
  codes of ethics, 16
  cultural differences, 102–3
  environmental issues, 179–80
  moral standards, 10, 16–17, 212, 215–16
Europe, Central and Eastern:
  development, 204–8
  free market, 9, 32, 193–4, 205–8
  privatization, 205–8
  transition to capitalism, 193, 195, 199
European Bank for Reconstruction and
    Development (EBRD), 193, 205
European Communities Act, 74
European Community (EC):
  competition rules, 73, 149, 154, 155–6
  consumer protection, 74
  Council of Ministers, 92
  directives, 74
  environmental issues, 179, 180
  Equal Pay Directive, 91
  Equal Treatment Directive, 91, 100
  and European integration, 102–3
  late payment, 140
  Single European Act, 92
  Social Action Programme, 93–4
  trade associations, 155
  Treaty of Maastricht, 90–102
European Court of Justice, 100
European integration, 102–3
European Trade Union Confederation
    (ETUC), 91

European Union, see European Community
Exemplary people, 17–19, 43–4, 45
Exemption clauses, 77
Extortionate interest, 66, 68, 75

Fair Trading Act, 73
Fair Trading, Office of (OFT), 65
Fairness and affordability, 220
Financial institutions:
  Central and Eastern Europe, 205
  information inequalities, 11, see also Insiders
  moral risks, 7
Financial Intermediaries, Managers and
    Brokers Regulatory Association, 125
Financial Services Act, 125
Flourishing, 46
Food Act, 74, 75
Food industry, and profits, 165–8
Food products:
  labelling, 32
  regulations, 74
Foot, Phillipa, 44–5
Fraternalism between competitors, 155–6
Fraud:
  Barlow Clowes, 4
  BCCI, 4–5
  Maxwell, 5
Free market, see Market
Friedman, Milton, 32
Friends of the Earth, 185

Gambling:
  and ethical investment, 132, 133
  shareholding as, 114, 119, 122, 123
Gender discrimination, 92–3, 100–1
  international differences, 211, 213
  sexism, 62
Generalist approaches to ethics, 8–10
Germany:
  environmental issues, 179
  Green Party, 190
  privatization, 207
  social market, 33
Good, 31
  greatest, 40–1, 51
Good practice:
  in competition, 153–4
  employee consultation, 109–10
  equal opportunities, 103–4, 107–8
Government, see State
Great people, 43–4, 45
Greatest good, 40–1
Greed, 197–8
Green issues:
  consumers, 78–82
  investments, see Ethical investment
  see also Environment
Green movement, 189–91
  deep green/light green, 185–6, 187, 189
Green parties, 81–2, 178, 190
Greenpeace, 180, 185
Grosfeld, I., 206–7
Groundwork Trust, 184

Growth, 198, 199–201, 213
Guest workers, 92
Gulliver, J., 3

Happiness, 35
Hare, P., 206–7
Hare, R.M., 42
Harm:
  to consumers, 60, 61, 64–5, 151
  and ethical investment, 131
  *see also* Risks; Safety
Hazards, *see* Harm; Risks; Safety
Health, harm to consumers, 64–5
Health and safety, Maastricht social chapter, 93–4
Health and Safety at Work Act, 74
Health services, and profits, 165–8
Heroic virtue, 43–4, 45, 49
Hindu ethics, 213
Hobbes, Thomas, 47–8
Holiday firms, codes of practice, 11, 15
Holiness, 44
Home or host country standards, *see* Cultural differences
Homeless people, companies' help for, 163
Honesty, 75, 88, 89
Horse-racing analogy with shareholding, 119, 122, 123
Host or home country standards, *see* Cultural differences
Hostile takeovers, 116–17
Housing, debts, 66, 69, 71
Howe Brown, A., 66–7, 70
Human rights, 38
Hungary:
  privatization, 205, 207
  *see also* Europe, Central and Eastern

Ideal utilitarianism, 42
Immigrant workers, 92
Immorality, irrationality of, 36–7
Import substitution, 203
Incommensurability, 41
Incorporation of green parties, 190
Indirect discrimination, 101–2
Individualism, 98
Industrial espionage, 148
Industrialization, developing countries, 201, 203–4
Inequality, and capitalism, 195
Inequality of opportunity, 105–6
Inertia selling, credit insurance, 71–2
Influence, and control, 122
Informal networks, recruitment, 106–7
Information:
  disclosure, 74, 124, 125–6, 217–18
  inequalities, 11
    and consumers, 58, 75
    and multinationals, 219–20
    and public opinion, 217–18
    and shareholders, 116, 124, 125–6
  takeovers and buyouts, 127, 128
  *see also* Insiders

misleading, 76
overload, 75–6
Inland Revenue, payments to, 144
Innovation, and competition, 149, 154, 155
Insiders, share dealing, 3, 7, 14, 116
Institute of Business Ethics, 67
Institute of Trading Standards Administration, 75
Institutional shareholders, 115–17, 121–3
Institutional Shareholders' Committee, 115, 116–17, 123
Insurance:
  of credit, 71–2
  disclosure of material facts, 74
Inter-company relations, 138–56
Interest:
  cultural differences, 213
  extortionate, 66, 68
  rates:
    APR, 70
    and overindebtedness, 68, 70
Interest groups:
  and politicians, 6
  *see also* Interests
Interests:
  conflict of, 15, 28
  contention of, 33
  corporate, *see* Corporate interest
  of directors, 129
  of managers, 127
  of shareholders, 28, 129
  *see also* Interest groups; Public interest; Self–interest
International business ethics, 210–23
International Finance Corporation (IFC), 194
International relations, 204
International rights, 220–1
International trade, and development, 200–1, 203–4
Investment:
  decisions, 118
  in ethical firms, 53, 129–35
Investment Management Regulatory Organization, 125
Investors, protection of, 12, 125
Irrationality of immorality, 36–7
Irresponsible lending, 70, 71, 77
Italy:
  late payment, 140
  scandals, 3, 5–6
  taxation, 42

Japan, bribery, 211
Japanese firms:
  employment, 86
  moral standards, 17
Job for life, 86
Joint ownership, 119–20
Joint ventures, public and private, 32
Jubilee Centre, 67
Judge, Paul, 126–7, 146–7
Justice, 45, 46, 119
  and corporate responsibility, 50
  social, 94

Kant, Immanuel, 23, 35–8, 212–13
Kantianism, 37–9, 49, 50, 51, 75, 81, 140, 212
Knowledge, *see* Information

Labelling, 32, 183
Landfill, 181
Language, and discrimination, 102
LAUTRO (Life Assurance and Unit Trust Regulatory Organization), 125
Law, 47
  and conflict of responsibility, 52
  consumer protection, 58
Laws, *see* Regulations, laws etc.
Lending, *see* Debt
Less developed countries, *see* Developing countries
Levitt, Theodore, 33
Life Assurance and Unit Trust Regulatory Organization (LAUTRO), 125
Life-time employment, 86
Light green/deep green, 185–6, 187
Limited liability, 48, 144–7
Liquidation, and phoenixing, 144–7
Loans, *see* Debt
Lobbying, *see* Interest groups
Long-term goals, 121, 188
Loyalty:
  of customers, 149
  of employees, 87–8
  of shareholders, 116–17, 121
  to suppliers, 139
Lying, 75, 88

Maastricht Treaty, *see* Treaty of Maastricht
MacGregor, Ian, 174–5
Magnificent people, 43–4, 45
Management:
  and privatization, 170–1
  and state ownership, 174–5
Management buy-outs (MBOs), 126–9
Managers, interests, 127, 128–9
Market:
  and capitalist realism, 197, 198
  Central and Eastern Europe, 9, 32, 193–4, 205–8
  and consumer choice, 168–70
  and corporate social responsibility, 31–2, 48–9
  and democracy, 199
  and efficiency, 168
  and ethics, 8–9
  newly industrialized countries, 195
  and poverty, 194
  and public services, 164
  and self-interest, 48–9
  social, 33
  *see also* Privatization
Market share, 72–3, 148
  dominant, 149–51
Marxist views of capitalism, 8–9
Masons, 3, 6
Mattioli, F. P., 5

Maxwell, Robert, 5, 6, 8, 200
Mergers, *see* Takeovers and mergers
Meta-ethics, 23–4
Mexico, debt, 202, 203
Militant greens, 190
Mill, J. S., 23
Minneapolis, 29, 30, 48
Misleading information, 76
Misuse of products, 60–1
Mixed economy, 208
Money Advice Support Unit, 65–6
Monopolies and Mergers Commission, 73
Monopoly:
  and capitalism, 195, 196
  public utilities, 173
  regulation of, 73
Moore, Pat, 83
Moral absolutes, 212–15
Moral aristocracy, 44
Moral behaviour, 36
Moral climate, 6–7
Moral codes, 11–16
Moral costs:
  of competition elimination, 151
  of consumer demands, 59–63
  of employee participation, 96–8
  of Maastricht social chapter, 93–4
Moral credit, 49
Moral culture, 16
Moral discredit, 49
Moral philosophy, 23–4
Moral prohibitions, 24
Moral purism, 35–6
Moral relativism, 212–15
Moral rhetoric, 19, 20
Moral risks:
  and codes of ethics, 15
  financial institutions, 7
  and size of firm, 7
Moral significance, 8–9
Moral theory, 19, 34
  and self-interest, 49–50, 51
Moral worth, 36
Morale, employees, 18
Morality, 23
  and self-interest, 34, 35, 42–3, 49–50, 51
Morally creditable, 31
Mortgage repayments, 66, 69
Motivation, 18
  and codes of ethics, 15, 16–17
Multinational corporations, 9, 200
  and cultural differences, 211
  and developing countries, 200, 201, 203, 219
  and information inequalities, 219–20
  responsibilities, 48
Mutual funds, ethical investment, 132–5

Nadir, A., 5
Nagel, Thomas, 105–6
Narrow ethics, 15, 16, 28–9, 38, 50, 51–2, 57–156
National Association of Boys' Clubs, 30

National Association of Citizen's Advice Bureaux, 66
National Children's Home, 53
National Consumer Council (NCC), 69–70, 71, 72
National Health Service, and profits, 165–8
National Insurance payments, 144
National Rivers Authority (NRA), 179–80
Nationalization, 115
Negligence, 75
Neo-Aristotelianism, 43, 44–6
Netherlands, environmental issues, 179
New Consumer, 79, 103–4, 107–8, 201, 202, 204
*New Consumer* (journal), 79
Newly industrialized countries, market, 195
Normative ethics, 23, 151

Objectivity of beliefs, 140
Obligations:
  moral, 23
  of shareholders, 115–23
  to shareholders, 114–15
Office of Fair Trading (OFT), 65, 75, 76
  credit regulation, 71
Old people as consumers, 82–3
Ombudsmen, 74
Openness and ethics, 218, 221
Opportunism, 78
Opportunities:
  equal, *see* Equal opportunities
  inequality of, 105–6
Others, 36–7, 47
Overbooking by airlines, 63–4
Overindebtedness, 67–72, 76–7
Ownership:
  of companies, 113, 115, 120, 121
  joint, 119–20
  moral desirability of, 135–7, 174
Oxfam, 204

Package holiday firms, codes of practice, 11, 15
Packaging, 30, 183
Part-time employees, 111
Participation:
  by employees, 94–9
  by investors, 134
Payment:
  in arrears, 66, 67–72, 139–44
  inability to pay, 140–1, 143, 144
  on time, 14
Pension funds:
  ethical investment, 132
  and Maxwell, 5, 6
Per Cent Club, 30, 160
Peru, debt, 202
Pharmaceutical industry, and profits, 165–8
Philosophy, 16, 19, 22, 34
  and conflict of responsibility, 52
  moral, 23–4, 35–52
Phoenixing, 144–7

Plato, 43
Pluralism, 33
Poland:
  privatization, 205, 206
  *see also* Europe, Central and Eastern
Political affiliations, and ethical consumers, 78
Political conditions and moral dilemmas, 222–3
Political costs:
  of employee participation, 97–8
  of Maastricht social chapter, 93–4
Politicians:
  and interest groups, 6, 12
  and public utilities, 175
Pollution, *see* Environment
Pollution Inspectorate, 180
Popular capitalism, 135
Pornography, 59, 61
  and ethical investment, 132
Positive discrimination, 104–7
Poverty, and capitalism, 194, 195, 207–8
Powdered baby milk, Third World, 61
Power generation, 180, 181
Pregnancy, 94, 100
Prices:
  collusion, 73
  and competition, 73, 149, 152, 154
  discriminatory, 149
  and environmental issues, 189
  and privatization, 206
  regulation, 74
  retail price maintenance, 72
  and social responsibility, 32, 33
Principles of ethics, 22
Private ownership, moral desirability of, 135–7
Private sector, Central and Eastern Europe, 193, 205, 206–7
Privatization, 115, 135, 136–7, 159
  Central and Eastern Europe, 194, 205–8
  and consumer choice, 168–70
  of public services, 163–73
  of state-owned businesses, 173–6
  and waste, 168–9
  *see also* Market
Professional associations, codes of ethics, 11–13
Profitability, obligations to shareholders, 114, 120, 125, 126
Profits:
  banks, 201–2
  ethics of, 8–9, 22, 25, 163–73
  glorification of, 195, 197
  from lending, ethics of, 66
  pollution by, 164–8
  public services, 163–73
  purification by, 168–72
  of share dealing, 118
  short–term, 121
Protection, of consumers, 58
Protestant ethics, 215

Public expectations of firms, 38
Public interest, 12, 15
Public opinion, and moral decisions, 217–18, 222
Public ownership, 115
Public Relations Consultants Association, 11–13, 15
Public sensibility, 8
Public services:
  contributions of business, 159–63
  privatization, see Privatization
  role of state, 159–61
Public utilities, privatization, 173–6, 206
Public virtue, 44
Publicity, for scandals, 6–7
Purism, moral, 35–6, 37
Purpose of companies, 114

Racial discrimination, 61–2, 91, 99, 102–3, 216
Rational behaviour by consumers, 76
Rational investment decisions, 118
Rationalization, codes of ethics as, 24–6
Reagan, Ronald/Reaganism, 200
Realistic critique of capitalism, 195–201
Receivership, and phoenixing, 144–7
Recruitment:
  and discrimination, 104–5, 106
  informal networks, 106–7
Recycling, 30, 181–2, 183, 189
Red revolutionary groups, 190–1
Redistribution of wealth, 130
Redundancy, 86, 111
Regulation:
  Central and Eastern Europe, 205, 206
  of competition, 72–3, 149–50, 151
  of credit, 71, 74
  of monopoly, 73, 196, 198, 205
  of privatized industries, 176
Regulations, laws etc:
  competition, 72–3, 149–50, 151, 154, 155
  consumer protection, 72–3, 74
  cultural differences, 217
  environmental issues, 180
  investor protection, 125
  racial discrimination, 99
  trade unions, 92
  trading standards, 73–5, 77
  see also Codes
Relativism, moral, 212–22
Religion:
  Christian ethics, 75, 81, 197, 212, 213, 215–16
  Islamic ethics, 213
  and moral values, 213, 215
Religious discrimination, 104, 216
Renewable resources, 183–4
Repayment of debt, 66, 67–72
Repossession by mortgagors, 66
Resale Prices Act, 72
Research and development cooperation, 155
Resources, renewable, 183
Respect:
  between employers and workers, 95, 96

  for cultures, 39
  for environment, 15
  for minorities, 103
  for persons, 36–7, 39
Responsibility, 36
  conflicts of, 28, 52
  of consumers, 78
  corporate, see Corporate social responsibility
  of employees, 87–9
  and privatization, 169, 170–2
  social, 48–9
  to suppliers, 138–9
Restraint in competition, 152, 153, 154
Restrictive Practices Court, 72
Restrictive Trade Practices Act, 72
Retail Credit Group, 68
Retail price maintenance, 72
Retailers:
  credit to customers, 68, 69
  'green' policies, 183
  Sunday trading, 111
Return on investment, 114, 115, 125, 126
Revolutionary groups, 190–1
Rhetoric, 19, 20
Rights, 220–1
Rimmer, Mary, 160–1
Risks:
  assessment, credit reference agencies, 71
  of harm to public, 65, 75, 88
  and return on investment, 121, 123
  see also Safety
River pollution, 179–80
Road Traffic Act, 74
Rome, Treaty of, see Treaty of Rome
Ronson, G., 4
Rubython, Tom, 146–7
Rule utilitarianism, 41–2, 81
Russia:
  privatization, 205
  see also Europe, Central and Eastern
Ryrie, William, 194–201

Sacrifice, 35, 49
Safety:
  employees' duty, 88
  in Maastricht social chapter, 93–4
  of products, 61, 75
  regulation, 74
  at work, regulations, 74
Safety nets, 198
St Helens (Lancs), 160
Saints/saintliness, 43–4, 49
Sale of Goods Act, 77
Salmonella in eggs, 64–5
Saunders, E., 3
Saving, and lending, 66–7, 70
Savings, ethical, 130
Scale:
  economies of, 138, 152
  see also Size
Scandals, 3–8

Schluter, M., 67, 72
Scotland, small firms, 154, 155
Securities and Futures Authority, 125
Securities and Investment Board (SIB), 125
Seduction of green parties, 190
Self-centredness, 47
Self-interest, 25, 196
  consumers, 75–6, 77
  enlightened, 31, 39, 54, 78
  and environmental issues, 189
  ethical egoism, 47–9
  and morality, 34, 49–50, 51, 77
  and opportunism, 78
  and social contract, 48–9
  see also Corporate interest
Self-sacrifice, 35, 49
Selfishness, 47
Selling:
  credit insurance, 71–2
  high-pressure, 76
Sensibility, public, 8
Service sector, Central and Eastern Europe, 206
Sex discrimination, see Gender
Sexism, 62
Share dealing, 3, 5, 7, 14
Share–owning democracy, 135
Shareholders, 113–37
  accountability of, 120
  individual/small, 118, 121–4
  institutional/large, 115–17, 121–4
  interests of, 28
    and employees' interests, 86, 88
  investment in ethical firms, 53
  loyalty of, 116–17
  obligations of, 115–23, 124, see also Ethical investment
  obligations to, 114–15, 124–6
Shareholding, moral desirability of, 135–7, 174
Sherwood, Louis, 122
Short-term goals, 121, 188
Side effects of actions, 151
Size of firm:
  and aggressive competition, 152
  and corporate social responsibility, 34
  and moral risks, 7
  and waste, 169
Slavery, 212
Small firms:
  and corporate social responsibility, 34
  and late payment, 140
  and moral risks, 7
  relations with competitors, 154, 155
  St Helens (Lancs), 160
Smith, Adam, 196
Smoking, see Tobacco
Social Action Programme (EC), 93–4
Social chapter, Maastricht Treaty, 90–102
Social contract, 48–9
Social derivation of morality, 214
Social engineering, 172–3, 208

Social fund, DSS, 71
Social justice, 94
Social market, 33
Social responsibility, 28, 48–9, 200, 203, see also Corporate social responsibility; Responsibility
Social Security, Dept. of, 71, 144
Socialism:
  and capitalism, 194–5, 198
  and public services, 164
Society, see Community
South Africa, 216, 222
  and ethical investment, 132, 133
Spain, environmental issues, 179
Specialization, 33
Sponsorship, 26, 31, 159, 162–3
Standards, see Codes; Regulations
Stanton, E., 68
State:
  intervention in economy, 195, 198
  role in public services, 159–61, 170, 172
  role in public utilities, 174–5
  role in welfare, 33
Statutes/statutory instruments, see Regulations, laws etc.
Steiner, Rudolf, 130
Sternberg, Elaine 117–23 passim, 131
Stone, Oliver, 7
Strategic alliances, 155–6
Strikes, 111
Subcontractors, see Suppliers
Sudan, debt, 202
Sugar markets, 203
  restrictive practices, 73
Sunday trading, 111
Suppliers:
  as creditors, 139–44
  minority-run, 104, 105
  as stakeholders, 138–9
Survival of firm, 115, 119
Sustainable development, 183–4, 200–1, 204

Takeovers and mergers:
  and competition, 149, 150
  hostile, 116–17, 124
  management buy-outs (MBOs), 126–9
  regulation, 149, 150
Tax credits and pollution, 182
Taxation:
  and capitalism, 198, 200
  Italy, 42
  payment of, 144
Temperance, 45
Testing of products, 79
Thatcher, M./Thatcherism, 135, 200
Theatre, moralizing, 7
Third World, see Developing countries
Timber trade/resources, 183–4, 204
Timeshare selling, 76
Tobacco, 59–60, 61
  and ethical investment, 132, 133, 134
Tour operators, codes of practice, 11, 15

Tourism, cultural and environmental effects, 15, 184
Trade, and development, 200–1, 203–4
Trade associations, 155
Trade Descriptions Act, 73, 75
Trade unions, 91–2
  and public utilities, 174–5
Trades Union Congress (TUC), 91–2
Trading standards, and consumer protection, 73–8
Trading Standards Service, 75
Training and education, 86, 111
  city technology colleges, 162
  Pilkington's role, 160
Transnational, see Multinational
Treaty of Maastricht, 90–102
Treaty of Rome, 73, 91, 92, 99–100, 101
Treuhand, 207
Trust, 78, 140

Unemployment:
  and capitalism, 195, 198
  and privatization, 173, 207–8
Unfair Contract Terms Act, 77–8
Unfairness, 171
  of consumers, 62–3, 77
Unit trusts, ethical investment, 132–5
United Kingdom:
  environmental issues, 179–80
  and social chapter, Maastricht, 94, 97–8
United States:
  codes of ethics, 15, 16
  equal opportunities, 103
  moral standards, 10, 17, 212
  positive discrimination, 104–7
Universalizability, 36, 37
Usury, see Extortionate interest
Utilitarianism, 23, 40–2, 49, 51, 75, 81, 131–2, 140, 141, 212

Valuation, for privatization, 206
Value of firm, maximization, 118, 120, 121
Values:
  conflicts of, 19–22, 215–22
  cultural differences, 212–15
  of environment, 186, 187

Victims, consumers as, 57–8
Violence, and environmental issues, 190
Virtue, 45–6, 212
  public, 44
Virtue theory, 24, 45–7, 49, 50, 51
Virtuous behaviour, 35, 43–4
Virtuous character, 23, 45–6
Voluntary codes, 13
Voting, 80–1

Wages:
  developing countries, 219, 220
  equal pay, 91
  and ethical investment, 132
War, 47
Waste, and privatization, 168–9
Waste management, 181, 182, 189
Water pollution, 179–80
Wealth:
  creation, 67
  inequalities, 200
  redistribution, 130
Weights and Measures Act, 74
Welfare, 33
  and charity, 4
  developing countries, 203
  of employees, see Employees
Welfare state, 159–63, 172, 174, 208
Which?, 78–9
Whistle-blowing, 88, 95
White people, Europe, 102–3
Whittaker, N., 30–1, 47
Wille, E., 13, 14
Women:
  equal pay, 91
  pregnant, 94
Workers councils, 91–2, 94–9
Working conditions, 91
Working environment, 91
Working hours, 98
World Bank, 194
World Development Movement (WDM), 201, 203, 204

ZBell (Arthur) and Son, 3